Readings in Schenker Analysis

and Other Approaches

Edited by Maury Yeston

New Haven and London, Yale University Press, 1977

Material in this book has previously been published in the *Journal of Music Theory*,
copyright © *Journal of Music Theory* 1959, 1961, 1966, 1968, 1969, 1971, 1975.

Chapter 1: *JMT* 3, no. 1 (1959); chapters 2, 8–10: *JMT* 12, no. 2 (1968);
chapter 3: *JMT* 5, no. 1 (1961); chapters 4, 15, 16: *JMT* 15, no. 1–2 (1971);
chapter 5: *JMT* 19, no. 2 (1975); chapters 6, 7: *JMT* 10, no. 1 (1966);
chapter 11 and part 3: *JMT* 13, no. 1 (1969); chapters 12–14: *JMT* 13, no. 1 (1969).

Preparation and layout by Lucinda Hill Gerson.
Set in IBM Selectric Journal Roman type.

Published in Great Britain, Europe, Africa, and Asia
(except Japan) by Yale University Press, Ltd., London.
Distributed in Latin America by Kaiman & Polon, Inc.,
New York City; in Australia and New Zealand by Book & Film
Services, Artarmon, N.S.W., Australia; and in Japan by Harper & Row,
Publishers, Tokyo Office.

Library of Congress Cataloging in Publication Data

Main entry under title:

Readings in Schenker analysis and other approaches.

    Bibliography: p.
    1. Schenker, Heinrich, 1868–1935. 2. Music—Theory—
Addresses, essays, lectures. I. Schenker, Heinrich,
1868–1935. II. Yeston, Maury Alan.
ML423.S33R4   781   76–40140
ISBN 0–300–02032–5
ISBN 0–300–02114–3 pbk.

Printed in the United States of America by
Alpine Press, South Braintree, Massachusetts.

Contents

Editor's Preface

This volume brings together for the first time for the general reader a large body of learned commentary deriving from the ideas of the Austrian music theorist Heinrich Schenker (1868–1935). Schenkerian analyses are contrasted here with numerous other approaches. The aim of the collection is to make Schenker's ideas more comprehensible and accessible than they have been and to portray them in the broadest possible context of tonal analysis. There is no intention to cast aspersions on the other excellent approaches that have been included here. As these latter approaches demonstrate, Schenkerian analysis is not the only way to probe sensitively into works of musical art in order to render more explicit their inner coherence.

Schenker's imagination was so fertile, and his theory so many-faceted in its references and applications, that any précis of it runs the risk of reducing the larger vision to one of its aspects or, worse, of distorting the theory in favor of the predilections of some other author. It is hoped that the present volume avoids these pitfalls by the sheer number of different points of view taken by its Schenker-influenced authors and by the diversity of topics that are addressed. Hence, Allen Forte's reasoned introduction to and defense of Schenker's fundamental ideas is followed by Schenker's own, somewhat polemical essay on sonata form. Ernst Oster's article on register subjects this aspect of compositional structure to close scrutiny and extends a discussion of a subject that was merely opened by Schenker in his essay on sonata form. John Rothgeb's discussion of middle-ground structure and foreground design is valuable not only for its revelations of tonal coherence but also because an awareness of the relationships he describes is a useful aid to the student of analytic technique. My own contribution is an attempt to expand the implications of Schenker's theories for rhythm and meter, and it also attempts to demonstrate the relevance of middleground structure to questions of performance.

The breadth of Schenker's thought and influence begins to show itself fully in the four analysis symposia that follow. Ernst Oster's analysis of a Mozart menuetto relates structure to style and suggests that Mozart may not have written the end of the composition. The colloquy between Messrs. Rothgeb and Schachter is a fortuitous demonstration of differences that can arise in the context of two Schenkerian approaches to the same piece, and it tends to refute the notion that this kind of analysis is dogmatic and insensitive to alternate readings. David Beach's consideration of a Beethoven sonata makes reference to the composer's autograph—a practice that is currently widespread and that was pioneered by Schenker. Finally, Edward Laufer's discussion of a Brahms song embraces the relationship of word and tone and, like the analyses mentioned above, demonstrates that a Schenkerian approach to a piece is not merely a disembodied graph.

Indeed, the contents of this volume, when taken together, reveal strikingly that Schenkerian analysis is far more than an arhythmic portrayal of long-range voice leading. It is, primarily, a means of uncovering organic unity within masterworks of tonal music, with "organic unity" understood not as an abstract aesthetic norm but rather as a demonstrably concrete relationship of part to whole. What makes this uncovering possible is the special mode of presentation that Schenker integrated into his system, since the very medium of discourse about the object under consideration—the work of music—is also music. In this respect, an analysis can aspire to the musical elegance of its object much in the same way that literary criticism aspires to the condition of literature.

The contributions of Howard Boatwright, Austin Clarkson, Matt Hughes, Lawrence Moss, and Robert Palmer are equally important inclusions in this volume, and they are as varied and as distinct from each other as each one of them is from a Schenkerian approach. In their considerable diversity, ranging from the purely quantitative to the literary-historical, they present a wide backdrop against which the reader can observe Schenkerian analysis in relief; in the valuable insights provided by their commentaries, they bring a balance and a perspective to this collection. Indeed, it is clear that all of the authors of this volume are united by a common passion for musical understanding and that no single approach, no matter how all-encompassing, can exhaust a musical masterpiece of its meaning.

It remains here to explain the function of the editor's short introductions. In some cases they update bibliographic references, but for the most part they are intended as an aid to the intermediate student—highlighting the authors' central points or relating disparate parts of this volume to one another. I would like to thank the class members of Music 53a at Yale College in this regard. They used this collection as a textbook for tonal analysis and kept me well informed as to which areas needed clarification for them.

I would also like to thank the editor of the *Journal of Music Theory*, Bryan Simms, for his cooperation in this project, my wife, Judy, and our son, Jake, for their love and patience, and an outstanding group of people at Yale University Press—Lucinda Gerson, Joanne Ainsworth, and Helena Bentz Dorrance—for their incalculable aid in editing the manuscript. (Ms. Dorrance, in particular, contributed at least as much as any of the authors.) Finally, I owe my thanks to the contributing authors, to John Rothgeb for his numerous suggestions, and especially to Allen Forte, whose teaching, creativity, and stimulation of the field of music theory are unending.

Contributors

David W. Beach is Associate Professor of Music Theory at the Eastman School of Music.

Howard Boatwright is Professor of Music at Syracuse University.

Austin Clarkson teaches at York University where he is Associate Professor of Music.

Allen Forte is Professor of the Theory of Music and Director of Graduate studies in music at Yale University.

Orin Grossman is Assistant Professor of Music at Fairfield University.

Matt Hughes is Assistant Professor of Music at Acadia University.

Edward Laufer teaches composition at the University of Toronto, where he is an Assistant Professor.

Lawrence K. Moss is Professor of Music and Chairman of the Theory-Composition Division at the University of Maryland.

Ernst Oster teaches at the New England Conservatory and at the Mannes College of Music.

Robert Palmer is Given Foundation Professor of Music at Cornell University.

John Rothgeb is Associate Professor of Music at the State University of New York at Binghamton.

Carl E. Schachter is Associate Professor of Music at Queens College and was, formerly, Dean and faculty member of the Mannes College of Music.

Maury Yeston is Assistant Professor of the Theory of Music and Director of Undergraduate Studies in music at Yale University.

PART 1

INTRODUCTORY ESSAYS

1. Schenker's Conception of Musical Structure

Allen Forte

Allen Forte's overview of Schenker's thought covers the subject from the influence of previous theorists upon Schenker to yet unresolved questions Schenkerian theory poses to present-day and future thinkers. Here the beginner will find careful definitions of Schenker's basic concepts and terms, as well as a detailed explanation of a typical analytic sketch.

There is one concept referred to in the text (p. 15) that often appears contradictory to beginning students: the consonant passing tone. This is a tone that is harmonized and made consonant on the foreground level but that appears as a dissonance at the middleground level. Students incorrectly assume that this is a violation of the logic of reduction since, ordinarily, one eliminates dissonant detail in order to reveal an underlying structure that is consonant. It should be remembered, however, that Schenker's reductive technique treats consonance and dissonance with respect to the particular harmony being prolonged at a given level (in this case it is a IV harmony functioning as a dominant preparation). Thus it is possible for a tone dissonant to that harmony (in this case a passing c-sharp) to be rendered superficially consonant on the foreground, and yet for the tone to remain dissonant to the IV harmony nevertheless. (An argument against Schenker's interpretation of this c-sharp appears in Arthur Komar's edition of Schumann's Dichterliebe *[New York: Norton, 1971], pp. 70–73.)*

At the end of the present article (first published in 1959) a series of unsolved problems in music theory was put forth by the author, and there has been considerable response. Work relating Schenker's theory to the study of rhythm has been done by Arthur Komar (Theory of Suspensions [Princeton: Princeton Univ. Press, 1971]), by Anne Alexandra Pierce ("The Analysis of Rhythm in Tonal

3

*Music" [Diss., Brandeis University, 1968]), and by the editor of the present volume (*The Stratification of Musical Rhythm *[New Haven: Yale Univ. Press, 1976]). The question of analyzing the history of tonality itself (and especially the development of chromaticism) using Schenker's ideas has received recent attention in Orin Grossman's "The Piano Sonatas of Jan Ludislav Dussek" (Diss., Yale University, 1975).—*Ed.

When Heinrich Schenker died on 14 January 1935, he bequeathed to the musical world a small number of students, a large body of work in theory, and a considerable amount of controversy. For the latter, no end is yet in sight—nor is this necessarily harmful, since disagreement has often been an important and stimulating adjunct to musical thought. But without first establishing criteria and agreeing upon conditions, issues cannot be clearly drawn, even provisionally satisfactory conclusions cannot be reached—in short, intelligent public discussion is impossible. Further, these requirements presuppose that all participants are more or less equally well informed about the subject. Clearly this latter condition is not fulfilled where Schenker's theory is concerned, for although a large porportion of his published work is available, many musicians remain uninformed regarding its extent, significance, and pertinence to current problems in music theory.

The purpose of this article is therefore to present an introductory account of his conception of musical structure, to explain why it should be recognized by serious musicians, and, beyond this, to indicate how it might contribute toward the solution of certain problems which stand before music theory today.

The boldness and the very comprehensiveness of Schenker's work guarantee that he will be a controversial figure for years to come. However, I hope that this review of his work, by providing accurate information to those who are unfamiliar with it, will serve to place future discussions on a somewhat more rational basis than they have been in the past. Yet, even as I write these words, I prepare myself to be misunderstood—such is the price of disputation long conducted in an atmosphere of general misunderstanding.

Why is Schenker's work not more widely appreciated? Is it recondite, unreasonably difficult, lacking in practical significance? The

following statements by two well-known musicians strongly support
a negative reply.

> The first work which made Schenker's name known in wider
> circles was his monograph on the Ninth Symphony of Beethoven.
> This book came into my hands quite by accident in the year
> 1911 at Lübeck, where as a minor conductor I was beginning
> my career. It immediately aroused my most intense interest.
> Although I was unable to endorse all of its details, and although
> the polemical posturing of the author went too far for me, the
> way in which questions were formulated and the conviction
> and insight with which these questions were answered were so
> unusual—indeed the whole was so far removed from the usual
> writings on music—that I was profoundly affected. Here for the
> first time were no hermeneutics; instead, the author inquired
> objectively and directly about that which actually stood before
> us in the work.[1]

> Only later [following unfruitful studies with Bussler] under the
> influence of the writings of the profound theorist and musical
> philosopher, Heinrich Schenker, did I become aware of what I
> had missed and begin to grasp theoretical problems, or, rather,
> they grasped me; they even fascinated me.[2]

Quite understandably, the absence of English translations of Schenker's main works[3] must be held responsible for a great many un-
desirable aspects of the present situation. But, you ask, what of the
books and articles in English which deal, to a greater or lesser extent,
directly with his work? I shall attempt to answer this question as
concisely as possible. Within the literature which has accumulated
around Schenker's theory we can distinguish three types. First, there
are surveys of his work. For the most part these are in the form of
book reviews where space limitations prevent any kind of thorough
coverage. Second, there are critiques of Schenker's concepts which
have been published in article form. These invariably presuppose at
least a partial acquaintance with his writings, permitting the author
to stress those parts of Schenker's theory which support his particular argument. Third, we have several more extended theoretical
works (in book form) which represent modifications or amplifica-
tions, or both, of his work, in part or whole. Unfortunately, these do
not always make clear the extent to which Schenker's ideas are
present in their original form. Therefore, broadly speaking, this
entire literature has not contributed significantly toward the understanding of Schenker's work *in his own terms.*[4]

A further obstacle to more widespread understanding of Schenker's theory is that its applicability to important current problems in music theory has not been sufficiently appreciated. Partly because of the unfamiliar language and representational means which are integral to it, it has been regarded as a purely "theoretical" system, jealously fostered by an inner circle whose members are completely at odds with the musical world at large. True, Schenker's proponents inevitably found themselves in conflict with the rigid and arbitrary constructs of what has come to be known as traditional theory. On the other hand, most musicians are unaware of the extent to which Schenker's ideas have penetrated and modified that theory in recent years.

Then, too, many serious musicians who are not specialists have remained uninformed during the quarter century following the completion of Schenker's work because there has been no professional journal devoted to disseminating information about music theory—an essential task which the present periodical has undertaken.

Finally, in considering reasons for the failure of Schenker's work to gain acknowledgement, we must recognize the problem which often arises upon initial contact with his work: even the well-trained musician who reads Schenker for the first time is apt to be thrown off his intellectual balance, for he is confronted with new interpretations of what he has come to regard as familiar events. He is faced with the task of learning a new terminology, a new set of visual symbols, and, most important, a new way of hearing music.

By this I do not intend to suggest that Schenker's theory is without faults. Further on, when I discuss its deficiencies, I shall make an effort to avoid duplicating other critical treatments of Schenker's theories. This is easier to do than one might expect, because earlier treatments tend to emphasize aspects of Schenker's work which are less problematic now.[5] A major reason for this change is to be seen in the general trend in thinking which has taken place during the past quarter century, a trend heavily influenced by the accelerated development of science. Even music has been affected to the extent that, for example, we can now regard the late nineteenth-century concept of "modulation" merely as a verbal inaccuracy. There seems to be no further need to worry about this or, I trust, such equally moldy bones of contention as the degree of correspondence between Schenker's theoretical formulations and what was "in the composer's mind" as he composed.

Before describing the content of Schenker's work in greater detail, I should like to survey his achievement in general terms. From the viewpoint of the present-day music theorist, this may be likened to a particular kind of high-level achievement in science: the discovery or development of a fundamental principle which then opens the way for the disclosure of further new relationships, new meanings. Regarded in this way, Schenker's achievement invites comparison with that of Freud. Just as Freud opened the way for a deeper understanding of the human personality with his discovery that the diverse patterns of overt behavior are controlled by certain underlying factors, so Schenker opened the way for a deeper understanding of musical structure with his discovery that the manifold of surface events in a given composition is related in specific ways to a fundamental organization. Over a period of years, Schenker's discovery gradually assumed a more distinct conceptual form which I shall refer to as the *concept of structural levels*. To articulate this idea Schenker invented a special vocabulary and devised a unique representational means. I will explain these further on.

I wish to emphasize at this point that the bases of Schenker's concept of structural levels, upon which his theory of music rests, are not to be found in abstruse speculation, nor in acoustical or metaphysical formulations (although Schenker was not averse to these), but in the organization of the music itself. Schenker consistently derived his theoretical formulations from aural experiences with actual musical compositions, and verified them at the same source.[6] Furthermore, his analytic techniques, as well as his analytic concepts, are directly related to performance and compositional practices which stand at the very center of the development of tonal music. I shall return to this often neglected facet of Schenker's work further on.

Schenker's achievement—which might be termed the deepening of musical understanding through the discovery of the principle of structural levels—spans a period of some forty years, during which time he was engaged in a wide variety of activities. Because these activities were all closely associated with his main task, the development of his theory of musical structure, I should like to devote a few words to a description of them, indicating how they provided an appropriate setting for his work. Schenker was never associated with an educational institution. He earned his living mainly by giving private lessons in theory and piano. He was able to bring all his instructional activities within the scope of his theoretical formulations through a single, central activity: analysis. This is evident in his attitude toward performance. Following the lead of C. P. E. Bach here as elsewhere, Schenker believed that a composition could be reproduced correctly only if the performer had grasped the composer's intentions as revealed by the score, and if he had developed an aural sensitivity to the hierarchy of tonal values which it expressed. His corresponding viewpoint toward music education should gladden the heart of every hard-pressed counterpoint teacher. According to Hans Wolf, Schenker once made the following remark: "If I had my way, every instrumentalist would have theory as his major study. It is not enough for him simply to play mechanically, as though he has Czerny exercises before him. They say they have practiced. . . . But what is the use of that? What *Geist* makes their practicing vital? In painting and poetry Czerny exercises do not exist."[7]

Schenker's pedagogical activities appear to have occupied a central position in his life. Almost all his writings are intended to instruct—in the most "practical" sense of that term. One sometimes overlooks the fact that his magnum opus, *Neue musikalische Theorien und Phantasien*,[8] is actually a self-contained series of textbooks which were published intermittently over a span of thirty-four years. Outwardly, the pedagogical goal of this series is direct, even old-fashioned—namely, to provide instruction in the traditional subjects of harmony and counterpoint. But—and here is Schenker's innovation—this instruction is so designed that it leads stage by stage to an understanding of the total work in all of its complexity. The boldness and uniqueness of this plan is hardly less striking today than it was a quarter of a century ago. Consider, for example, that in the first volume of his *Kontrapunkt* Schenker relates rudimentary species counterpoint exercises to the elaborate structural events in composed works, and that the relationships established are not of the obvious and transitory nature so often encountered in textbooks but are far-reaching, cogent, and, in the best sense, musical.

To continue this short account of Schenker's activities, I turn to his work as editor. It is perhaps not exaggerating to say that, in his explanatory editions of the late Beethoven sonatas, Schenker gave a major impetus to the entire modern movement toward better editing practices. In preparing that edition (published 1913–20) as well as the complete edition of the Beethoven sonatas, the C. P. E. Bach sonatas, and the J. S. Bach Chromatic Fantasy and Fugue, he employed the procedure, now standard, of consulting autographs and first editions in order to arrive at the best possible reading. Whenever they were available, he also studied compositional sketches and copies revised by the composer.

Autograph study played an especially important role both in Schenker's editions and in his analyses. He regarded the autograph not only as an authoritative source (in conjunction with the first edition) for making decisions about the externals of the music (notes, slurs, etc.), but also as an indicator of more elusive properties—for example, rubato, dynamics, and phrasing. As is the case with other aspects of his work, Schenker's contributions to the field of autograph study have not been widely acknowledged by the profession. Fortunately, Schenker (never one to conceal his accomplishments) took the precaution of securing credit for himself by means of a single sentence in *Der freie Satz* (p. 33) where he claims the honor of being "the founder of the science of autograph study."

However, it is in the application of his theory of musical structure to the analysis of a wide variety and large number of compositions by means of unique procedures that Schenker is most outstanding.[9] The most important and definitive segment of Schenker's analytic work is contained in the "Anhang" to *Der freie Satz,* a collection of 550 illustrations drawn from the literature of tonal music. These include examples of details as well as analytic sketches of complete movements from extended works. Here the representational devices developed by Schenker reach a degree of refinement which renders lengthy verbal explanation unnecessary.[10] Since these sketches use the symbols of standard musical notation, augmented by arrows, brackets, dotted lines, etc., much of the information they present is readily accessible to the musician, although he may not read German, provided he has had some instruction in interpreting the signs with relation to Schenker's thought. Further on I shall provide a commentary upon an analytic sketch, which is designed to introduce the reader to Schenker's notational devices as well as to his ideas of musical structure. First, however, I would like to complete this brief survey of Schenker's life work by mentioning two projects which interested him considerably, but which he did not live to complete. One of these was an instruction book on form, apparently intended to supplement the final chapter of *Der freie Satz,* where the subject is given only a cursory treatment. The second was a book on interpretation ("Die Kunst des Vortrags"). However, this did reach a certain state of completion and I understand it is to be published in Germany under the editorship of Oswald Jonas.

I can think of no more satisfactory way to introduce Schenker's

ideas, along with the terminology and visual means which express
them, than to comment at some length upon one of his analytic
sketches. For this purpose I have selected from *Der freie Satz* a
sketch of a complete short work, the second song from Schumann's
Dichterliebe (ex. 1.1). I shall undertake to read and interpret this
sketch, using, of course, English equivalents for Schenker's terms.[11]

Here in visual form is Schenker's conception of musical structure:
the total work is regarded as an interacting composite of three main
levels. Each of these structural levels is represented on a separate
staff in order that its unique content may be clearly shown. And to
show how the three levels interact, Schenker has aligned corresponding elements vertically. I shall first make a quick survey of this
analytic sketch and then give a more detailed explanation.

The lowest staff contains the major surface events, those elements
that are usually most immediately perceptible. Accordingly, Schenker
has designated this level as the *foreground*. In deriving his foreground
sketch from the fully notated song, Schenker has not included all its
actual note values. Those which he does include represent in some
cases the actual durational values of the work; but more often they
represent the relative structural weight which he has assigned to the
particular tone or configuration. This sketch omits repeated tones
and shows inner voices in mm. 8–12 only, indicating that there they
have greater influence upon the voice-leading.

On the middle staff Schenker has represented the structural events
which lie immediately beyond the foreground level. These events,
which do not necessarily occur in immediate succession in relation to
the foreground, comprise the *middleground*. It should be evident
now that the analytic procedure is one of reduction; details which
are subordinate with respect to larger patterns are gradually eliminated—in accordance with criteria which I will explain further on.

Finally, on the upper staff, he has represented the fundamental
structural level, or *background*, which controls the entire work.

Now let us consider the content of each level in some detail. This
will provide an opportunity to examine other important aspects of
Schenker's thought, all derived from his central concept.

A series of sketches such as this can be read in several directions.
For the purpose of the present introductory explanation it would
seem advantageous to begin with the level which contains the fewest
elements and proceed from there to the level which contains the
most—thus, reading from top to bottom or from background to fore-

Example 1.1

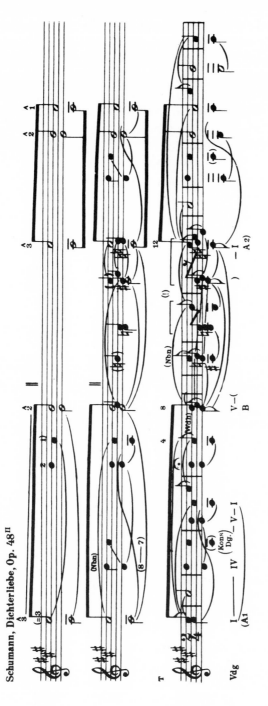

Figure 22a from the "Anhang" to *Der freie Satz*. Reprinted with permission of Universal Edition, Vienna.

ground. By reading the sketches in this order we also gain a clear idea of Schenker's concept of *prolongation:* each subsequent level expands, or *prolongs*, the content of the previous level.

The background of this short song, and of all tonal works, whatever their length, is regarded as a temporal projection of the tonic triad. The upper voice projects the triad in the form of a descending linear succession which, in the present case, spans the lower triadic third. Schenker marks this succession, which he called the *Urlinie*, or fundamental line, in two ways: (1) with numerals (and carets) that designate the corresponding diatonic scale degrees, and (2) with the balken which connects the stemmed open notes (I shall explain the black noteheads shortly). The triad is also projected by the bass, which here outlines the triadic fifth, the tonality-defining interval. Schenker calls this fundamental bass motion *Bassbrechung*, or bass arpeggiation. Like the fundamental line, it is represented in open noteheads. The fundamental line and the bass arpeggiation coordinate, forming a contrapuntal structure, the *Ursatz*, or fundamental structure, which constitutes a complete projection of the tonic triad.[12] Thus, to Schenker, motion within tonal space is measured by the triad, not by the diatonic scale.

Observe that in this case the most direct form of the fundamental structure would be the three-interval succession in the outer voices:

fundamental line, $\hat{3}$–$\hat{2}$–$\hat{1}$

bass arpeggiation, I–V–I

The background sketch shows that this succession occurs consecutively only in the last part of the song. The song begins unambiguously with $\hat{3} \atop I$; however, it does not progress immediately to $\hat{2} \atop V$ and from there on to $\hat{1} \atop I$; instead, the first interval is *prolonged* as shown in the sketch: the upper voice C-sharp first receives an embellishment, or diminution, in the form of the third-spanning motion, C-sharp–B–A (represented in black noteheads), and then moves over a larger span (shown by the beam) to B on the last eighth note of m. 8, where it is supported by the bass V. (This V is not to be equated with the final V (m. 5), which effects a closure of the fundamental line.) Schenker then shows how this initial prolongation is followed by a restatement of $\hat{3} \atop I$ and the completion of the succession $\hat{3}$–$\hat{2}$–$\hat{1} \atop I$–V–I.

To recapitulate, there are two prolongational classes shown in this background sketch. The first includes diminutions, or prolongational tones of shorter span (represented by black noteheads); the second includes the larger prolongational motion from $\hat{3}$ to $\hat{2}$ (connected by the beam), which comprises the controlling melodic pattern of the first phrase. Schenker regards this larger prolongational motion as an *interruption* of the direct succession, $\frac{\hat{3}-\hat{2}-\hat{1}}{I-V-I}$, and represents it by placing parallel vertical lines above the staff following $\frac{\hat{3}-\hat{2}}{I-V}$. The fundamental structure, which is in this case the uninterrupted succession $\frac{\hat{3}-\hat{2}-\hat{1}}{I-V-I}$, therefore may be considered as the essential content of the background.[13] In reading Schenker's analytic sketches a distinction must often be drawn between the background level in toto, which sometimes includes prolongations of primary order as in the present case, and the essential content of that level, the fundamental structure. Thus *fundamental structure* designates a specific contrapuntal organization which assumes several possible forms, whereas *background* is a term which may include other events in addition to the fundamental structure, as in the present instance, where it includes two prolongations, each belonging to a different structural order. This distinction, not always clearly drawn by Schenker, is indispensable to the full understanding of his sketches and commentaries. In this connection I point out that within each of the three main structural levels several sublevels are possible, depending upon the unique characteristics of the particular composition.[14]

The idea of the interrupted fundamental line provides the basis for Schenker's concept of form. For example, in the typical sonata-allegro form in the major mode, interruption of the fundamental linear progression at the close of the exposition normally gives rise in the development section to a prolongation which centers on V. Of course, the prolonged fundamental line component varies, depending upon which form of the fundamental structure is in operation and upon which specific prolongation motions occur at the background level.

Before explaining the middleground, I should like to direct attention again to the diminution which spans the third below C-sharp (black noteheads). By means of the numerals 3, 2, 1, enclosed in parentheses, Schenker indicates that the motion duplicates the large descending third of the fundamental line. This is an instance of a special kind of repetition which Schenker called *Uebertragung der Ursatzformen* (transference of the forms of the fundamental structure). Throughout his writings he demonstrates again and again that tonal compositions abound in hidden repetitions of this kind, which he distinguishes from more obvious motivic repetitions at the foreground level.

We can interpret the content of the middleground most efficiently by relating it to the background just examined. The first new structural event shown at the middleground level is the expansion of the smaller prolongational third (black noteheads) by means of the upper adjacent tone[15] D, which serves as a prefix. The sketch shows how this prolongational element is counterpointed by the bass in such a way as to modify the original (i.e., background) third. That is, the figured-bass numerals in parentheses indicate that the second C-sharp (black notehead) is a dissonant passing tone and therefore is not to be equated with the initial C-sharp, which serves as the point of departure for the fundamental line. The adjacent tone D recurs in m. 14, where Schenker assigns more structural weight to it, as indicated by the stem. I reiterate that conventional durational values are used in the analytic sketches to indicate the relative position of a given component or configuration in the tonal hierarchy—the greater the durational value, the closer the element to the background.

In addition to the prolongation described in the preceding paragraph, the middleground contains the essentials of the prolongational middle section (mm. 10–12), which appears in more detail in the foreground sketch. Schenker regards this entire middle section as a prolongation of the background fifth formed by $\frac{\hat{2}}{V}$. Its main feature is the inner voice which descends from G-sharp to E, a middleground duplication of the fundamental line's third. The bass which counterpoints this inner voice arpeggiates the tonic triad, E–C-sharp–A. Schenker shows how the arpeggiation is partially filled in by the passing tone, D, and by slurring E to A he indicates that he considers that motion to be the controlling bass motion, within which the C-sharp functions as a connective of primarily melodic significance.[16] Here we have an example of the careful distinction which Schenker always draws between major bass components, or *Stufen*, which belong to the background level, and more transient, contrapuntal-melodic events at the foreground and middleground levels.

A brief consideration of three additional events will complete our examination of the middleground level. First, observe that the diatonic inner-voice descent in the middle section, G-sharp–E, is filled in by a chromatic passing tone, G. Schenker has enclosed this in parentheses to indicate that it belongs to a subsidiary level within the middleground. Second, observe that just before the inner-voice motion is completed on the downbeat of m. 12, the G-sharp, its point of departure, is restated by an additional voice which is introduced above it. Schenker has pointed out that in "free" compositions, particularly instrumental works, the possibility of more elaborate prolongation is greatly increased by introducing additional voices, as well as by abandoning voices already stated. The final event to observe here occurs in the middle section: the motion from B, the retained upper voice, to C-sharp on the downbeat of m. 12. This direct connection does not actually occur at the foreground level, but Schenker, feeling that it is strongly implied by the voice-leading context, encloses the implied C-sharp in parentheses and ties it to the actual C-sharp, thereby indicating that it is an anticipation.

In the foreground sketch Schenker represents for the first time the metrical organization of the song. As I have already mentioned, he shows there some of the actual durational values, in addition to using these as sketch symbols. This reveals the position assigned to meter and rhythm in his system: he considered them to be important structural determinants at the middleground and foreground levels but subsidiary to the fundamental tonal organization, which, he maintained, was arhythmic. I shall return to this further on when I consider the general problem of constructing a theory of rhythm for tonal music.

Let us now examine some of the relationships which Schenker has shown in his sketch of the foreground, this time beginning with the bass. In m. 3 he encloses the bass note A in parentheses and marks it with the abbreviation Kons. Dg. (*Konsonanter Durchgang*, or "consonant passing tone"). By this he indicates that the tenth which the bass A forms with the upper-voice C-sharp transforms the latter, a dissonant passing tone at the middleground level, into a consonance at the foreground level. In this way he also intends to indicate the function of the chord at that point. Since it supports a passing tone in the upper voice it is a passing chord. In addition, it belongs only to the foreground and therefore is to be distinguished from the initial tonic chord, a background element. Two of Schenker's most important convictions underlie this treatment of detail: (1) that the study of strict counterpoint provides the indispensable basis for a thorough understanding of the details, as well as the larger patterns of a composed work, and (2) that the function of a chord depends upon its context, not upon its label. This can be seen in his notation of the chords in this sketch. Although he uses the conventional roman numerals, he provides them with slurs, dashes, and parentheses to show their relative values in the tonal hierarchy. Thus, the long slur from I to I indicates that the IV and V chords lie within the control of that chord, while the abbreviation Vdg. *(Vordergrund)* shows that the succession belongs to the foreground. And in the middle section, mm. 8–12, the parentheses show that the chords between V and I are subsidiary chords. These arise as part of the prolongational complex at that point and stand in contrast to the stable background chords I and V.

Now let us turn to the melody. We can most efficiently examine its structure by first comparing each foreground prolongation (slurred) with the larger middleground prolongation immediately above it, and then by relating both the foreground and middleground to the background. In this way we see that the foreground prolongation of the first section spans a descending third twice, thus duplicating the successively larger thirds at the middleground and background levels. In the middle section the melody undergoes more elaborate development. There, by means of connecting beams, Schenker shows how the upper voice skips down to the inner voice and back again. The ascending skips comprise a sequence of two fourths, which are marked by brackets and emphasized by a typically Schenkerian exclamation point. This sequence lends support to his reading of the implied anticipation of C-sharp in the upper voice of m. 12, mentioned earlier.

The foreground of the middle section provides a good example of Schenker's concept of "melody" (he avoided the term in his writings) as a self-contained polyphonic structure. This valuable aspect of his theory[17] —an aspect absolutely indispensable to any kind of intelligent melodic analyses—is well substantiated by compositional practice. There are many passages in the literature where polyphonic melodies, implied at one point (often the beginning), are subsequently realized in full, for example in the first movement of Mozart's Sonata in A Minor, or in Brahms's Intermezzo in B-flat Major op. 76 no. 4; and, of course, we find a special development of this concept in Bach's compositions for solo violin and for solo cello.[18] Here, in the foreground sketch of the middle section, the diagonal beams show that the vocal melody shifts back and forth between two lines, the lower of which belongs to the accompaniment. It is evident that this section contains the most intricate upper-voice prolongation.

It also contains the most elaborate bass motion. The sketch shows how the bass provides counterpoint to the upper-voice (foreground) prolongation of B, bass and upper voice comprising the interval succession 5–10–5–10–5, which is enclosed within the middleground outer-voice succession, $\frac{\text{B–C-sharp}}{\text{E–C-sharp}}$. Observe that the upper voice alternates between an upper adjacent-tone prolongation of B (marked Nbn.) and the skips into the inner voice which were explained in the preceding paragraph. The lowest voice in this passage is subordinate to the voice which lies immediately above it, E–D–C-sharp, the latter succession being the actual bass line (cf. middleground sketch). Nor does its registral position above the foreground bass lessen its importance as the main motion-determinant in the lower voices. Therefore, the foreground bass which displaces or covers it registrally might be termed a "pseudo-bass."[19]

One final aspect of the foreground sketch deserves mention: the form. Schenker indicates this with the customary letters and exponents. The foreground form therefore corresponds to the form-generating interruption at the middleground and background levels as follows:

Statement	Interruption	Restatement and Closure
A^1	B	A^2

It should be apparent that an analysis of this kind embraces all the information generally included under the heading "form and analysis" but that it goes far beyond to interpret the relationships to the background which are revealed during its initial phases, where the main concern is to achieve an accurate reading of foreground and middleground.

A summary of this analysis should properly include a classification of the chromatic chords in the middle section of the piece and a more precise explanation of the coordination of linear intervals at the foreground level, the descending thirds and fifths (which latter take the form of diminished fifths and ascending fourths in the middle section). However, because of space limitations, I shall not undertake a summary here but instead shall go on to discuss other aspects of Schenker's work. If the preceding commentary has succeeded in demonstrating some of Schenker's more important ideas, as well as clarifying some of the vocabulary and visual devices which he employs to express those ideas, it has fulfilled its purpose.

I turn now to the development of Schenker's theory and to its sources in musical practice. The concept of structural levels, which, as I have pointed out, is central to Schenker's theory, was first set forth in the analyses published in *Der Tonwille* (1921–24). However, the idea of the background and its essential content, the fundamental structure, did not emerge clearly until many years later; not until the publication of *Der freie Satz* (1935) was it definitively stated. Schenker was very much aware, in retrospect, of the development of Ursatz concept and the representational means which he so closely associated with it. Thus, in the introduction to *Der freie Satz* he remarks (with characteristic pride): "Since the task of being the first to discover the background world in music devolved upon me I was not spared the difficulty of finding symbols which would represent it, a task which required many years. Furthermore, the engravers did not always display the requisite degree of understanding. For these reasons the illustrations in, for example, the issues of *Der Tonwille* and in the Jahrbücher[20] have not always revealed the final structure."

Although Schenker explained his relationship to theorists of the past in considerable detail (his *Kontrapunkt* for example includes quotations from Fux, Albrechtsberger, Bellermann, Cherubini), he did not spell out the basis in musical practice of his main tool, the reduction technique, with which he revealed and articulated tonal organization. Possibly he was unaware that it required explanation or justification. However this may be, subsequent misunderstanding of his work, allegations of arbitrariness, and failure to recognize his direct link with the traditions of music suggest that an explanation is in order. In brief, the analytic technique of reduction derives from the compositional technique of variation, as it developed during the tonal period.[21] At the risk of oversimplifying, I point out that reduction is approximately the reverse of variation. By means of variation techniques a basic structure becomes more elaborate, in terms of increasing number and variety of melodic-rhythmic events. Reduction accomplishes the reverse; detail is gradually eliminated in accord with the traditional distinction between dissonant and consonant tones (made with reference to the tonic triad, the elemental consonance) so that the underlying, controlling structure is revealed.[22] Although Schenker amplified and refined this procedure, it is far from being his innovation. Reductions of a rudimentary kind are to be found in, for example, many of the sixteenth-century textbooks on diminution, in the seventeenth-century writings of Bernhard, and in the eighteenth-century tome on figured-bass by Heinichen (see note 18). The latter author makes extensive use of reductions to explain the process of Verwechslung (prolongation, in Schenker's terms) as well as to analyze certain passages purported to be "incorrect" by colleagues. All of these treatises lend strong support to Schenker's musical thought and, on the negative side, demonstrate the extent to which nineteenth-century theorists obscured the relationship between theory and practice so firmly established at the close of the eighteenth century.

In Schenker's early analyses, the reduction technique served to reveal only the sublevels within the foreground and to a certain extent the middleground. Thus, the Urlinie of 1921 is not the Urlinie of *Der freie Satz*. The latter is a single linear progression which spans the whole work under specific contrapuntal conditions. The Urlinie of 1921 corresponds more closely to what Schenker ultimately would designate a *Zug* (linear progression) at the middleground level. Thus, with the development and refinement of the concept of structural levels, Schenker, probing ever more deeply into musical structure, went beyond mere reduction and description; he began to interpret the reduction with reference to a unique conception of structural coherence, a bold and imaginative formulation of the organizing forces of triadic tonality. While doing this, he greatly enlarged the traditional notions of harmony and counterpoint and at the same time made them far more specific. These are embodied in the Ursatz, where the fundamental line represents the contrapuntal-melodic dimension and the bass arpeggiation represents the harmonic.

Critics of Schenker seem to fall into two general categories: in the first are those who reject his attitude toward music and music study, and in the second are those who reject either part or all of his theoretical system.[23] Of the latter group of critics, by far the largest number question the validity of the Ursatz, the fundamental structure.[24]

The fundamental structure can be justified on perceptual grounds. Relevant to this, Furtwängler has called Schenker's great accomplishment the discovery of *Fernhören* (literally, "distance-hearing"). And the fundamental structure can be justified on historical grounds. I have already explained its direct connection with traditional practices in composition and performance. But it is also, and perhaps most importantly, justifiable on methodological grounds. By this I mean that if, in analysis, the fundamental structure is regarded as a generalized characteristic of the composed music of triadic tonality, if it is regarded as a structural norm, as a construct which is always subject to modification when the structural events of a particular work do not support it, then surely a number of objections disappear. Understood in this way, the fundamental structure is one norm—at a high level of abstraction—among a number of others (such as root progression by fifths, sonata-allegro form, stepwise resolution of dissonance) which are now widely utilized, generally without question. It should be remarked here that some of Schenker's critics are not always explicit as to whether they reject only *his* structural norms or structural norms altogether. This makes communication difficult, if not impossible.

Although Schenker came very close to constructing a complete system, further refinement and amplification are required if it is to fulfill its promise. Superficial criticism is particularly damaging to efforts along this line. Specific deficiencies are only obscured when it is alleged that faults in Schenker's theory can be traced to his rigidity and arbitrariness. These characteristics, which are by no means typical, are symptomatic rather than causal. The important deficiencies in his system arise from his failure to define with sufficient rigor the conditions under which particular structural events occur. An instance of this, in my opinion, is the upper-voice event which Schenker called *Anstieg*, an initial stepwise, usually ascending "space-opening" motion to the first tone of the fundamental line. Schenker, in failing to describe fully the conditions under which this event occurs, opened the way for inaccurate readings, even of entire works. Its nature becomes clear when the following factors are taken into consideration: (1) the triadic tone which is the goal of motion; (2) the nature of the bass and inner voices (chords) which support the upper voice; (3) the duration of the motion (with respect to tempo, note values);[25] (4) when $\hat{5}$ is the final tone, the mode. The coherent completion of the space-opening prefix depends upon a motion tendency usually taught in elementary strict counterpoint: the tendency for a given melodic tone to progress upward or downward to the diatonic tone adjacent to it at the distance of a semitone, provided that the setting (bass and chord) affords proper support, and, of course, in consideration of the functional relationship between tonic and dominant degrees, which may modify this tendency. In amplification, there follows a brief account of the conditions necessary for space-opening motions to 3̂ and to 5̂.

Example 1.2 presents models of unprolonged space-opening motions to 3̂. In both modes the bass and chords which support the ascending motion are I–V–I. Observe the horizontal interval succession in the upper voice of example 1.2a (major mode); two whole steps. In the absence of semitones, the passing tone A thus serves to connect G and B without tending strongly toward either one (except insofar as a slight preference is given to the tonic G, the point of melodic closure). But in the minor mode (ex. 1.2b), we encounter a different situation. There the horizontal interval succession contains a semitone between the passing tone A and 3̂. This semitone connection therefore tends to make the ascent to 3̂ stronger, more coherent in the minor mode.

Example 1.2

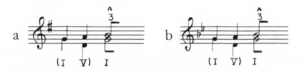

The space-opening motion to 5̂ entails more problems. In place of the second degree, the fourth degree serves as the connective to the final tone. In the minor mode (ex. 1.3b) this degree stands at the distance of a whole tone from both the third and fifth degrees. Thus, there is no obstacle to a strong ascending connection from 4 to 5̂, provided, of course, proper support is given by bass and chords, such as is shown in the model. However, in the major mode (ex. 1.3a) the fourth degree stands at the distance of a semitone from the third scale degree and thus tends to relate downward to that tone, rather than upward to 5̂. A space-opening motion to 5̂ therefore requires that the fourth degree be chromatically raised to create the necessary semitone connection between 4 and 5̂. This chromatic inflection is

Example 1.3

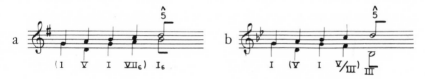

usually supported by a secondary dominant chord, so that the ver-
tical situation at the conclusion of the motion is $\frac{\hat{5}}{V}$ (ex. 1.4). You may
ask how one accounts for a motion of this kind in the major mode—
one that ascends to the fifth degree but does not include the raised
fourth degree. Example 1.5 provides the answer: the motion is then
read as a space-opening to $\hat{3}$, followed by a prolongational motion
within the third above $\hat{3}$.

It appears that Schenker was somewhat aware of the problem of
the space-opening motion to $\hat{5}$ in the major mode, for in *Der freie*

Example 1.4

$$I \quad (V_6 \quad I \quad V^3\!/_V) \quad V$$

Example 1.5

$$I$$

Satz he makes the following comment: "The space-opening motion
to $\hat{5}$ is particularly well-suited to the employment of the raised
fourth degree. By this means the $\hat{5}$ achieves a special effectiveness,
especially when the chromatic alteration in the foreground results in
a modulation[26] to the key of the dominant." However, he did not
realize that the alteration constitutes a necessary condition for the
motion. This particular deficiency in Schenker's work may serve to
explain an instance of an incorrect and somewhat arbitrary reading,
his analysis of the well known Air in B-flat by Handel, which first
appeared in *Der Tonwille* in 1924 and was subsequently included in
abbreviated form in *Der freie Satz,* where it is used to illustrate both
a special foreground melodic technique (unfolding) and also uninterrupted, or one-part, form. Example 1.6 presents the minimal sketch
which Schenker used in *Der freie Satz* (fig. 103, 6). In example 1.7
I have constructed a different sketch of the same work, which, on
the basis of the conditions set forth above for the space-opening
motion to $\hat{5}$ in the major mode, is a more accurate representation of

its structure. A brief comparison follows. In example 1.6 (Schenker's sketch) the first tone of the fundamental line is $\hat{5}$; in example 1.7 it is $\hat{3}$. His misreading is to be attributed to his failure to recognize that the motion to $\hat{5}$, lacking the raised fourth degree, is not conclusive. But, having decided that the fundamental line operates within the space of a fifth, he then forces his reading to conform. He locates the descending passing tone $\hat{4}$, which is required to close the fundamental line, on the third beat of m. 6, and thus shows an uninterrupted descent: $\hat{5}$–$\hat{1}$. Compare example 1.6 with example 1.7. The latter shows a space-opening motion to $\hat{3}$, not to $\hat{5}$. The triadic fifth degree is represented directly above the main melodic tone $\hat{3}$ and is enclosed in brackets to show that it belongs, conceptually, in the register an octave lower. After the double bar, C undergoes a diminution, which spans the third, C–E-flat. This E-flat (m. 6) serves as an upper adjacent tone to the restated $\hat{3}$ which follows. According to Schenker, the E-flat in question is the passing tone $\hat{4}$ in the descending fundamental line, clearly an erroneous reading, since it is exclusively an adjacent tone in the foreground. Whatever passing-tone implications it may have are so weak as to be inconsequential. Therefore, on the basis of this reading, the form of the piece is two part ($\hat{3}$–$\hat{2}$ $\hat{3}$–$\hat{2}$–$\hat{1}$), not one part as Schenker maintained.

Example 1.6

Example 1.7

It is to be hoped that, as Schenker's work becomes more widely recognized, serious music theorists will make further applications of his ideas.[27] With the view to indicating the direction such applications might take, I should like to devote the following paragraphs to a discussion of five unsolved problems in music theory, indicating in each case how Schenker's ideas could contribute toward a solution. Four of these deal with music written prior to 1910,[28] and a single but very important general problem involves music written after that year. Here, then, are the five problems:

1. Constructing a theory of rhythm for tonal music

Hardly any aspect of tonal music is more obscure than that of rhythm. To be sure, we have a number of studies on the subject, but for the most part they are lengthy descriptions of obvious surface events, taking prosodic practices or exotic music as points of departure, or they are metaphysical treatments which have little significance to the theorist whose proper concern is with the structural role of that which we ordinarily designate as "rhythmic," those relationships which determine the temporal ordering of compositions. (There is, of course, a certain amount of verbal self-deception involved in the separation of rhythmic from tonal events.)

Schenker's work in the theory of rhythm was fragmentary and oftentimes obscure; yet the basis of his thought, particularly as expressed in *Der freie Satz*, is clear: the concept of structural levels. Consider, for example, these unique and provocative statements:

> In the fundamental structure, rhythm exists no more than it does in a cantus firmus exercise.

> Only when linear progressions arise within prolongations in the upper and lower voices of the middleground does it become necessary to counterpoint the voices against each other in a rhythmic ordering. All rhythm in music comes from counterpoint, only from counterpoint.

> In the middleground every individual sublevel has a unique rhythm which is in accord with its contrapuntal content. Thus rhythm progresses through various prolongational stages until it reaches the foreground, just as do meter and form, which also represent consequences of a progressive contrapuntal differentiation.[29]

Schenker's highly significant observations suggest the following questions, which might well serve as points of departure for extended studies in rhythm: (1) At what structural level do rhythmic events begin to determine the tonal structure of a given work? (2) What is the nature of the relationship between the constituent rhythmic levels in a given work? Clearly, the analytic techniques developed by Schenker would be indispensable to the answering of these questions. And his structural concepts would be invaluable, if, as one might reasonably expect, such investigations were to lead to the formulation of a general theory of rhythm in tonal music.

2. Determining the sources and development of triadic tonality

A technical history of triadic tonality has yet to be written.[30] When it is, it will have to demonstrate historical continuity in other than poetic terms. Again, here, the concept of structural levels is invaluable. If, for example, it can be shown that underlying structural levels in works from various periods carry similar tonal events, and that these have undergone an orderly transformation, a major step will have been taken toward the establishment of the convincing historical picture which is now so clearly lacking.[31]

Within this large problem are smaller ones. For example, the development of chromaticism has not yet been traced in any detail. The facile generalizations which have circulated for years in the musicological literature and the statistical studies of chromaticism which are based upon very rudimentary concepts of musical structure offer little of value to serious music theorists.

Schenker, particularly in his Jahrbücher and in *Der freie Satz*, laid the groundwork for fruitful studies in chromaticism. Indeed, his fundamental principles have already been accepted—but not acknowledged—by all but the most atavistic circles. Thus, it is now generally recognized that the meaning of a particular chord is dependent upon its function in a particular context. But it has not yet been widely recognized that Schenker long ago specified the functions of various contexts. Even with regard to diatonic chords, Schenker early in his career recognized the necessity for clearly differentiating harmonic from contrapuntal functions. In his counterpoint book (1911) he drew the following sharp analogy to those theorists who are unable to make this distinction:

> We are all familiar with the way a child carries on with its doll. Now the doll is this or that friend, now an aunt—in short, everything that the child needs for its play is represented by the doll. The child speaks to the doll and receives an answer (one, of course, provided by itself). The theorists who write "harmony textbooks" carry on in the same way with their "tone-dolls." Here the doll represents this or that "degree progression," now only a suspension, here a "harmonic degree," there this or that

voice-leading, in short, to everything that they demand, and in whatever condition they demand that it be, their tone-dolls answer, yes![32]

3. Gaining information about compositional technique

As long as the only determinants of compositional choice are thought to derive from the composer's desire to achieve a balance between "unity" and "variety" or some other similarly profound impulse, very little information about his technique can be gained. As a result the serious student is often led to believe that the composer's technical grasp of music is either quite ineffable or is "obvious," even "mechanistic," and he remains unaware of that which can be gained from a deeper study of compositional problems. The composer stands to benefit from information about compositional determinants not so much by making direct applications to his own work as by coming to understand how underlying structural forces shape compositions, what it means for a work to begin to establish its own terms, its own conditions. To the non-composer such knowledge is also advantageous. He becomes more aware of the unique characteristics of the work, he comprehends the reasons for deviations from an established pattern, unusual rhythmic occurrences, and so forth.

Unfortunately, Schenker's views regarding compositional technique often have been misunderstood. Because he writes freely about compositional choice, occasionally drawing inferences with respect to the way in which ideas develop, he sometimes offends those who for one reason or another deal with the problem of compositional choice only at the most trivial level. But although he did not hesitate to set forth requirements for a good composition, he did not presume to tell anyone how to go about composing. And despite the implication of its title, *Der freie Satz* ("free composition") is an instructional book not on composition but on analysis. Let there be no doubt on this point, Schenker was outspokenly against any efforts to use the concept of fundamental structure for the purpose of composing music. To him, music study, represented at the highest level by analysis, makes an essential contribution to composition, but the latter activity lies only in the province of the gifted and is essentially unteachable.

Schenker approached compositional problems mainly through the principles of strict counterpoint, in the conviction that these under-

lay the intricate works of the major composers. This belief was supported by his knowledge of the training received by Haydn, Mozart,
Beethoven, and others. Nowhere is this fundamental aspect of Schenker's thought more apparent than in the first and third sections of
Der freie Satz, which comprise a condensed reinterpretation of principles formulated years earlier in *Kontrapunkt.*

With the aid of this methodologically valuable norm, Schenker was
able to investigate many aspects of compositional technique which
otherwise would have remained inaccessible. Again and again he
demonstrated that foreground detail, with its multiple meanings,
could be understood only in relation to the middleground and background, which provide definition in accord with the principles of
strict counterpoint. As a study technique he occasionally considered
alternate solutions in order to reveal compositional determinants
more clearly. To illustrate this, I shall undertake to explain the
structural factors which determined Schumann's choice of the secondary dominant (A^7) chord in mm. 12–13 of his song analyzed
earlier (ex. 1.1). (To avoid misunderstanding, I point out that this
discussion is not directly related to Schenker's sketch.) In view of the
strong tendency of the preceding C-sharp-major chord to progress to
an F-sharp-minor (VI) chord, the A^7 chord seems abrupt, has the
effect of a discontinuous element, and therefore requires special
explanation. True, it leads to the upper voice adjacent tone, D, an
essential foreground element which, in accord with the rhythmic
pattern already established as well as with the consistent association
of the adjacent-tone motive (D–C-sharp) with the verbs in the poem,
must occur on the downbeat of m. 13. But, as shown in example 1.8,
the alternate solution, this tone could also be reached without the
aid of the A^7 chord. This indicates that the upper voice did not determine the choice of the A^7. When the alternate solution (ex. 1.8) is
considered, the more important function, hence the raison d'être of
the A^7 becomes clear. This alternate passage omits the A^7 but retains

Example 1.8

the essential features of its immediate context: the preceding C-sharp chord and the upper-voice D which follows it. The alternate begins by fulfilling the tendency of the C-sharp chord to resolve to F-sharp minor. From there it moves through an E chord back to $\frac{\hat{3}}{1}$ in m. 14.

What features of the original passage are most noticeably missing from the alternate? First, it is apparent that the upper-voice D on m. 14 lacks the support of the IV chord, which was impossible to reach logically beginning from the VI. But the most striking omission in the alternate version is the chromatically descending inner voice, which, in the original version, begins with the G-sharp carried by the C-sharp chord, moves through A to G-natural in the A^7 chord, descends to F-sharp–F over IV, and finally moves through E to D–C-sharp over V^7–I. Observe that this striking inner-voice line concludes in m. 15 with a statement of the characteristic upper adjacent-tone motive.[33] We can therefore infer that Schumann selected the A^7 chord in question not only because of its secondary-dominant relation to the IV at m. 14, but primarily because the A^7 chord carries G-natural, an essential component in the long descending line just described. Using Schenker's concept of structural levels as a criterion we can therefore say that the contrapuntal-melodic reason for the A^7 chord is more important here than the harmonic (fifths relationship) reason. Obviously, expression of the secondary-dominant relationship does not require the presence of the seventh, G; but by "more important" I mean here that G is a component in a configuration which belongs to a higher structural level than does the secondary-dominant relationship.[34] In amplification of this, example 1.9 shows how the inner-voice component A is stated at the beginning of the song, prolonged by the lower adjacent 7 tone, G-sharp, in the middle section, then in m. 12 begins the descent to C-sharp. In Schenker's terms, this linear progression is the composing-out of an interval,

Example 1.9

not a random interval, but in this case the composing-out of the sixth, A–C-sharp, the inversion of the triadic third which controls the upper-voice motion of the entire song. This third, stated vertically at the very outset of the piece, is also expressed in the bass succession

III–I, a means of associating the outer voices at all levels.

In attempting to ascertain the major compositional determinant in this instance, I do not disregard the influence of the form of the poem and its internal associations. Doubtless Schumann wanted to set the words *und vor deinem*, which begin the last section, with the same C-sharp used at the beginning with the words *aus meinem*. Also I do not overlook the fact that the chromatic descent of the inner voice in the final measures repeats the inner voice and bass diminutions of the middle section, an additional means of unification.

Not only are Schenker's concepts and techniques valuable in the study of such details in completed works, but they also provide the means for interpreting compositional sketches, rough drafts, revisions, notated improvisations, and so on. For example, many of Beethoven's otherwise perplexing sketches become clear and significant when they are examined with reference to a thorough structural analysis. At present a large amount of such material awaits investigation by music theorists.

4. Improving theory instruction

We all recognize that the serious student of music today is faced with an enormous task. He is expected to know the literature and structure of the music of the past, as well as the ever increasing literature of the present with its diverse and often problematic compositional systems. In order to relieve this situation we would do well to emulate science education, where, thanks to the continual refinement of concepts, students cover traditional material more and more efficiently. In my opinion, the intelligent and serious music student could cover the basic, traditional curriculum within two years, and then go on to more advanced studies in music of all periods—provided the instructional methods and concepts used were adequate to the task. Here Schenker has much to offer. Consider, for example, the unreasonable amount of time ordinarily spent on the relationship between fugal subject and answer. But when these are regarded as thematic expressions of the tonic-dominant relationship—within a single key[35]—and when necessary adjustments in the answer are explained in terms of relationships between structural levels, the student quickly grasps the underlying principles and is able to cope intelligently with details. Instruction of this kind, extended to all aspects of traditional theory, could lead to far greater efficiency without sacrificing thorough coverage.

In more general terms, ineffective theory instruction often can be attributed to a failure to recognize the importance of nonconsecutive relations. The student's hearing is directed only to the immediate connections in the foreground, which provide an exception to every rule, and he soon comes to feel that concepts derived from his theoretical studies are incapable of explaining with any degree of precision the organization of actual compositions. Schenker has suggested that Brahms so vehemently repudiated his formal studies for this very reason. He makes clear that the significance of Brahms's collection of examples of parallel fifths and octaves[36] lies in the composer's recognition of the contradiction between a theory which dealt with immediate relationships only, often of a transient nature, and his own highly refined sense of hearing, which encompassed large spans.

5. Understanding the structure of problematic modern works

It is no secret that Schenker detested modern music. Indeed, his concern about the current state of affairs in music seems to have been an important motivation for all of his writings. At the beginning of the first volume of his *Kontrapunkt* (1910) he declaims:

> We stand before a Herculaneum and Pompeii of music; musical civilization is obstructed! The tonal material itself is destroyed, those essentials of music which were created by artists, who, working with their own resources, went far beyond the meager indications of the overtone system.[37] [My translation]

Nor did time modify his opinion. Some sixteen years later in Jahrbuch II he undertook an analysis of a passage from Stravinsky's Piano Concerto, concluding:

> My analysis gives me the right to say that Stravinsky's work, despite its slight suggestions of linear progressions, which have to do with the folk-like elements it contains, is altogether bad, inartistic, and unmusical. [My translation]

In view of these and other statements, it seems contradictory that Schenker's work should contribute significantly to the solution of certain problems in advanced contemporary music. Yet his general concept of structure, apart from his specific formulations of triadic tonal events, lends itself to modern thought regarding music.[38] For example, the idea of the "totally organized" work, now become quite fashionable, was clearly set forth by Schenker (but without reference to Webern!). He even recognized the structural role of orchestration and demonstrated this in his analyses, notably in those of the Scherzo to Beethoven's Third Symphony and the G-Minor Symphony of Mozart. Relevant to this, he writes in *Der freie Satz:*

> In the masterworks, orchestral colors are not combined according to [the composer's] mood and applied haphazardly. They are subject to the laws of the total composition.[39] [My translation]

More specifically, Schenker's theory established two basic requirements for analysis which are applicable to modern music: first, an analysis should undertake to explain the essential relationships within a composition, their genesis, ordering, interaction, and relative importance to the parts and to the whole of the work; second, as part of the analytic undertaking, there should be developed a representational means and vocabulary which are in accord with the unique characteristics of the work.[40]

But beyond these values—the point of view and the general requirements—Schenker's theory offers a specific study tool, the reduction technique, which can be used to good advantage in analyzing certain modern works.[41] The long-range goal of such analytic studies should be kept in mind. If it can be demonstrated that contemporary compositions, particularly those of the problematic 1910–25 period, reveal significant similarities at other than the surface level, and if these similarities can be interpreted in an orderly fashion, while at the same time accounting satisfactorily for differences, a beginning will have been made toward a genuine technical history of contemporary music.

Many of the works composed during this period have achieved the status of standard repertoire items, insofar as a modern work can achieve that status. And yet, by and large, even these "standard" works are little better understood now than they were at the time of their composition.[42] It has been demonstrated that Schenker-derived concepts and techniques can be used to good advantage here, provided each work is examined in its own terms. This means that, even though Schenker's concept of structural levels is used, the general content of each level cannot be predicted as it can in tonal works where we know in advance the underlying organizational principles and the function of detail.

Obviously there is a danger of reading triadic characteristics into a work which is based upon nontriadic premises. Therefore, the initial problem in the analysis of a work from the period under discussion is to discover a clue which will reveal its basic structural terms. To illustrate the application of Schenker-derived techniques toward the solution of this problem, I present here a partial analysis of Debussy's *La Cathédrale Engloutie* (1910), a work which is familiar and relatively uncomplicated, but which deviates considerably from triadic norms despite certain external triadic characteristics.

A careful examination of the first measure, in the course of which all doublings are eliminated to show the basic components in their most condensed form, yields an incomplete succession of parallel fourths above a sustained "bass" note (ex. 1.10a). The fact that the lower line in this succession is incomplete compared to the upper, suggests that it will eventually complete itself—that is, E will ascend to F-sharp, thus paralleling completely the motion of the upper voice. This provides a clue, at least, to the melodic structure. The tendency of E to ascend is strengthened with each repetition and with the placement of the succession D–E in the upper register at the end of every melodic group; yet the implied motion is not completed. At m. 6 the E achieves a certain stability, supported by the bass E and embellished by C-sharp and D-sharp. To clarify the structure of this section, the melodic tones are arranged vertically, in accord with Schenker's concept of polyphonic melody. The result is a succession of parallel fourths like that at the beginning. This succession prolongs the central tones, E and B (ex. 1.10b). Observe that, unlike the opening succession, the lower voice of the succession is complete.

At m. 13 the bass continues its descent, arriving at C. Following this, the initial parallel fourths succession is repeated (mm. 14–15), reinforced here by another parallel succession, A–B, added in the lower staff. Finally at m. 16, the melodic connection from E to F-sharp, suggested at the very outset, is completed, and as the inner voice ascends to F-sharp, the bass descends to B. Example 1.10c summarizes the first section of the piece showing how the implied motion is ultimately realized. This sketch also shows that the F-sharp is followed by G-sharp, suggesting a further ascent by whole steps, which, of course, does occur.

A comparison of the horizontal and vertical intervals tells us something about the interaction of the various structural levels as the piece unfolds. A number of symmetries appear. To illustrate, example 1.10d represents the third within which the upper voice operates, and the sixth—the inversion of the third—which is simultaneously composed-out in the bass. In contrast to the thirds, which

Example 1.10

are associated with the horizontal unfolding at the middleground level, the vertical fourths belong exclusively to the foreground. The most active element in the composition, on the basis of this incomplete analysis, is the ascending inner voice, which demands attention at the very outset. Example 1.10e shows how it slowly unfolds a whole-tone progression over the span of an octave. Thus, to use Schenker's terms, the structural content of the upper voice at the middleground level is an ascending whole-tone scale.

There are diverse elements at the foreground and middleground levels further on in the piece which require explanation before the background can be discussed intelligently. I shall not take time for that here, in the hope that the partial analysis already given has served its purpose: the demonstration of Schenker-derived concepts and techniques applied to problematic modern music.

It would be foolish to assert that Schenker's concepts and techniques can be applied with equal effectiveness to all music. For example, the reduction technique is not suitable for the analysis of 12-tone music, nor is it required there in order to explain structure. The 12-tone system has its own history, its own terminology and analytic technique.[43] Certainly, as music continues to be composed, performed, and studied, music theory is responsible for developing new concepts and new analytic procedures which will contribute toward the understanding of that music. But at the same time, we should recognize that the possibilities for applying Schenker's technique have by no means been exhausted.

There are those who feel that Schenker's concepts are of questionable validity because they do not apply to all music. The implications of such an unreasonable criterion are disturbing, since a general theory which would apply to music in the many periods even of occidental history, each with its own structural principles and extensive literature, would very likely be of such a rudimentary and primitive nature as to be—for all practical purposes—valueless. (It may well be that a theory of this kind is already implicit in the musicological literature of the past quarter-century.)

In many respects Schenker's work provides us with a model of what the work of the music theorist should be—one searches in vain for a comparable effort. And yet Schenker did not regard himself as a theorist or as a musicologist, but rather as an artist. He has indeed the artist's traits of courage and perseverance combined with intellect and insight (which we also associate with the true scientist), traits which set him apart from the bigoted pedant who, all too often in Schenker's day, bore the name of music theorist. It is to be hoped that, as his ideas are more widely understood and applied, the image of Schenker as a visionary will be replaced by one of a unique, original, and highly gifted person. For the conceptual framework which he expounded, as well as for the vast amount of information about specific musical structures which he provided, he deserves recognition by all intelligent musicians.

NOTES

1. Wilhelm Furtwängler, *Ton und Wort* (Wiesbaden: Brockhaus, 1954). My translation.

2. Bruno Walter, *Theme and Variations* (New York: Alfred Knopf, 1946).

3. Only his *Harmonielehre* (1906) has been made available in English: *Harmony*, ed. Oswald Jonas, trans. Elizabeth Mann Borgese (Chicago: University of Chicago Press, 1954).

4. An exception to this is Milton Babbitt's excellent condensed survey of Schenker's work included as part of a review of Felix Salzer's *Structural Hearing* in the *Journal of the American Musicological Society* 5:260–65. The best extended introduction to Schenker's theory is in German: Oswald Jonas, *Das Wesen des musikalischen Kunstwerks* (Vienna: Saturn-Verlag, 1934).

5. To the best of my knowledge the most recent extended critique of Schenker in article form is Michael Mann's "Schenker's Contribution to Music Theory," *Music Review* 10:3–26.

6. A certain amount of confusion in this regard may be attributed to Schenker's frequent indulgence in lengthy ontological justification of his concepts.

7. Hans Wolf, "Schenker's Persönlichkeit in Unterricht," *Der Dreiklang* 7:176–84. My translation.

8. Heinrich Schenker, *Neue musikalische Theorien und Phantasien*, 3 vols.: vol. 1, *Harmonielehre* (Vienna, 1906); vol. 2 (part 1), *Kontrapunkt* (Stuttgart and Berlin, 1910);

vol. 2 (part 2), *Kontrapunkt* (Vienna, 1922); vol. 3, *Der freie Satz* (Vienna, 1935).

9. On this point Milton Babbitt has written: "Schenker has contributed . . . a body of analytical procedures which reflect the perception of a musical work as a dynamic totality, not as a succession of moments or a juxtaposition of 'formal' areas related or contrasted merely by the fact of thematic or harmonic similarity or dissimilarity" (in *Journal of the American Musicological Society* 5:260–65).

10. I stress the adjective "lengthy" here. Obviously a certain amount of verbal explanation is required.

11. The rendering of Schenker's technical expressions into English presents a number of problems, not the least of which is the fact that there are already, in some cases, two or more published versions of the same term. It is to be hoped that with the publication of *Der freie Satz* (now being translated) a standard nomenclature will be established.

12. Each tonal work manifests one of three possible forms of the fundamental line, always a descending diatonic progression: 3–1 (as in the present case), 5–1, and 8–1. Variants upon these forms arise when the bass arpeggiation disposes the fundamental line components in different ways.

13. It should be apparent that Schenker's major concept is not that of the Ursatz, as is sometimes maintained, but that of structural levels, a far more inclusive idea.

14. Undoubtedly Schenker compressed many of his sketches in consideration of the practical requirements of publication. Ernst Oster, who has in his possession a large number of Schenker's unpublished materials—which he plans to present along with commentaries at a future date—has brought this to my attention. Schenker's unpublished sketches of Brahms's *Waltzes* op. 39, for example, are executed on several superimposed staves, so that each structural level is shown distinctly and in detail.

15. Schenker's abbreviation "Nbn" stands for *Nebennote*, or in English, "adjacent tone" (not "neighbor tone").

16. "The bass executes an arpeggiation, descending through the third, but without terminating the interruption" (*Der freie Satz*, p. 89). This is one of Schenker's few comments upon this sketch.

17. A highly interesting application of this concept is to be found in Schenker's essay "Das Organische der Fuge," (Jahrbuch II; see note 20, below), where he employs his technique of synthesis, or reconstruction, to demonstrate that the subject of Bach's C-minor Fugue (*The Well-Tempered Clavier*, book 1) implies a complete, self-contained contrapuntal structure.

18. Cf. Johann David Heinichen, *Der General-Bass in der Composition* (Leipzig, 1728), pp. 558ff.: "Das 2-stimmige Harpeggio," "Das 3-stimmige Harpeggio," etc.

19. Relationships of this kind occasionally cause students to be confused; by assigning a structural event to the wrong level they necessarily arrive at a misreading. The technique of reconstruction serves as a corrective in such instances.

20. Schenker usually referred to the three volumes of *Das Meisterwerk in der Musik* as the Jahrbücher ("Yearbooks"), abbreviated Jhrb. (Munich: Drei Masken Verlag, 1925, 1926, 1930).

21. This development is interestingly documented in Ernest Ferand's anthology, *Die Improvisation in Beispielen aus neun Jahrhunderten abendländischer Musik* (Cologne: Arno Volk Verlag, 1956). Ferand's illustrations and commentary substantiate Schenker's conviction that variation procedures are shared by formal composition and extempore composition.

22. Curiously enough, Schenker did not explain in his writings how to carry out a reduction. Whatever his reasons for this may have been, he is probably being sarcastic when he suggests in *Der freie Satz* that the reader who wishes to arrive at the deeper structural levels need only apply the method of reducing more extended diminutions which is taught in all schools and textbooks. Such an undertaking, even supposing that student grasped the bare essentials, would be like translating from a foreign language word by word, mechanically, without understanding its syntax or idioms. At the Mannes College of Music, where Schenker's theory has been taught since Hans Weisse introduced it in 1931, students normally require a full year of instruction before they achieve the kind of facility which enables them to deal with more complex works.

23. Implicit here is a distinction between Schenker as theorist and Schenker as philosopher-historian. Schenker's interpretation of music history rarely demonstrated the same clear, rigorous thinking which is evident in much of his theoretical work. I therefore find myself at odds with Michael Mann, who has based an extensive article (see note 5) upon the thesis that "the dogma on which Schenker's descriptive music theory is based cannot be judged apart from his outlook on music history." In my opinion this is fallacious. The same criterion applied to Freud's outlook on anthropology in relation to his psychological theories would yield curious results indeed.

24. In reply to one criticism of the Ursatz, Milton Babbitt has written: "Nothing could be less accurate than Daniskas' characterization of Schenker's method as embodying a 'static' notion of tonality" (in *Journal of the American Musicological Society* 5:260–65). Babbitt refers to John Daniskas's *Grondlagen voor de analytische voormleer der musik* (Rotterdam, 1948). Leonard B. Meyer echoes Daniskas's erroneous opinion in his *Emotion and Meaning in Music* (Chicago, 1956).

25. This motion presents no problems when it is executed rapidly and receives no support from bass and chords.

26. By "modulation" Schenker means "tonicization," which is conceptually quite different from the erratic changing of key usually designated by the former term.

27. The extent to which Schenker's ideas have already been absorbed, perhaps unconsciously in some instances, is truly remarkable, particularly in view of the failure of his work to gain acknowledgement. When, for example, William Reynolds writes of the possibility of "reducing the melody to a more skeletal background in which the actual structural linear movement is laid bare," and points out that "many melodies may be bi-linear or even poly-linear," surely we can detect Schenker's influence ("Re: Unity in Music," *Journal of Music Theory* 2:97–104).

28. I have selected 1910 as the approximate year when such major composers as Stravinsky, Bartok, and Schoenberg began to abandon the system of triadic tonality in their works.

29. *Der freie Satz*, par. 21. My translation.

30. To the best of my knowledge there are only two books which deal directly with this subject, and they only in part: Felix Salzer, *Sinn und Wesen der abendländischen Mehrstimmigkeit* (Vienna: Saturn Verlag, 1935); and Armand Machabey, *Genèse de la Tonalité Musicale* (Paris: Richard Masse, 1955). Schenker's own treatment of the subject is, in my opinion, desultory.

31. Felix Salzer's *Structural Hearing* (New York: Charles Boni, 1952) and Adele Katz's *Challenge to Musical Tradition* (New York: Alfred Knopf, 1945) both contain information pertinent to this problem. A striking instance of Schenker-derived analytic technique

revealing a unique relationship between works of different periods is to be found in Ernst Oster's article "The Fantasie-Impromptu: a tribute to Beethoven," *Musicology* 1:407–29.

32. Schenker, *Kontrapunkt* (part 1), p. xiii.

33. As in mm. 3–4 (7–8) Schumann here requires the accompanist to interlock the hands in such a way that this motive is naturally stressed.

34. Here I disagree with Schenker's sketch, which shows the A^7 chord supporting $\hat{3}$. In my opinion $\hat{3}$ is supported by the tonic triad in m. 14 .

35. The notion of "modulation" is particularly confusing to students here.

36. Johannes Brahms, *Octaven und Quinten*, edited by Heinrich Schenker (Vienna: Universal Edition, 1933).

37. Schoenberg, in the first edition of his *Harmonielehre* (1911), took exception to this as follows: "Dr. Heinrich Schenker (I hear) writes in a new counterpoint book of the art of composition and maintains that no one can compose any longer. Certainly Dr. Schenker is a thinker whom one must take seriously (even though nothing correct is to be gained from it), for he is one of the few who strive for a system. And if he makes the same mistake as others, one must nevertheless value him for other merits. But what he says is hardly better than the remarks of the senile about 'the good old days!'" In the 1922 edition Schoenberg changed his remark about "nothing correct to be gained" to read "although he brings nothing to full clarity." Schenker reciprocated by attacking Schoenberg's *Harmonielehre* in Jahrbuch II (1926).

38. Roger Sessions recognized this as early as 1935 when he wrote: "Although Schenker remained bitterly hostile to all that is contemporary in music, his work and his ideas nevertheless embody very clearly certain aspects of contemporary musicality. . . ." ("Heinrich Schenker's Contribution," *Modern Music* 12:170–78).

39. *Der freie Satz*, 2d ed., 1956, p. 34. My translation.

40. Schenker was aware of the problem of verbalizing music. In *Der freie Satz* he remarks: "As a verbal connection, a name always indicates at once a logical connection and an essential unity." Thus, he rejected the terms "melody," "motive," and the like, because he felt that they lacked significance with respect to more comprehensive events such as "fundamental line."

41. Applications to modern works have already been made in the books of Salzer and Katz cited earlier and in *Contemporary Tone-Structures*, by the present writer, Allen Forte (New York: Bureau of Publications, Teachers College, Columbia University, 1955).

42. The familiar terms "atonal," "polytonal," etc., do not constitute explanations but are merely labels, somewhat shopworn, which usually serve only to obscure really significant structural events. Unfortunately, the currency of these terms has given them the aura of genuine technical language, with the result that many people, even some musicians, are under the impression that the organization of contemporary music is fully comprehended.

43. Milton Babbitt has made original, highly significant contributions to the theory of 12-tone music. See, for example, his article "Some Aspects of 12-tone Composition," *The Score* 12:53–61. Important work has also been done by George Perle. See his book review in the *Journal of the American Musicological Society* 10:55–59.

2. Organic Structure in Sonata Form

Heinrich Schenker
Translated by Orin Grossman

In the following essay, the reader can easily observe the passion and enthusiasm which often accompanied Schenker's theoretical explanations. It should be emphasized that, at the time of writing (1926), Schenker was finding extraordinary relationships among concealed motives in compositions (such as the four-note configurations of examples 2.4 and 2.5), and that his observations were entirely new and unrecognized by others. He was, in effect, perceiving similarities within sonatas in precisely those areas where others perceived only differences. This led him to discount, perhaps too hastily, theorists who concentrated on those differences, since he blamed them for overlooking aspects of compositional unity. Schenker's revelations of formal coherence in this essay, however, more than make up for his rhetorical excesses. —Ed.

To effect an agreement between general concepts and specific details is one of the most difficult tasks of human understanding. In order to reduce the world of appearances to only a few concepts, knowledge must seek general truths. At the same time, one must examine the particulars to the last detail, in all their secrets, if one wishes to grasp correctly these general concepts, which are, after all, supported by particulars. The task is difficult because generalities, however arrived at, easily mislead men into a premature satisfaction which spares any further effort concerning specifics. Through continuous disregard for detail, knowledge of general truths is impaired; it does not ripen into truth but remains limited to a schema.

Thus it was not really difficult for theorists to gather together the

This essay was originally published in *Das Meisterwerk in der Musik* (Jahrbuch II) (Munich: Drei Masken Verlag, 1926), pp. 45–54. I am indebted to Allen Forte and Ernst Oster for their numerous suggestions, almost all of which have been incorporated into the translation.

general characteristics of many sonatas.* They believed that the last generality had been found and they left it for the composer to apply their theory in actual composition. They were so sure of the correctness of their definitions that the theory dismissed every doubt. Even when sonatas composed along these outlines had obviously unmasked their idea of sonata form, rather than revise their concepts, they concluded that sonata form as such was obsolete. The theory was satisfied too quickly with an inadequate abstraction, even before it had developed the ability to cope with those particulars which are the distinctive features of a work of genius. Otherwise recognition of those particulars would certainly have prevented the formation of that schema and facilitated a more accurate grasp of the general truths.

Of course it has been observed that the tendency toward a three-part division with a modulation and a contrasting key in the first part is characteristic of the sonata form. But the true significance of this has not yet been grasped. The concept of sonata form as it has been taught up to now lacks precisely the essential characteristic—that of organic structure [*organischen*]. This characteristic is determined solely by the invention of the parts out of the unity of the primary harmony [*Hauptklang*]†—in other words, by the composing-out of the fundamental line [*Urlinie*] and the bass arpeggiation [*Bassbrechung*]. The capacity to have such a perception of the primary harmony is a prerogative of genius, derived from nature. Genius transforms the triad into the melodic progressions of the fundamental line and at the same time, into a few basic chords [*Einzelklänge*] which are subdivided again and again. This perception cannot be developed in an artificial way, which is to say that only what is composed with the sweep of improvisation [*aus dem Stegreif*] guarantees unity in a composition. Therefore in order to express the general idea more clearly, one should add to the concept of sonata form that the whole must be discovered through improvisation if the piece is to be more than a collection of individual parts and motives in the sense of a schema.[1] As confirmation of the crucial hallmark of improvisation, I wish to add the following particular examples to the many which I presented in the *Tonwille* pamphlets and the first Jahrbuch.

*Schenker is referring to the rather sterile and academic descriptions of sonata form by such nineteenth-century theorists as A. B. Marx.

†By this term Schenker means the tonic triad, which governs both the fundamental line and the bass arpeggiation.

Haydn's Piano Sonata in G Minor op. 54 no. 1 [Hoboken (XVI) no. 44] reveals the following fundamental structure [*Ursatz*] (see ex. 2.1).* To be sure, example 2.1b makes use of the customary indications of formal parts: first theme, modulation, second theme, development, and recapitulation. However, the sketch also reveals the deeper significance of the motion, since this motion derives from the first composing-out of the fundamental structure (ex. 2.1a). It is not enough just to enumerate the key changes as they occur in the foreground, as conventional theory does; it is also necessary to know what force brings about the modulation and assures the unity of the whole. Haydn knew no treatises on form as we know them today. It was the life of his spirit which generated the new life of his music. The fundamental line and bass arpeggiation governed him with the power of a natural force, and he received from them the strength to master the whole as a unity. Where in the prevailing theory do we find even a hint of such a path to unity? To be sure it preaches tirelessly about organic structure, but only with cheap words, which are no more than a pious wish. Actually, theory does not yet comprehend the nature of organic structure in music and therefore cannot specify those phenomena which contribute to it.

Let us go on, however, to the diminutions in this sonata. The direction which the master's fantasy takes in the first part is briefly shown in example 2.2. Scarcely is d^2 played on the upbeat, when it ascends by a fourth to g^2 on the downbeat of m. 1. The question is, should d^2 or g^2, $\hat{5}$ or $\hat{8}$, be the first note of the fundamental line? In mm. 1–2, in spite of the higher g^2, there develops the motion of a sixth downwards, from d^2 to f-sharp^1 (see ex. 2.3), a descent which supports the claim of d^2, that is, $\hat{5}$, as the first note. The two neighbor-note motions d^2–e-flat^2–d^2, which hover above the progression of a sixth, also lend credence to this claim. However, in m. 3, there suddenly appears a b-flat^2 above the g^2; this entrance weakens the first supposition, particularly since a progression of a third, b-flat^2–a^2–g^2, is formed in m. 4. Already the first arpeggiation of the bass is at an end and we still grope in darkness.

In m. 5 the voice leading rises surprisingly out of the deep with the

---

*Although there are problems associated with Schenker's analysis of this sonata, they do not detract from the central point of the essay. One must realize that Schenker was in the process of formulating many of his ideas at the time this essay was written and that the analyses contained herein do not represent his ideas in their final form.

Example 2.1   Haydn, Piano Sonata in G Minor op. 54 no. 1

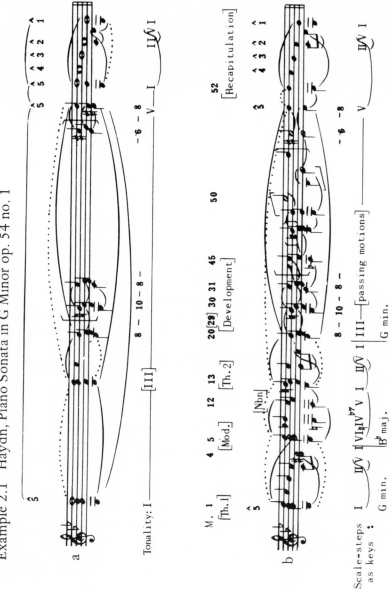

Example 2.2

Example 2.3

arpeggiation d^1–g^1–b-flat^1. We immediately recognize a shortened repetition of the previously traveled path. A chain of overlapping motions [*Übergreifzüge*] leads upward to d^3 in m. 8. Subsequently this d^3 descends through d-flat^3 in mm. 9–12, to c^3 in m. 12. With the greatest atonishment we finally recognize here that, although c^3 is not once expressly stated, the whole content of mm. 1–12 is only the octave transfer from d^2 to d^3 an octave above. Thus d^2, not g^2, is the first note of the fundamental line. Furthermore, this one ascent creates an arc which connects all the formal parts designated by the prevailing theory with the terms first theme, consequent, and modulation!

This knowledge is confirmed by the further course of the voice leading. In mm. 12–17, there occurs the upward arpeggiation f^2–b-flat^2–d^3. The d^3 harkens back to the d^3 in m. 8, and from here it descends through c^1 to b-flat^1 in mm. 17–20—the $\hat{4}$, $\hat{3}$ of the fundamental line (in the foreground key of B-flat major). The second arpeggiation coincides with the second theme of the accepted theory. Has conventional theory even considered, however, what function such an arpeggiation serves—that it not only holds together the second theme as a unity but also recognizes and expands upon the organic structure of the first idea by imitating the first arpeggiation through the parallel structure and the motion to the same high point (d^3)? Has the theory even suggested such a function for the second theme? Has it not rather demanded the opposite from the second theme? It follows that Haydn could never have written this sonata if he had had to conform to our theories, which have allegedly thoroughly explored the essence of sonata form.

Now we come to the main question: Would it have been possible for Haydn to compose both arpeggiations in such a manner if the sweep of improvisation had not shown him the way? The downbeat has scarcely indicated d^2 when in m. 1 the arpeggiation begins. Surely this idea must have necessarily been present from the first. Where, in the work of a non-genius, is there a similar motion, a similar arpeggiation, which bridges several formal parts?

If theory were to take cognizance of these relations it would have to value the arpeggiation as a motive of the highest order (Jahrbuch I, pp. 64ff.). Only then would it have to deal with the less significant motives which are there: the linear progressions of a sixth in mm. 1–2, of a third in mm. 3–4, of a seventh from d-flat^3 to e^2 in mm. 10–11, and of a rising sixth in conjunction with a 5–6 replacement pattern in mm. 14–17. There is also the change of diminution in m. 5 and mm. 6–8 (here, the chain of overlapping motions), as well as the second theme at m. 12 and following. Does the theory follow such a procedure? No. For conventional theory, melodic successions are important at best as motives which sooner or later reappear in exact repetition.

Thus in example 2.3, for example, the important motives would be the upbeat triplet and the following eighth notes on the first and second beats of m. 1. On the other hand, the theory would not be able to deal with the neighbor-note motive in these measures. Observe the bracketed notes in example 2.3. The middle group employs the lower neighbor note for the sake of contrast. The last group extends into the next neighbor-note group, thus binding together the two smallest formal parts. The theory does just as poorly with the remaining contents because it does not recognize such repetitions and does not grasp the motivic nature of the higher ranking motion of a sixth from d^2 to f-sharp^1.

The present theory also does not recognize the unity of the motive, for example, in the neighbor-note formations of mm. 5–12 (see ex. 2.2). The overlapping, the ascending register transfer, and the linear progression of a seventh in these measures obscure the more central c^2 to b-flat^2 in mm. 6–8 and the d^3–(d-flat^3)–c^3 in mm. 8–12, not to mention the fact that the theory could observe the same neighbor-note motive in the second theme. There, for example in m. 13, f^2–e-flat^2 and d^2–c^2 are placed together to form a fourth (Haydn suppressed the c^3 in m. 12 on account of the d^2 to c^2 in m. 13). The theory does not hear the connection between the fourths d^2 to g^2 from the upbeat to the downbeat of m. 1 and at the change from m. 2 to m. 3, and the fourth f^2 to b-flat^2 at the change from m. 12 to m. 13. As a result, it perceives no motivic significance for these fourths.

I believe that I have been clear enough. Nevertheless I will state my conclusion once more. Until now, theory had no way of dealing with the organic structure of sonata form. The characteristics which the theory stresses do not deal with the inner nature of sonata form. The heart of the theory is lifeless, and works which have been nourished by it are stillborn. In short, until now theory has lacked the means for discussing the improvisation-derived driving force [*Stegreif-Zug*] in sonata form.

Here is another example—the first part of the first movement of

Beethoven's Piano Sonata op. 10 no. 2 (see ex. 2.4). The present theory uses the standard designations even for contents such as these. It only describes the state of the developed material [*den Zustand des Gewordenen*] in a superficial and shallow way and clearly reveals that it knows nothing about the principle of development of particular characteristics [*Gesetz des besonderen Werdens*]. Yet the general specification of form depends solely on that principle. Even a fleeting glance at the sketch (ex. 2.4h) suffices to reveal that here, just as in the Haydn example already cited, the first theme, consequent, modulation, and antecedent of the second theme are elevated to the status of an organic whole by the force of the melodic progressions and arpeggiations. The first fifth-progression, f² to b², extends up to m. 31 and alone unites the first theme, consequent, modulation, and antecedent of the second theme. Since this fifth represents a motion into an inner voice, f² is established as the main tone of the fundamental line. Therefore the top voice begins new progressions from the f² (see ex. 2.4i): the second fifth-progression (mm. 39ff), which spans the consequent of the second theme, and the third progression (mm. 47ff) [actually a fourth-progression], which finally includes the tones 7̂, 6̂, and 5̂ of the fundamental line. It is the succession of all these motions which creates coherence out of the parts and the organic nature of the contents. This succession is called into being by the law of retention of the main note.

It should be said here that it is possible to invent such a progression of a fifth as in mm. 1–31 only through improvisation. The first fifth inspires the next progression, so that we hear this storm of spontaneity with true devotion as it rushes along creating life and coherence from progression to progression.

To this we shall add the figurations, which offer further proof of that natural force. Individual arpeggiations unfold the chords and unite them (ex. 2.4g). A four-note motive enlivens the arpeggiations (see the brackets in ex. 2.4h). It also encompasses contractions in example 2.4i and is even interwoven with the large scale neighbor-note motion of the development section [ex. 2.5]. Thus everything is, level after level, a world in itself. This unity cannot be explained, however, except by the miracle of improvisation, which creates the whole as one configuration.

Has the theory spent even a word on this natural phenomenon of organic structure? Can its designations of form specify even the limits of the second theme or the contents of the development section? Has

Example 2.4   Beethoven, Piano Sonata op. 10 no. 2, first movement

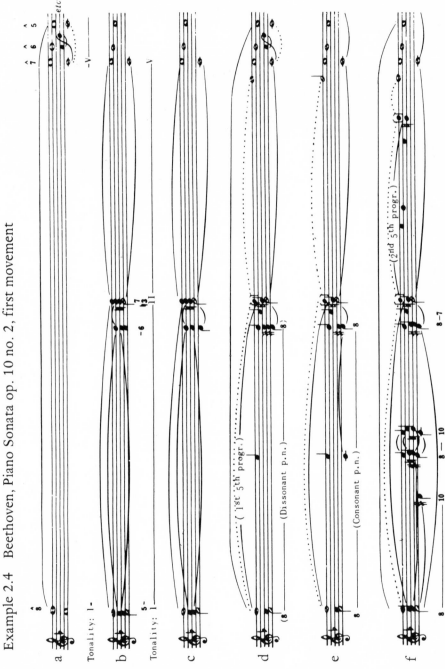

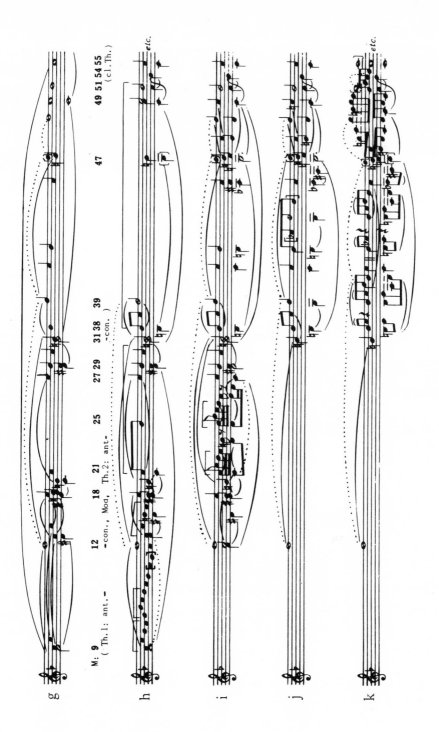

Example 2.5   Beethoven, op. 10 no. 2, first movement, development

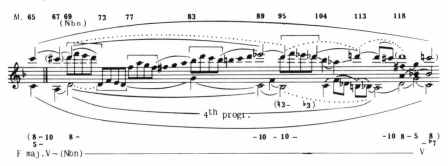

a performance of this sonata ever impressed upon us this miracle?

In the first movement of the Piano Sonata op. 10 no. 1, Beethoven wrote [what appears in ex. 2.6]. In spite of the differences between legato, staccato, etc., the relationship between all the skips from m. 28 (see ex. 2.6b) can be seen at a glance. However, the one who is really able to recognize the relationship is the one who sees the derivation of the skips from those in the first theme (see ex. 2.6a and compare with Jahrbuch I, p. 189, fig. 2). Only this person will perceive the unity of the diminutions from the shape of the whole.

We see that the diminutions could not possibly blossom into such unity—the unity and synthesis of the whole which flows from the fundamental line and the bass arpeggiation—were it not for the miracle of improvisation!

If this were not concealed, as is every miracle, conventional theory long ago would have seized upon more than the few superficial characteristics which it has applied to every situation. If the theory has not even a hint of this motive of the leap, how is it supposed to encompass the organic structure of the whole?

In the development section of the first movement of Beethoven's Sonata op. 109, the composer establishes the following high points (see ex. 2.7): The manner in which Beethoven suddenly abandons the high g-sharp³ in m. 21 and jumps down to d-sharp² has puzzled everyone. What could this leap, this sudden change, signify? Even if one grapples with the problem of discovering a relationship between such widely separated high points, namely the ascent from g-sharp³ to b³ (m. 42), which is to be the main note of the recapitulation, one has not yet gained the highest degree of insight. Understanding results much more from the following connection (see ex. 2.8): The impro-

Example 2.6 Beethoven, op. 10 no. 1, first movement

Example 2.7   Example 2.8

visational fantasy of the master pursues both tones of the upbeat in the development and in the coda! He must drive after them. They signify to him a motive—the key to a world of unity and coherence. What does the theory of sonata form care about such a miracle? And yet, the substance of this movement develops only through this miracle.

History and experience teach us that the improvisational gift comes very infrequently.[2] It will not be otherwise in the future. Let it be said that only he who is granted the power of intuitive creativity will be able to fulfill again the idea of sonata form like the old masters and create an organic unity. He who does not possess it can still form some notion of this particular natural gift. We often see someone with a modest talent for this or that instrument. By means of continuous practice, such a person reaches the point where he can play a great number of notes easily in a minute and can—with regard to stress, touch, shadings, and tempo—handle the notes with ease according to the composer's directions and (more frequently) according to his personal conception. On a higher level of musical invention, the image of the spirit of genius shows a similar situation. This spirit of genius, creating mysteriously out of the background of a fundamental structure, masters all the arpeggiations of the many individual harmonies and all the diminutions of the linear progressions in the composing-out process.

This conception of composition, however, seldom satisfies the hasty person. A composition presents itself to the observer or performer as foreground. This foreground is, so to speak, only its "present" [*Gegenwart*], taking the dictionary sense of the word. We know how difficult it is to grasp the meaning of the present if we are not aware of the temporal background. It is equally difficult for the student or performer to grasp the "present" of a composition if he does not include at the same time a knowledge of the background. Just as the demands of the day toss him to and fro, so does the foreground of a composition pull at him. Every change of sound and of figuration, every chromatic shift, every neighbor note signifies something new to him. Each novelty leads him further away from the coherence which derives from the background.

Particularly today, when the superficial, raucous, hedonistic life is exalted as the highest goal of existence—even though we would do better to consider how we might save our lives from chaos—particularly today this disposition to the present has become a barrier to the understanding of a work of genius. Such a work differs from life, however, in that its material is derived from improvisation, which gives an unequivocal meaning to the whole. Therefore it is a contradiction, for the sake of life and the present, whose plan remains concealed from man, to deny the existence of a background structure in a work of art. Even if we can not force anyone to understand such a plan, even if we must let the unwilling and incapable move about in the foreground of a masterpiece just as he moves about in a chaotic, superficial day-to-day existence, at least we can force him to realize that a true masterpiece has no connection with his superficial mindless life.

If we merely point out the themes and melodies in a sonata the way we pursue gratifying moments in life, we are only reflecting a point of view derived from the superficial aspects of life. The layman desires melody as a fulfillment of the moment. Progressions of a fourth, fifth, or sixth, for example, would not constitute a melody for him, although such motions, being horizontal realizations of vertical ideas, are nevertheless also melodies in a higher sense (see ex. 2.3). The layman demands still more composing-out, more decorations. He surmises therefore that the art of music—of course he always means only the melody—consists of an abundance of details. But the limitations of his spirit set the boundaries for such an abundance; a large-scale compositional process which he cannot comprehend is not a melody for him. He can only hear so much, and that much is what he calls melody!

It should not astonish us now that the prevailing theory shares the viewpoint of the layman and also looks for themes and motives understood in the vague sense of the uninitiated. The theory has not yet advanced to a true conception of melody encompassing a whole composition or large sections. It does not recognize the shape of the whole, or the diminution levels and their motives. Therefore it does not know how its concepts of themes, melodies, and motives contradict true sonata form.

Melody, in the inappropriate way it is usually understood by the layman and theoretician, derives from the smallest most rudimentary relationships of art. On the other hand the sonata represents a realization of the largest conceivable world of related tones in the most complex form of a highly developed era.[3] Only a few geniuses were able to meet the demands of organic structure in sonata form. What they accomplished for this structure was because of improvisational gifts. This art was neither perceived nor was it teachable. When the era of the masters had past, there followed talents without the gift of improvisation, who could no longer attain sonata form. The Italian opera and its melodies were degenerating. Just at this time, however, the ambition of these talents strove after higher and higher goals. They wished to create sonatas and symphonies even greater than those by the masters. And so the inevitable occurred. The talents strove after melodies and sudden effects, thinking that they could fulfill the demands for an organic formal structure if they only filled their supposed form with melodies and themes. The result was sufficiently deplorable. Instead of organic works of art, they created works whose parts are comparable to raisins placed in dough—even in a baked cake the raisins are clearly distinguishable. The sonata, however, is no cake; it is a tonal mass formed from a unitary material in which the raisins are not distinguishable.[4]

After this there developed a misconception fostered by Wagner. To be sure his leitmotiv technique was in accord with a world used to categorizing melodies. On the other hand, because of his overemphasis on the musical foreground (Wagner was no background composer!) due to theatrical requirements, he introduced a heaviness which previously had not existed at all in music. People imagined that they heard a similar heaviness also in the improvisational works of our masters. The desire strongly arose to escape from this heaviness. They clamored for "melody"!

Lack of understanding of this improvistory quality had disastrous consequences. On the other hand those who like to listen to a whole evolving from a whole rejoice over the radiance of the improvisational genius in, for example, the late string quartets and symphonies of Beethoven. In these pieces, melody stands in the shadows. Beethoven truly remained to his last breath a composer of connected tones, a producer of tonal wholes which created luminous and floating coherence.

The so-called melodies, themes, and motives of the present theory do not constitute sonata form. The examples cited above, along with many others, have shown what we mean by diminutional motives in sonata form. This process involves, among other things, the composing-out of arpeggiations, octave couplings [*Oktavkoppelungen*], and unities of a higher order established through repetition (e.g., the neighbor-note shapes examples 2.3, 2.4h, 2.5).

Without understanding the motive in this sense, we could not attain the breadth and expanse of improvisation,[5] which alone creates the organic structure of sonata form. A tradition of sonata form is entirely lacking. How could it ever have arisen when the general musical opinion as well as the general instinct was unable to cope with exactly that characteristic, the intuitive, improvisational process, which unites the parts of the form by means of progressions?[6] The sonata form of the masters, however, will remain preserved for all time by virtue of the integrity of the improvisational style.

NOTES

1. Compare Jahrbuch I, p. 127, where I wrote on "Sonaten-Atem."

2. See Jahrbuch I, p. 11ff.

3. *Tonwille* 2:3–6.

4. We might also offer the following analogy: The attempt to hear melodies in the sense of the layman and theorist resembles the attempt of certain utopians to transfer the morals, customs, and habits of a small group of men to entire nations. They do not realize that for a greater mass of people, new demands and difficulties accompany new suppositions—difficulties which are not found in smaller groups. The same is true for that ever more popular desire to return to the first primitive state of nature. Only one who is incapable of dealing with the higher demands of culture would abandon it for Nature.

5. *Tonwille* 5:54–57.

6. When someone cites a motive from this or that sonata, for example, and thereby purports to know it thoroughly, this reflects anything but tradition. When an amateur, who has played this or that masterpiece in his youth, later resists going back to it and asserts that he has already done that piece, this also does not demonstrate a tradition. Why should there be talk of a renunciation of a tradition when one does not exist?

3. Register and the Large-Scale Connection

Ernst Oster

Here, Ernst Oster begins with a reference to the Beethoven Piano Sonata op. 109 previously mentioned by Schenker in his essay on organic form. Note that the long-range repetition of motive in the Beethoven example is only one kind of compositional technique associated with register. Equally compelling is the completion of typical pitch resolutions within isolated registers, such as the long-range $\frac{d\text{-}c\text{-}sharp}{g\text{-}sharp\text{-}a}$ resolution of example 3.8. Note too that this essay does not confine itself to the uppermost register but provides, in addition, examples of significant types of pitch relations confined to middle and low registers.

The reader may observe further examples of the structural significance of register (especially obligatory register) later in this volume. It plays an important role in David Beach's analysis of Beethoven's Piano Sonata op. 53, Introduzione (see examples 13.1, 13.3, 13.5), in Carl Schachter's commentary on Schubert's op. 94 no. 1 (ex. 10.6), and in Edward Laufer's analysis of the Brahms Song op. 105, no. 1 (ex. 16.18). This last essay provides a fascinating detail: a high d-sharp is left unresolved in the upper register in conjunction with the sung word, schwebt *("hovers").*—Ed.

In an essay, "Vom Organischen der Sonatenform,"[1] Heinrich Schenker writes:

> In the first movement of the Piano Sonata op. 109, Beethoven establishes the following high points in the development section:

> After reaching the high g-sharp³ he suddenly abandons it and leaps down to d-sharp². What is the meaning of this perplexing leap? Even if we were finally to have recognized a relation between these two widely separated climaxes . . . we still would not

54

have gained the ultimate clarity. The latter is provided by the
following relations:

Schenker goes on to say that Beethoven pursues these two tones also
in the development section and in the coda. To the master, they have
the meaning of an actual motive and are "a clue to a world of unity
and coherence."

This feature of the first movement of opus 109 demonstrates in
brief the topic of our discussion. Two tones which, viewed superficially, have nothing to do with each other enter into a relationship
merely through the register in which they appear. In this case,
register becomes one of the main elements of composition and
is on an equal footing with harmony, counterpoint, and thematic
development. The consideration of register is indispensable to the
true understanding of the main feature of this development, namely
the preparation of the first two tones of the recapitulation in the
three-line octave.

It is surprising that Schenker was the first to draw attention to the
significance of register in composition. As far as is known to me, the
only other reference to registral significance was made by Schenker's
pupil Oswald Jonas in his book *Das Wesen des musikalischen Kunstwerks*, published in Vienna, 1934.

Schenker, in *Der freie Satz*, devotes a chapter to what he calls
obligate Lage (obligatory register).[2] By this is meant that the fundamental line, as well as the bass, appears in a single and primary
register which is maintained through the composition, despite frequent necessary excursions to higher or lower octaves. A magnificent
confirmation of this view is to be found in the C Major and C Minor
Preludes of the first book of *The Well-Tempered Clavier*. These preludes first appear in Friedemann Bach's *Clavierbüchlein,* although in
a shorter version. In this earlier version, after beginning in the two-
line octave, they both end in the one-line octave. When Bach incorporated these preludes into *The Well-Tempered Clavier,* he lengthened
them and made little improvements here and there. In addition, he
apparently felt that it was necessary or at least desirable to return to
the initial register at the end of each composition. One can easily see
at which points in the added sections Bach regained the higher octave,

thus fulfilling the "law of obligatory register." A detailed analysis of the C Major Prelude appeared in Schenker's *Fünf Urlinie-Tafeln,* published in Vienna, 1932, while an analysis of the C Minor Prelude appeared in his essay, "Das Organische der Fuge" (Jahrbuch II). Excerpts from both are included in *Der freie Satz.*

Strangely enough, Forkel considered these shorter versions to be improvements made on the ones appearing in *The Well-Tempered Clavier.* And more recently, Siegfried Borris has tried to show that the shorter versions in the Friedemann Bach *Clavierbüchlein* were arrangements of the ones in *The Well-Tempered Clavier,* made by Bach himself to adapt them for the little hands of his son.[3] Among other things, this argumentation disregards entirely the question of register, which is of paramount importance in judging the relative value of the different versions.

It is not the purpose of this article to go further into the question of obligatory register in its broadest aspect as it pertains to an entire composition. Our aim is rather to show a number of instances where register contributes in an essential way to clarifying certain contrapuntal, structural, or thematic-motivic connections and relations. It is not intended to show the historical development of the use of register for artistic purposes. Our approach must necessarily be more or less unsystematic, and we will simply proceed from one example to the next.

Before presenting examples in which the bass shows large-scale progressions, we should like to discuss one of the relatively rare cases in which a middle register plays an essential role. In the middle section of the Adagio of Mozart's Piano Sonata in D major K. 576, the main melody notes are doubtless a^2, b^2, a^2 in mm. 17, 18 and 19 respectively. Yet if we follow up the initial c-sharp^2 of m. 17 we hear that it describes a slow turn-like motion c-sharp^2–d^2–c-sharp^2–b-sharp^2–c-sharp^2 during these measures. In example 3.1a these notes are connected by heavy lines between the staves. Since c-sharp^2 is also the very first tone of the Adagio, and since it reappears in m. 5 and in m. 13 we understand the c-sharp^2 of m. 17 simply as another occurrence. Of course there is nothing remarkable about a middle section beginning with the same tone as the main section. Numerous instances of this are to be found, for example, in Chopin's Mazurkas op. 24 no. 4 and op. 30 no. 1, taken at random. What gives the c-sharp^2 in our Mozart excerpt such significance is the fact that both in m. 1 and in m. 17 it is followed by a turn, the second one enlarged,

Example 3.1 Mozart, Sonata in D Major K. 576, Adagio

a

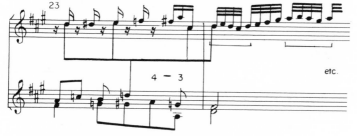

b

c

adapted to F-sharp-minor, and hidden under the higher melody tones. It permeates the first four measures, thus relating and linking the F-sharp-minor part closely to the beginning. The point we want to make here is that despite the turn's motivic relationship, which can easily be seen on paper, this relationship is perceivable only through the identity of register.

Further, example 3.1a shows that in m. 23 the turn starts on d^2 (note the suspension of d^2 on the third beat which corresponds to the suspension of c-sharp^2 in m. 19!) and that it "comes out into the open" in thirty-second notes at m. 24. Example 3.1b shows that the entire middle section is governed by the same turn, with b-sharp–c-sharp appearing an octave lower, for pianistic reasons. Significantly, Mozart does not write a turn in m. 39—although it would have been due here—a turn based on f-sharp instead of c-sharp^2 or its auxiliary note d^2. However, he makes amends for this missing turn. At the very last moment before the return of the main section, he manages to insert c-sharp^2–b-sharp^2 between the seventh d and its resolution c-sharp^2 in the reprise so that at this point we hear once more the turn motive (ex. 3.1c). Since we already are on the V^7 chord of A major and expect the tonic momentarily, the turn with its b-sharp sounds like a last farewell to the events of the middle section. In the subsequent measure it is replaced by the turn with the initial, normative b-natural.

Two more instances in which the middle register plays a leading role are to be found in Brahms's Intermezzo in E Major op. 116 no. 4 and in the Scherzo of Beethoven's Sonata in A-flat Major op. 26. In the Brahms work, the idea appearing in m. 1 is continued to d-sharp^1 at the pianissimo, three lines before the end, and from there to e^1, nine measures away.

Beethoven's Scherzo opens in an unusual way (ex. 3.2). The top voice outlines the A-flat triad but the bass enters on f^1, the auxiliary note of e-flat^1 in m. 2. Later this f^1–e-flat^1 becomes the first motive of the Trio. Although the F-minor triad in m. 1 is of a merely contrapuntal nature, Beethoven nevertheless begins the reprise (m. 45) as if the piece were actually written in F minor, introducing it by a V^7 harmony on C which lasts no less than twenty-one measures. Thus, f^1, which in m. 1 clashes so sharply with the tonic triad outlined by the top voice (see the sforzato), determines the entire course of the composition. Because f^1–e-flat^1 is of such pre-eminent importance we can understand the beginning of the Trio as a reiteration of mm.

1-2 of the Scherzo. It is as if f¹ at last comes into its own when it becomes the third in D-flat major. In passing, it should be mentioned that f^1-e-flat¹ played a certain role even in the first movement, especially in the middle section of the theme and at the beginning of the last variation.

As an example of bass progressions which are made to stand out by means of low register we cite mm. 52–124 in the first movement of Bach's Italian Concerto (ex. 3.3). It is noteworthy that Bach's keyboard extended as far as the low A (see the Finale); thus he could have written B-flat and A in m. 60 and in m. 74 an octave lower, had he so desired. Yet he reserved this register for the main structural tones C–D–B-flat–C, of which C–B-flat–A is only a prolongational motion.

Example 3.2   Example 3.3

Bass progressions brought into prominence in a manner similar to that described above occur fairly frequently. For example, in Chopin's Etude in F Major op. 10 no. 8, the bass line D–C–B-flat–A (mm. 29–41) stands out because of the register. Domenico Scarlatti was particularly ingenious in using the extreme registers—especially the low bass—very sparingly, and chiefly at the main structural points. Examples of this as well as examples of the use of register for other purposes can be found in abundance in his sonatas. When one examines the sonatas for features of this kind one gradually comes to realize that the beauty of Scarlatti's keyboard style—and that of other composers too—is at least partly due to masterly treatment of register.

Turning now to registral features of the top voice, we should first like to mention Beethoven's Bagatelle in G Minor, and its coda in particular (ex. 3.4). A coda was probably necessary in this piece,

Example 3.4

perhaps because it needed a stronger ending after the almost literal repetition of the first section. But what would be the tonal content of the coda? The E-flat major middle section starts out from g^1, gradually works its way up to g^2, then ends as shown in example 3.4, with c^3 and b-flat^2 superimposed above the descent g^2–f^2–e-flat^2.

The superimposed c^3 and b-flat^2 are touched upon only once, and our desire for their continuation—perhaps as in mm. 19–20, where we heard the same situation an octave lower—remains unsatisfied. But the desire is satisfied in the coda. By means of a long ascent, c^3 and b-flat^2 are reached again. This time they are led down stepwise to g^2, in a stronger, more definite fashion and supported by cadential bass steps. Thus, here the high register which was only briefly suggested previously is restated, and that which was lacking in the middle section is finally fulfilled. But although the two points in question, the one in the middle section and the other in the coda, have been associated by means of register, they are not structurally connected. The c^3 and the passage that follows in the coda are merely a repetition of something we have heard before, the repetition of a musical idea even though its meaning is changed. Thus the association is necessarily loose and was possible only in a composition as simple in character as this Bagatelle.

In contrast to the situation described above, the registral connection between m. 17 and m. 20 of Bach's Chromatic Phantasy is very close (ex. 3.5). If we eliminate the arpeggiations and two subsidiary

Example 3.5 Bach, Chromatic Phantasy

chords, we reveal the auxiliary note motion, 9–8, over A. This is perhaps so obvious that one need not call special attention to it. However, we wish to emphasize that the principle is exactly the same whether we deal with a group of four measures or with connections over much larger spans such as those to be examined below: register is the chief element which makes the two points in question stand out and thus be related and connected.

The excerpts from Brahms's Capriccio in D Minor op. 116 no. 7 presented in example 3.6 do not require comment. The parentheses indicate that in the intervening measures the lower register is prev-

Example 3.6   Brahms, op. 116 no. 7

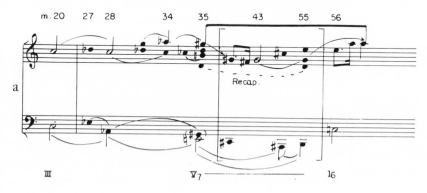

alent. There is marked similarity between this type of piano style, with the higher register appearing at only a few strategic points, and that of Scarlatti. Through the ages the external appearance of music had changed immensely, of course, but the principle of writing for keyboard instruments remained the same.

The Menuetto of Schubert's Quartet in A Minor, specifically its recapitulation, is probably unique in the entire literature (ex. 3.7). Upon arriving at the V^7 chord in m. 35, there is a sudden halt, followed by a recapitulation based on C-sharp minor instead of in the expected A minor, with the register dropping a full octave. (Actually, C-sharp on which the recapitulation begins is merely a connective between E and A-sharp which lies within a prolongation of the dominant extending from m. 35 to 55.) Furthermore, the motives shown in example 3.7b are also continued at this point and the previous forte is resumed. All these factors contribute to the linking of m. 35

Example 3.7   Schubert, Quartet in A Minor

with m. 56, but probably the most obvious factor involved is the abandonment and resumption of the high register at m. 35 and at m. 56, respectively. The beginning of the recapitulation is interpolated between these two points. It is subordinate to larger events of a higher order, or, to use an image, an arch is formed over it by the main progression shown in example 3.7a and specifically by g-sharp^2–a^2. One might almost describe it as having been composed in a parenthetical manner. To be sure, the C-sharp minor recapitulation is thematically important and does initiate the third section of the composition. However, its importance is minimized by the other events which bypass it. In consequence of all this the middle and the third sections are closely linked together, much more so than would have been the case if the recapitulation had started in a normal manner. This bypassing of an otherwise important event by means of registral connections can be found occasionally in the works of the great masters. Wherever it occurs, it constitutes one of the most remarkable features of the particular composition.

In the Brahms Capriccio in D Minor (ex. 3.6), the return of the first section in m. 62 is inserted or interpolated in a manner similar to that described above. And in the Rondo of Mozart's Violin Sonata in A Major K. 526 (ex. 3.8), the tenth a^1–c-sharp^3 in m. 183 (note the beautiful slur!) is derived from and continues the diminished fifth g-sharp^1–d^3 outlined in the ending of the previous E-major section (mm. 161–164). Thus the intervening recurrence of the main

Example 3.8 Mozart, K. 526

rondo theme in the lower register sounds incidental to this large-scale linkage of the E-major section with the one starting at m. 183. Here again we have a link that is perceivable only through the abandonment and resumption of the three-line octave. It should perhaps be mentioned that, of course, the diminished fifth has resolved to a–c-sharp in the A-major section of m. 167—but in the lower octave. As far as register is concerned—and this is what matters here—d^3 is continued to its tone of resolution only in m. 183.

After having followed the previous examples, a longer passage from the Finale of Mendelssohn's Quartet in E Minor will be easily understood (ex. 3.9a). Measures 288–331 all lie within the one-line octave. In m. 332, the e^2 of m. 287 continues to d-sharp². It is preceded by e^2 which joins together the two separated measures. Thus the half note e represents a huge suspension spanning forty-five measures

Example 3.9 Mendelssohn, Quartet in E Minor

(ex. 3.9b). And five measures later when d-sharp² returns to e^2, the notes marked by a bracket show a slightly changed enlargement of the motive appearing in mm. 286–87, the point at which the high register was interrupted. Thus these two distant points are closely linked together, primarily by means of register, and in addition, by contrapuntal means (suspension) and motivic relation. Bypassing of the kind described was occasionally used by Bach even in fugue writing. Measures 6–8 of the Fugue in C Minor from book 2 of *The Well-Tempered Clavier* which we quote in example 3.10a are of particular interest in this regard. According to Schenker,[4] Beethoven made a copy of this fugue for himself and marked the B in m. 7 with a large cross. Schenker remarks that this B contains a most significant clue to organic fugue writing and that at the same time it points up an essential difference between the fugal art of Bach and the fugue writing of others. We quote:

> Although this fourth entrance, obviously in comes form, should normally appear in G minor, Bach deprives it of this key by altering B-flat chromatically, thus incorporating it into the main key of C minor. Of course, Bach did this not to be different but because he wished to fulfill the overall tonality also in fugue writing. . . . Beethoven noticed this particular detail; this and similar features are the reason why Beethoven studied and emulated Bach. [My translation]

Example 3.10 J. S. Bach, Fugue in C Minor (*The Well-Tempered Clavier*, book 2)

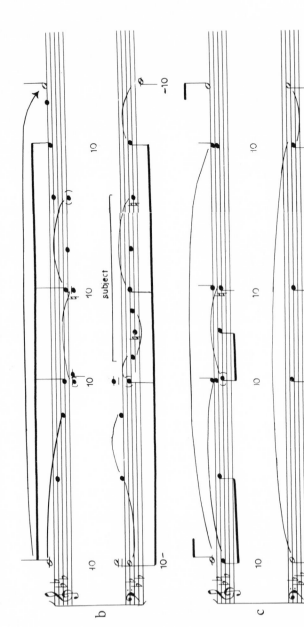

Thus far Schenker. A detailed analysis of the fourth entrance and its immediate surroundings reveals this passage to be even more remarkable. Example 3.10b shows the main voice-leading progressions, with the notes written in the registers in which they actually appear and with a few implied notes in parentheses; example 3.10c presents a further reduction with the various registers disregarded. It becomes apparent that up to and including the second beat of m. 8 we hear a progression of parallel tenths between bass and top voice. Consequently, the beginning of the fourth subject entrance (m. 7) occurs at the second tenth e-flat–g which is merely passing through. We even have to hear an E-flat triad at the beginning of this measure. As to the top voice, the discontinuation of the high register and its resumption in m. 8 show clearly that the first tenth f–a-flat^2 finds its real continuation only with E-flat–g^2 on the third beat of m. 8, well after the fifth entrance has begun. The true goal of the overall motion is therefore the C-minor-sixth chord in m. 8, not the C-minor triad in m. 7. Because of this the fourth entrance is weakened in three different ways: the B deprives it of the G-minor quality, the key in which it should have appeared; it is merely inserted between several passing tenths; and the registral connection of the top voice makes it sound almost parenthetical. We wait for the continuation of a-flat^2, and when g^2 finally appears as its continuation, the fourth entrance is a thing of the past. This passage is a striking example of Bach's art of subordinating fugal entrances to the broader scheme of the composition and making them an integral part of the whole. To achieve this end, he often made the entrances so inconspicuous that they pass by almost unnoticed. A good example of this is the entrance in m. 11 of the same fugue, although Bach uses means other than registral to achieve this. Other instances of Bach's use of register can be found in the Fugue in C-sharp Major, from book 1 of *The Well-Tempered Clavier*, mm. 13–16, and in the big Organ Fugue (BWV 547) in C Major which is altogether a miracle of this type of fugue writing. One is reminded of Robert Schumann's somewhat facetious remark:

The best fugue will always be that which the public takes for a Strauss Waltz; in other words, where the artistic technicalities are covered as are the roots of a flower, permitting us to see the blossom only. I know of—the case is real—a connoisseur of music, by no means contemptible, who mistook a Bach Fugue for a Chopin Etude—to the honor of both.

As additional examples, we refer the reader to mm. 21–41 of the first movement of Mozart's Piano Sonata in C Minor, where the first part of the E-flat major section is "bridged over." We also suggest mm. 14–23–27 of the first movement of Mozart's Quartet in D Minor, which are somewhat similarly constructed, or mm. 83–108–120–132 of Schubert's *Wanderer* Phantasy, where the beginning of the E-flat-major theme is inserted between a-flat^3 and a-flat^3–g^3 in m. 108 and in m. 120. Lack of space makes it impossible to go into detailed analyses of these compositions. They would reveal beautiful motivic and other relationships and connections besides the ones expressed solely by register. A few more interesting examples can also be found in Jonas's book published in Vienna, 1934, *Das Wesen des musikalischen Kunstwerks*, examples 116, 118, 119, 194; and in Schenker's *Der freie Satz*, examples 40, 7; 62, 3; 62, 4; 101, 6.

One might well ask why in the course of this discussion no examples from orchestral compositions were cited. The reply is that in orchestral compositions register plays a less significant role in pointing out or providing large-scale connections than it does in keyboard compositions. The reason may be that the orchestra, with such a great variety of means at its disposal, does not require the use of register to the same extent as the more poorly endowed keyboard instrument. A similar reason may account for the lack of examples from such an outstanding composer as Chopin. His richly developed piano style apparently gave rise to new techniques of writing which probably replaced older ones. Besides, one may say that from the very beginning of any of his major compositions all the registers of the keyboard are simultaneously present, as it were. Even so, register connections and relations are to be found in his compositions. In many cases, however, they are not quite as clear cut as the ones in earlier piano music and were therefore not as suitable for the first presentation of the subject.

As the last example to be presented we have chosen the first movement of Beethoven's Piano Sonata in C Minor op. 13, the *Pathétique*. Clearly, this movement extends in various ways far beyond anything the young Beethoven or anyone else had written before. One of the most striking features of this magnificent piece of music is the reappearance of a part of the introduction at the beginning of the development section, and again at the beginning of the short coda. A similar use of the introduction within the Allegro section is to be found in Haydn's Symphony in E-flat Major no. 103, which Beethoven probably knew at the time he wrote his Sonata in C Minor. Beethoven had employed a similar procedure once before: in the *Kurfürsten* Sonata in F Minor, written at the age of twelve, he introduced the recapitulation by a free repetition of the initial introduction. In opus 13 his intention was different: to make the introduction an integral part of the entire first movement. The combination of elements of the first subject and of the introduction at the beginning of the Allegro in the development (mm. 137–41) serves the same purpose. Also the melodic relationship between certain elements of the introduction and certain passages of the Allegro is quite apparent and has been described repeatedly. Thus as far as thematic material is concerned the composition is a unified whole.

When we turn to an examination of the structure of the exposition, we will first of all have to clarify the harmonic and contrapuntal meaning of mm. 51–88 (ex. 3.11). There can be no doubt that this section is to be considered the second subject. This is because when we arrive at E-flat major, III of C minor (m. 89), we have the impression of already being at the beginning of the coda of the exposition. This impression is created mainly by the fact that the ascending chromatic line of mm. 89–98 bears a resemblance to the first subject. The resemblance becomes still closer in the analogous place in the recapitulation (at m. 253).

Example 3.11 Beethoven, op. 13

It is surprising that even Tovey considers the second subject to be written "in E-flat minor." By no means can the six-four chord at its beginning be considered an inversion of an E-flat minor triad. Nor is there any E-flat minor triad or sixth chord to be found, except for one in m. 79. This, however, is merely a passing harmony between D-flat and F in m. 75 and in m. 83. The second subject should be understood as taking place within an extended prolongation of the B-flat harmony, the dominant of III which finally enters at m. 89.

The bass, represented in example 3.11a shows an arpeggiation of the B-flat minor instead of the B-flat major harmony, the minor third D-flat appearing in m. 75. Thus it becomes evident that the initial "E-flat minor" six-four chord has nothing to do with E-flat minor; rather, it is related to the D-flat chord arising in m. 75, and this in turn is part of the larger B-flat minor harmony. The g-flat^1 is an auxiliary note of f^1 in m. 43 and serves as consonant preparation of the seventh g-flat in m. 64. It then returns to f, as shown in example 3.11a. This makes it clear that the first E-flat harmony is reached only after the second subject has passed by: in m. 89, at the beginning of the coda of the exposition. Instead of bringing in the second subject on III, which is the normal procedure, Beethoven starts it on B-flat, that is, during the motion towards E-flat. The purpose of this overlap of structural and thematic events is to achieve a tighter connection between the different sections. In an earlier work, Sonata in F Minor op. 2 no. 1, Beethoven had based the second subject on the dominant of III. However, the prolongation of that dominant was simpler and briefer than the instance in opus 13. Turning now to the function of register in this remarkable treatment of theme and harmonic progression, we see with the aid of example 3.11b that the main bass progression from the beginning of the exposition to the beginning of the coda consists of C–B-flat–E-flat.

Note against note, above this bass progression, the top voice moves from c^3 in m. 15 to d^3 in m. 45 and finally to e-flat^3 in m. 98. This ascending third in the upper voice thus spans the entire exposition, unfolding in a single register. In relation to it the second subject is an interpolation, an episode between the passing tone d^3 and its goal e-flat^3. Truly, a greater triumph in the use of register for large-scale connections could hardly be imagined.

In addition it must be remarked that the rising third c–d–e-flat represents more than just the lower third of the C-minor triad: it is thematic in character, constituting a huge enlargement of the same third in m. 1 of the introduction. The introduction itself shows a first enlargement of this third, with the same bass as later in the Allegro, in the one-line octave in mm. 1, 4 (end), and 5. This enlargement then prepares the ground, so to speak, for the second and most extended enlargement in the exposition.

In the recapitulation it was not possible for Beethoven to duplicate the effect he had created with his treatment of the second subject in the exposition. Obviously he could not base it on the dominant, *G*, and begin it with a six-four chord on this tone. To provide at least some harmonic contrast and achieve an effect similar to the suspense created by the B-flat harmony in the exposition, he begins the second subject on the F-minor six-four chord, the subdominant (m. 221), which then leads to V and to I. This six-four chord is, for once, a true inversion since it is followed by the F-minor-sixth chord.

This was a satisfactory solution for matching the harmonic appearance of the second subject in the exposition. But how could an equivalent be found for the bypassing of the second subject by means of the high register? Since the recapitulation begins and ends in C minor—not, as does the exposition, on different harmonies—this was impossible. But Beethoven found a "substitute solution," one which is as impressive as his use of register in the exposition. We find that the development section concludes in m. 187 with a V^7 chord. The resolution of the seventh f^3 to e-flat^3 seems not to be forthcoming. The recapitulation begins, the entire first subject passes by, still no e-flat^3. The second subject begins on the subdominant, as described above; then in mm. 231–32 the melody leaps, unexpectedly and strikingly, to f^3. This f^3 takes up the preceding, unresolved f^3 of the development; it becomes a seventh over the following dominant and finally resolves to e-flat^3 in m. 239, in the tonic six-four chord. This is the "substitute solution": Instead of bypassing the second subject with the high register so that it would sound parenthetical, the beginning of the recapitulation itself is bypassed and appears incidental to the progression V^7–I^3 (f^3–e-flat^3), which extends far into the second subject. In the Menuetto of his Quartet in A Minor, Schubert carried out the same idea but by different means, as previously discussed and illustrated in example 3.8.

Example 3.12a shows Beethoven's general plan (an octave lower) and explains also why the six-four chord in m. 239 must be considered a tonic six-four, not an embellishing chord of any kind.

Example 3.12b includes f^3 of the second subject. This note appears first as a consonant sixth which prepares and reintroduces the seventh f^3. One can hardly consider it as structurally, contrapuntally connected back to f^3 of the development. Rather, f^3 forms what one might describe as a prefix to e-flat^3. It is associative in character,

Example 3.12

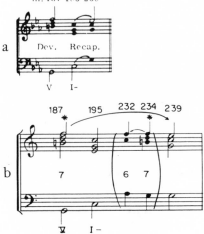

reiterating f³ of m. 187 for the purpose of underscoring the large progression f³–e-flat³.

In a looser way even the introduction of opus 13 is connected to the Allegro by means of the high register. Its climax is also a V⁷ chord with f³. This f³ does continue to an e-flat³, but since e-flat³ appears in a six-four chord on the dominant, it is a passing tone moving on to d² in the next measure, not a true resolution. In the strictest sense, then, f³ resolves in the three-line octave only at m. 98, towards the end of the exposition. This huge arch subordinates the first and second subjects of the exposition, just as f³ of the development section moves to e-flat³ of the second subject and bridges everything in between.

But even if we wanted to attach more importance to e-flat³ in m. 10—it certainly gives more definition to the ending of the introduction than is found at the end of the development section—the fact would remain that the three-line octave is abandoned at this point, that no d³ as the tone of resolution appears, and that e-flat³ is taken up only in m. 98. Consequently, the picture drawn in example 3.13 would not be essentially altered. Corroborating our reading is the striking resemblance of mm. 9–11 to mm. 187–95, with passages rushing down to the beginning of the first subject.

One can safely say that the grandiose use of the high register for creating large-scale connections and for tying various sections closely together constitutes one of the main features of this movement. If

Example 3.13

we compare this movement to later compositions of Beethoven, it is fair to say that it equals them in scope as far as the use of register is concerned. In other respects, such as complexity of content or subtlety of expression, Beethoven's later compositions probably surpass the Sonate *Pathétique.*

In closing we point out that the purpose of this article has been to indicate the important role which register can play in establishing the larger connections in a musical composition. We have seen that in some works, particularly in piano works, register assumes a significance as great as that of harmonic and contrapuntal texture or the unfoldment of thematic-motivic relationships. Its importance as one of the structural elements of music should not be overlooked in composition and analysis.

NOTES

1. In Schenker, *Das Meisterwerk in der Musik*, vol. 2 (Munich: Drei Master Verlag, 1926), hereafter cited as Jahrbuch II.

2. Schenker, *Neue musikalische Theorien und Phantasien*, vol. 3, *Der freie Satz* (Vienna: Universal Edition, 1935 and 1956), sec. 268–70.

3. Siegfried Borris, "Das Bearbeitungsverfahren bei den 11 Präludien in Friedeman-Bach-Buch," *Die Musikforschung* 5 (1952).

4. Schenker, *Der Tonwille*, 10 issues (Vienna: A. Gutmann Verlag, 1921–24), 3:43.

4. Design as a Key to Structure in Tonal Music

John Rothgeb

The method by which an analyst relates the structure of a piece to its constituent levels is often obscured by the simplicity and apparent ease of the solution. John Rothgeb's essay addresses the difficult area of how to go about doing an actual analysis from the beginning.

The reader is urged not to pass too lightly over his description of examples 4.1 and 4.2, in which "the durational unit remains constant throughout; the only rhythmic articulation is that which results from purely tonal processes." An understanding of these "tonal processes" (harmony, counterpoint, texture, and design) is thus an indispensable prerequisite for analysis.

Here the point should be made that Schenkerian theory is not an alien system superimposed upon pieces of music. Rather, good conclusions one may draw about tonal compositions are the outgrowth of a solid grounding in principles of harmony, figured-bass, compound line, and strict counterpoint. David Beach's description of Schenker's main writings, at the end of this collection, makes it very clear how Schenker arrived at his most mature thought in the context of his long study of basic harmony, counterpoint, and form. (See also John Rothgeb's article "Strict Counterpoint and Tonal Theory," JMT 19:2 (1975), pp. 260–84, which specifically describes the relationship of Schenkerian principles to species counterpoint.)—Ed.

It has long been recognized that simple and basic principles of voice leading are operative in the masterworks of tonal music. These principles give a foundation of coherence upon which the most elaborate configurations of the musical surface acquire significance; they are the source of musical direction, climax, closure, and other phenomena that we associate with structure on the large span. This has been demonstrated repeatedly, and the principles themselves—the theoretical bases—are relatively easy to grasp; yet their application to practical analytical problems remains extremely difficult. Perhaps this is to be expected, for as Milton Babbitt has observed, "anything vital is problematical; the nonproblematical is static." Nevertheless, it is surprising that there have been so few attempts to specify procedures for the derivation of musical analyses. There is still no textbook in which pedagogically satisfactory techniques of analysis are presented.[1]

I do not propose to offer here a general solution to the problem, but rather to discuss one aspect of the totality of musical structure—namely the design of the surface—and its implications for the study of voice leading. In particular, I shall cite a number of examples which illustrate the following general principle: Changes in surface design usually coincide with crucial structural points, and accordingly such changes must be given the most thoughtful attention in deriving or verifying an analysis.

It is appropriate to begin with two examples from Bach that show the greatest economy of articulative resources on the musical surface. In both examples there is little change of texture, and since the durational unit remains constant throughout, the only rhythmic articulation is that which results from purely tonal processes. The first work is the Presto from Bach's first unaccompanied violin sonata, in G minor. Example 4.1 shows a synopsis of the events in the first twenty-five measures. At m. 9 the head tone b-flat^2 is established after an ascent from g^2; m. 9 functions as a nodal point, becoming at once the point of departure for the next motion, which reaches the dom-

Example 4.1 Bach, Violin Sonata in G Minor

inant at m. 12. Measure 13, a rhythmically strong measure,[2] begins a "sequential" passage that lasts until m. 17, where we find a significant change of design and the beginning of a different "sequence" which ends at m. 25, where a new design group begins. Let us consider the purpose of these design changes in m. 17 and m. 25. We are all familiar with the usual textbook admonitions against carrying on a "sequence" too long, but we are rarely shown exactly why the boundaries of such passages fall where they do. Bach does not change design just because a continuation would be "monotonous" (see mm. 121–26 of this same movement, where a melodic pattern occurs no fewer than six times in succession moving upward in steps); he changes design at points where a structural unit is completed and a new one begins; that is, in order to clarify underlying structure. In the Presto example, m. 13 shows a beginning on the tonic with the original b-flat[2] transferred down an octave to b-flat[1]; at m. 17, an E-flat triad has arrived and a stepwise ascending progression with the typical 5–6 alternation leads to the long range goal, a B-flat harmony (as III of G minor) which is first reached at the next design change, m. 25, and thereafter confirmed by a cadence at m. 32. How clearly these design groupings express the underlying counterpoint between m. 13 and m. 25 is shown in example 4.2. The change at m. 17 points

Example 4.2

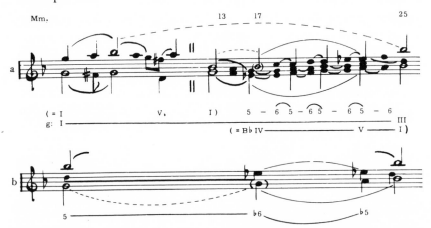

out the E-flat harmony, which represents basically a change from 5 to ♭6 above a bass tone G (see example 4.2b); just before m. 25 this ♭6 becomes a diminished fifth of the bass passing tone A and returns to d[2] within the B-flat harmony at m. 25. Bach's concern for the longer span is now made apparent as the original b-flat^2 returns simultaneously with the arrival of III.

The technique of "modulating" from I to III in minor as shown in the Presto, mm. 13–26, is common enough and is certainly the simplest and most obvious contrapuntal solution to the problem. But it is marvelous to see the care that Bach takes to change details of the continuity, always avoiding the schematic or mechanical, and achieving the utmost clarity and coherence. In the D Minor Prelude from book 1 of *The Well-Tempered Clavier* we find exactly the same basic procedure used in mm. 2–4; the aim is again the I–III progression, here in D minor. The sixth, B-flat, arrives on the second beat of m. 3, again locally expressed as a root-position triad, and there follows precisely the same type of ascending progression with the 5–6 alternation that we saw in the Presto, mm. 17–25 (see example 4.3).[3] The remarkable feature here is the change of register in the left hand within the rising sequence that began on B-flat. On the last beat of m. 3, just at the arrival of d^1 in the left hand, Bach writes an octave instead of the third that would have been expected; this change of register results in a connection to the original d in mm. 1–2, which now moves through the passing tone e to f in m. 4. The reader can easily see the other obvious ways in which features of design and detail determine and are determined by the voice leading prototype.

Another example of the interaction of design with basic plan is provided by mm. 10–13 of the same prelude. Bach's bass line has moved from F as III, confirmed by a cadence at m. 6, through G (mm. 7–8) to A, the dominant, at m. 10. Since the first part of the bass arpeggiation (the motion from root to fifth within D minor) is completed at m. 10, we would naturally expect a change of design, and one does indeed occur. Now the structural problem is to return from the fifth to the tonic, but first the minor dominant must become major; Bach accomplishes this by a descending passage in which the bass moves from A, m. 10, to g, m. 12, where a G-minor chord appears as a neighboring-tone harmony returning to the dominant (now major) in the middle of m. 12; the completion to I follows immediately at m. 13. (The passage from m. 10 to m. 12 also gives Bach an opportunity to regain the two-line register which was left in m. 4 and to introduce the structural $\hat{4}$, g^2, as a consonant octave of the neighboring-tone harmony in m. 12.) From m. 10 to m. 12 the bass really moves down through a ninth, articulated as four thirds, but because of various octave leaps the result is merely the

Example 4.3 Bach, D Minor Prelude (*The Well-Tempered Clavier*, book 1)

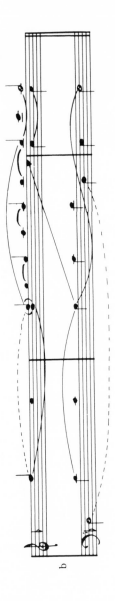
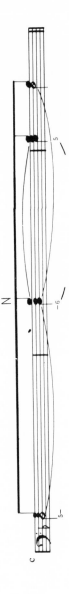

descent of a second (the basic idea to begin with). Now it is an error rather common among beginning students in analyzing this piece to read the arrival of the D-minor tonic at m. 11, where there is in fact a D-minor chord, and at first glance one can see some design features that support such a reading: the low D on the first beat of m. 11 and the change of register in the upper part. These changes, however, are overridden by the fact that bass and soprano fundamentally move in parallel tenths (with 9–10 suspensions) with a repeated inner voice configuration all the way from m. 10 to m. 12 (see example 4.4). Admittedly the regaining of the high register in m. 12 plays an important role in clarifying the meaning of the passage, but the continuity of the descending tenths from m. 10 to m. 12 alone should prove immediately that any event within that span must be regarded as transient, as a passing event within a larger structural unit.

Occasionally the most subtle of foreground changes provides clarification of the meaning of harmonic events. Bach's small Prelude in C Minor BWV 999 (usually printed as the third of *Twelve Little Preludes*) is not a closed composition, ending as it does on the dominant of C minor. (A condensed score is given in example 4.5.) In m. 13 a G-minor harmony arrives, introduced by a diminished-seventh chord on F-sharp; at m. 17 a dominant-seventh chord built on D is reached, which ultimately resolves to the G-major chord that ends the piece. Even Schenker, in an early published analysis,[4] regarded the G minor of m. 13 as the arrival of the dominant, within which the minor third was converted to a major third at the end, and he accordingly explained the $D_{\sharp}^{7}$ of m. 17 as the *Oberquintteiler* ("dividing dominant") of the G: thus m. 13 to the end would represent basically a prolongation of G. One would have to be suspicious of this reading just because of the weight given to the extended $D_{\sharp}^{7}$ in mm. 17–32, and one's doubts would be confirmed by the progress of the upper voice from m. 1 to m. 17. The initial tonic prolongation occurs in mm. 1–8 by a connection from the principal tone g^1 ($\hat{5}$) to the inner voice e-flat^1; the latter tone is retained until the arrival of the G minor at m. 13, where it moves to d^1. There follows a strong connection in the bass of E-flat (m. 15) to D (m. 17), and just as the E-flat enters, the upper voice again takes over the first tone g^1 from which it moves to f-sharp^1 in parallel tenths with the bass. The regaining of g^1 ($\hat{5}$) at this point establishes a connection with the very

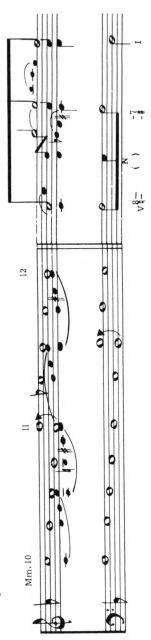

Example 4.4 Bach, D Minor Prelude (*The Well-Tempered Clavier*, book 1)

Example 4.5 Bach, Prelude in C Minor BWV 999

beginning and suggests that the intervening G-minor chord, rather than being the arrival of V, is really a passing chord. Indeed, the G-minor chord supports large-scale passing tones in thirds, d/b-flat, moving to c/a-natural, as shown in example 4.6. So the basic motion of the whole piece is I–II$^7_\#$ (or V of V)–V♮ in mm. 1, 17, and 32 respectively—and the G minor at m. 13 is a chord of purely contrapuntal origin. In my opinion, all other things being equal, it would be hard to escape this reading even if the literal soprano did not skip back to the original g^1 at m. 15, but this small feature of detail makes the total structure crystal clear, and otherwise it might not have been so.

Example 4.6

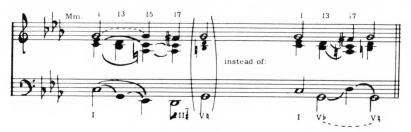

A more difficult example is found in the third of C. P. E. Bach's "demonstration" sonatas that accompanied the *Versuch über die wahre Art das Clavier zu spielen* (1753 and 1762). The third movement of this work, in E major, already shows most of the important features of sonata-allegro form, including a development section and a complete recapitulation. The text of the development (mm. 25–48), which begins with the opening theme in the dominant, is given in ex. 4.7 (see p. 82). It is a complex composition, but again the basic plan is clearly indicated by variations in the surface design. Among the problems that are solved by the design groupings is the meaning of the E-major harmony in mm. 29–31. The E triad here surely does not represent the structural return of I, for if it did we would have to understand these measures as the beginning of the recapitulation. (Incidentally, they are identical to the opening measures in all respects excepting only the bass in the first half of m. 29.) This E major, then, must fit into the larger plan as a transient event, a connective from the B of m. 25 to some later harmony.[5] The first step in discovering the solution is to observe that mm. 29–32 are composed as a transposition of mm. 25–28, so the total group is homogenous from the design standpoint. At m. 33, however, there is a significant change, introducing a new group that lasts until the arrival of an F-sharp-minor harmony at m. 37. As a result of these groupings the basic motion is clarified, and we see the connection between b^1 over B at m. 25 and a^2 over c-sharp at m. 33. The outer voices, an octave, have simply moved in a step to a sixth. In the process, b^1 was transferred up an octave to make the registral connection. (If we want to be very precise contrapuntally, we might also read an inner voice f-sharp^1 (m. 25), g-sharp^1 (m. 31), a^1 (m. 33), and thereby complete the explanation of the E harmony as a support for the passing tone g-sharp.) Further events in the course of this development are more difficult, but there is still a remarkable transparency of structure as a result of the surface design. To describe the course of events briefly: mm. 33–36 again form a design unit expressing the basic voice leading $\begin{smallmatrix} 6-5 \\ \natural - \sharp \end{smallmatrix}$ above the c-sharp bass with the seventh, b, returning at the end; thus a^2 of m. 33 was only a passing tone to g-sharp, and the original b^2 is retained, resolving the lower register to a^1 at m. 37. The dramatic F-sharp-minor section, with its syncopated rhythm and dynamic changes, restores the two-line register, bringing a^2 as the continuation of the original b^2 from m. 32 (and earlier, in the exposition). This a^2, first brought in as a consonance about f-sharp, becomes a dissonant diminished seventh above B-sharp and moves (implicitly) to g-sharp over c-sharp at m. 41. There are many details here that would merit further discussion, but I leave them for the reader to discover. Three levels of structure for mm. 25–46 are shown in example 4.8 (see p. 84).

Even more contrast in surface design is shown in Mozart's A Minor Sonata K. 310, development section. The main structural points are given in example 4.9. At m. 50 the development begins with the first theme, which is the principal source of motivic content until m. 70, where the content changes significantly. At m. 73 there is another important change, with the left hand descending quickly in quarter notes to the dominant in the following measure. Thus the total motion expressed in the development is the continuation of the triadic bass arpeggiation from C, the third step of A minor, to E, the fifth, with the most striking internal change occurring at the arrival of a D-minor triad in m. 70. The structural weight that thereby accrues to this D minor is perfectly logical and understandable when we consider the underlying voice leading: the bass fills the space from c to e with the passing tone d, while the upper voice counterpoint moves from g^2 through f^2 (above the bass tone d) as a passing tone, arriving at e^2 simultaneously with the bass at m. 74. The resulting structure is shown in example 4.10. Further insight is provided in the following remarks by Oswald Jonas:

[At m. 70] the upper voice has arrived at f^2, and the bass at the passing tone d. Both voices should now converge on the octave e. At this point a motivic problem arises for the forthcoming recapitulation. The first theme of the sonata began with an appoggiatura d-sharp^2. But here the upper voice comes directly from f^2, the bass from d. This could have resulted in a purely mechanical quoting of the appoggiatura; but Mozart instead composes an exchange of voices wherein the bass tone d is taken over by the upper voice as d-sharp^2, while the f^2 of the upper voice is transferred to the bass, thus introducing the appoggiatura tone d-sharp organically, really composing it in the large.[6]

The exchange of voices is indicated by arrows in example 4.10; it is carried out by means of a passing tone e^2 in the upper voice with an A-minor harmony as consonant support.

Jonas's observations on the motivic problem, the large-scale composing of an embellishment, apply equally well to a somewhat more

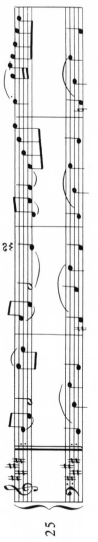

Example 4.7 C. P. E. Bach, Sonata III, third movement, development

Example 4.8 C. P. E. Bach, Sonata III, third movement, development

Example 4.9 Mozart, K. 310

complex passage in Mozart's A Minor Rondo K. 511, mm. 64–74.
The music is shown in example 4.11. This example moves basically
from the end of an F-major "episode" to the dominant of A minor in
preparation for the return of the rondo theme. Because the top voice
of the closing F-major chord is the octave of the bass F, there is the
additional danger of parallel octaves between soprano and bass as the
latter moves to the dominant e. Mozart solves this problem, and at
the same time composes an enormously enlarged version of the turn
which opens the rondo theme, by moving the soprano through a
passing tone e (transformed to a consonance by an A-minor chord,
just as in the preceding sonata example) to d-sharp at the end of
m. 73 (see example 4.12).[7]

We have already seen in the Bach D Minor Prelude (*The Well-
Tempered Clavier*, book 1) an example in which register is an indispensable guide to subsurface structure.[8] In the exposition of Mozart's
D Minor String Quartet K. 421, register and other aspects of design
combine to clarify long-span voice leading and at the same time to
foreshadow the second theme in a most remarkable way. The transi-

Example 4.10 Mozart, A Minor Sonata K. 310

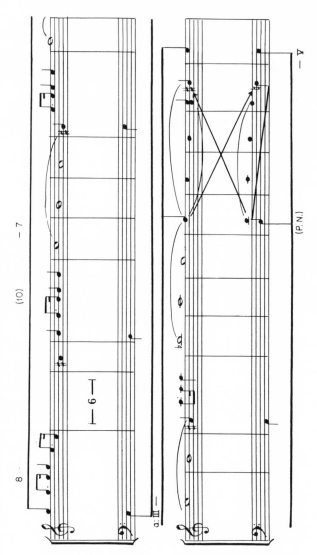

Example 4.11 Mozart, K. 511

tion to the second theme begins in m. 9 and features a descending
melodic fourth, a^2–g^2–f^2–e^2; at m. 12 the fourth is compressed by
suppression of the passing tones and is presented in four different
registers by the four instruments in succession. As the cello arrives at
E, forte, the original upper voice a^2 moves up a step to the neighboring tone b-flat^2, giving a 6/5 chord over E and thus the dominant of
III where the second theme will appear. But instead of resolving the
b-flat^2 immediately in its own register, Mozart drastically changes
register and dynamics (the latter to piano). In the middle of m. 16
the 6/5 chord is regained, but now in the middle register. It is prolonged to m. 18, with the upper voice moving basically b-flat^1–a^1–

Example 4.12 Mozart, K. 511

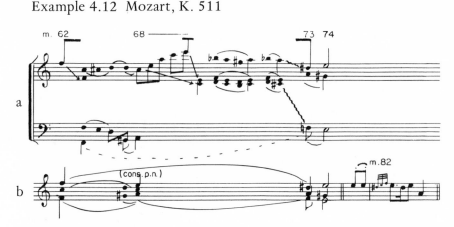

g^1, with the passing tone a^1 made consonant as the third of an F chord. Example 4.13 shows roughly the contents of mm. 14–18. Now in m. 19 a new two-measure group begins which has the effect of introducing c^2 in the top voice; in mm. 21 and 22 the c^2 descends through b-natural^1 to b-flat^1, and it is just following this, in m. 23, that the high register reappears and the resolution of b-flat^2 to a^2 occurs. If the motive in the first violin at m. 23 had imitated exactly

Example 4.13 Mozart, K. 421

the previous occurrences in mm. 20–22, it would have begun with an octave leap c^2–c^3, but Mozart alters this beginning so that the total motive, g^2–c^3–b-flat^2–a^2, repeats in a compressed form the basic shape of the upper part from the phrase ending at m. 18 to the b-flat^1 at m. 22.[9] This is remarkable enough in itself, but it takes on added significance in relation to the second theme, which fashions itself along the same lines, opening with the figure f^1–b-flat^1–a^1–g^1, which is then repeated a step higher. Example 4.14 graphically illustrates these relationships.

  In the second movement of C. P. E. Bach's third demonstration sonata, an important motivic clarification is provided by the dy-

Example 4.14   Mozart, D Minor String Quartet K. 421

Example 4.15 C. P. E. Bach, Sonata III, second movement

namic markings. The text of mm. 15–26 is included in example 4.15. The movement is in A minor, and at m. 14 a cadence to C major completes the first part of the large bass arpeggiation I–III–V. At m. 19 an E-major harmony arrives, but it probably does not yet represent "the" dominant (although this is debatable), because the bass continues another step to f at m. 21. Observe that precisely in m. 20 at the tone b the dynamic abruptly drops to piano, with forte returning at the f in m. 21. This has the effect of unifying the fifth descent from c^1 at m. 19 to the next true bass tone, f; it gives the impression of a 5–6 motion above the bass e at m. 19 such that the sixth, c^1, ties across to become the fifth of f. But the return of forte in m. 21 also points out the figure f–d-sharp–e, a motivic shape that has permeated the texture of the work in its detail, appearing (sometimes inverted) both as three eighth notes within a beat and also as an eighth-note upbeat plus two eighths in the following beat. In the excerpt quoted the reader will immediately find several such instances. He will also note that an even larger augmentation (see example 4.16) of the motive is presented in mm. 23–26; and this is quite an impressive compositional feat, for mm. 23–26 form a transposed recapitulation of an earlier section, mm. 9–12. In its earlier occur-

Example 4.16

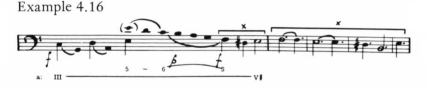

rences, however, the passage had quite a different meaning, having been approached in a different way. The ability to recapitulate a section and to make it appear logical and convincing in a different way in its new environment shows a thorough compositional mastery.

One final example, the Brahms Waltz op. 39 no. 11, will show again how dynamics and expression marks sometimes coincide with, and therefore clarify, structural connections. This waltz (see example 4.17), a ternary form, opens in B minor, but the final *A* section is composed in B major, and it is this section, mm. 25–40, with which we are concerned. The bass fundamentally ascends stepwise from the tonic to the cadential dominant, reached at m. 39; the stepwise ascent is elaborated by chromatic passing tones (B–B-sharp–C-sharp, etc.), and these give rise to secondary dominants to the triads on C-sharp and D-sharp. The literal bass descends a third each time to the root of the secondary dominant, which contrapuntally represents the sixth of the preceding bass tone, and thus the familiar 5–6 voice leading. As soon as D-sharp is reached, however, the melodic direction changes; the melody, having been forced upward, so to speak, by the ascending bass, now begins its descent, and Brahms accordingly changes the design of the bass. Instead of another descending third, D-sharp–C-sharp–B, in mm. 34–36, Brahms inverts the third and expresses it as an ascending sixth: D-sharp–F-sharp–B. As a result the expected 5–6 above D does indeed occur; now, to clarify the connection of D in m. 34 to E in m. 37 (and also for reasons derived from the melody), Brahms writes "piano, dolce." The placement of this dynamic and expression mark corresponds also to the distribution of harmonic weight, since m. 37 represents really the beginning of the cadence, the cadential II^6 (see example 4.18).

One of the chief sources of the beauty of tonal masterworks is the simplicity, elegance, and precision of the principles of harmony and voice leading upon which they are based. Those principles are realized in a different way in each individual work, and to understand exactly how they are realized requires the closest attention to detail and design. Conversely, as the structural basis of a work begins to be under-

Example 4.17   Brahms, Waltz op. 39 no. 11

Example 4.18

stood, the surface associations acquire new dimensions; so perhaps a necessary complement to this paper would be one entitled "Structure as a Key to Design in Tonal Music."

NOTES

1. This is not to deny the existence of pedagogically valuable descriptions of musical structure, but only to observe that such descriptions almost never concern themselves with procedures by which an analysis can be derived or critically evaluated.

2. In the manuscript Bach clearly indicates the basic two-measure groupings by writing long bar lines at the beginning of each odd-numbered measure and short bar lines elsewhere.

3. The analysis may seem strange at first glance, since it almost appears that Bach arrives at F (III) on beat 1 of m. 3; but the reader should consider the metric structure of the first four measures: the strong beat at the beginning was displaced by one beat, thus falling on beat 2, and beat 2 remains the strongest beat of each measure until m. 5. Therefore the counterpoint in mm. 2–3 should be read as descending 10ths, f^2/d^1, e^2/c^1, d^2/b-flat, as shown in example 3.

4. *Der Tonwille* 5 (1923):3–4.

5. The appearance of a pseudo tonic early in the second part of a sonata movement is, of course, quite normal. (See for example, the Allegro from Handel's Suite II in F, mm. 17–18, or Haydn's Sonata in F, Hob. 23, I, mm. 52–53.) Such "tonics" always function as intermediate points in a larger motion.

6. *Das Wesen des musikalischen Kunstwerks* (Vienna, 1934), p. 143.

7. To appreciate fully the significance of this enlarged turn one should be aware of the extraordinarily important motivic role of turns throughout the work, and particularly in the F-major section. (See O. Jonas, "Mozarts ewige Melodie," *Der Dreiklang* 3 [1937]:84–92.)

8. For an excellent discussion of the structural use of register see Ernst Oster, "Register and the Large-Scale Connection," Chapter 3, this volume.

9. It is clear from the manuscript (published in facsimile by the Robert Owen Lehman Foundation, New York) that Mozart did in fact write the octave c^2–c^3 first, substituting g^2 for c^2 only afterward.

5. Rubato and the Middleground

Maury Yeston

The following essay merely touches upon a problem that remains far from being solved—the analysis of rhythmic levels and an understanding of their interaction. The position taken here is that meter cannot be accepted as a functioning "given" in a composition but that it must be indicated and supported by tonal relationships. As illustrated in example 5.5 below, no single level of motion carries the meter by itself. Indeed meter would appear to grow out of a relationship between rhythmic levels much in the same way that tonal coherence is an outgrowth of relationships between pitch levels.

An additional aspect of temporal relations in the context of pitch levels can be seen by observing the rhythmic values associated with middleground events. In this regard see Ernst Oster's note 5 at the end of his analysis of Mozart's Menuetto K.V. 355 in this volume (p. 140).

Tempo rubato may be generally described as a practice whereby a performer deviates, by tempo variation and other means, from the notated rhythmic values of a score. The effect of this practice poses some interesting problems for music theory, particularly in the context of metrical music. To what extent does a performer's informality with regularity of tempo and prescribed durational values risk obscuring the metric structure of a piece? How much and what kind of change is permissible? And finally, should a specific meter survive through a highly distorting rubato treatment, what are the inherent structural aspects of a musical work that provide for such survival?

There has been substantial variation in the precise meaning of rubato over the past four hundred years. The practice is likely to have begun with subtle applications of interpretive rhythmic alteration in the context of vocal music. Probably the earliest written suggestion to take some cognizance of tempo and some liberty with rhythm in the performance of a work appears in Luis Milán's *El Maestro* (1535), where the lutanist is exhorted to play *a espacio* ("slowly") or *a priesa* ("quickly") during the chordal or embellished passages respectively.[1] In the early seventeenth century, Caccini and, later Frescobaldi urge some rhythmic freedom upon the performer in order to heighten the expression of affect and to achieve a *parlando* style.[2]

It is in the theoretical writings of the eighteenth century, however, that rubato gains rather specific definition. Both C. P. E. Bach's and Leopold Mozart's concepts of the practice lend primacy to the etymology of the term, tempo rubato literally meaning "stolen" or "robbed" time. This can be seen in their consistent reference to rubato only in the context of an accompanied soloist or, on the keyboard, of a right-hand melodic figure accompanied by the left hand. In either case the accompanist, or the accompanying left hand, is cautioned to maintain strict tempo. Since it is against a strict metric support that the rubato part plays, the length of the bar is clearly meant to remain substantially the same. Thus any note that is given added duration in the rubato part will likely "steal" its temporal increment from another note that is correspondingly shortened. Here, L. Mozart:

> Many, who have no idea of taste, never retain the evenness of tempo in the accompanying of a concerto part but endeavour always to follow the solo part. . . . But when a true virtuoso who is worthy of the title is to be accompanied then one must not allow oneself to be beguiled, by the postponing or anticipating of the notes which he knows how to shape so adroitly and touchingly, into hesitating or hurrying but must continue to play throughout in the same manner, else the effect which the performer desired to build up would be demolished by the accompaniment.

Here, Mozart adds a footnote:

> To a sound virtuoso he certainly must not yield, for he would then spoil his tempo rubato. What this "stolen tempo" is, is more easily shown than described. But on the other hand, if the accompanist has to deal with a *soi-disant* virtuoso, then he may, after an adagio cantabile, have to hold out many a quaver the length of half a bar, until perchance the latter recovers from his paroxysms.[3]

C. P. E. Bach's definition closely resembles the one above and appears to draw distinctions even more narrowly. Note that his prescription for rubato playing calls for an alternate level of regular motion that plays against the normal metric division of the bar.

This brings us to the tempo rubato. Its indication is simply the presence of more or fewer notes than are contained in the normal division of the bar. A whole bar, part of one, or several bars may be distorted in this manner. The most difficult but important task is to give all notes of the same value exactly the same duration. When the execution is such that one hand seems to play against the bar and the other strictly with it, it may then be said that the performer is doing everything that can be required of him. It is only rarely that all parts are struck simultaneously.[4]

Again, there is no suggestion of radical tempo-altering initiatives that might be taken by performers. The actual duration of the bar is clearly preserved, and Bach stresses a characteristic equality of note values in the rubato part as he continues:

As soon as the upper part begins slavishly to follow the bar, the essence of the rubato is lost, for then all other parts must be played in time. Other instrumentalists and singers, when they are accompanied, can introduce the tempo much more easily than the solo keyboardist. The reason for this is the one just stated (i.e. it is easier for two performers to play in contrived disagreement than it is for the two hands of a single performer). If necessary the solo keyboardist may alter the bass, but not the harmony. Most keyboard pieces contain rubato passages. The division and indication of these is about as satisfactory as can be expected. He who has mastered the tempo rubato need not be fettered by the numerals which divide notes into groups of 5, 7, 11, etc. According to his disposition, but always with appropriate freedom, he may add or omit notes. [p. 162]

One line, almost hidden in the above citation, should be brought out here: "the solo keyboardist may alter the bass but not the harmony." Bach's proscription can be read two ways, both of which are relevant. First, there is the implication that the bass may be somewhat altered (e.g., its figuration may be changed, or a chord may be represented by one of its inversions) but that an actual change in harmony is an abuse of the harmonic structure of a piece. Secondly, there is the possibility that Bach sees a change in harmony as a danger to the rhythmic-metric structure of a piece, especially since the warning is couched in a section that describes the limits of rhythmic liberties and that is directed towards preserving metric order.

There are other sections of Bach's treatise that implicitly address the interaction of altered rhythm with pitch and meter. Significantly, these passages describe rhythmic practices that Bach did not subsume under the rubato heading but that were later to be included as rubato practices by zealous (and overzealous) interpreters of Romantic music: accelerations, ritards, pauses, elongations of durations, changing meters—in short, the musical "paroxysms" feared by Leopold Mozart.

Here, then, is a historical anomaly that bears underlining. Tempo rubato has come to mean the opposite of its eighteenth-century counterpart. Where the earlier practice could occur only alongside another part that is required to retain metric regularity at all costs, the more modern practice stretches, contracts, and generally challenges the elasticity of meter since all parts of the music may be made subject to the same rhythmic deformation. In effect, the newer rubato can be achieved by doing what Bach and Mozart, in their definitions, specifically say not to do. Hence, those sections of Bach's treatise that deal with what he considered to be nonrubato rhythmic alterations are the ones that are relevant to later practice.

In a short paragraph, Bach first recognizes the importance of general tempo alterations, and he limits them to solo performers or small ensembles.

> In order to avoid vagueness, rests as well as notes must be given their exact value except at fermate and cadences. Yet certain purposeful violations of the beat are often exceptionally beautiful. However, a distinction in their use must be observed. In solo performance and in ensembles made up of only a few players, manipulations are permissible which affect the tempo itself; here, the group will be less apt to go astray than to become attentive and adopt the change; but in large ensembles made up of motley players the manipulations must be addressed to the bar alone without touching on the broader pace. [pp. 150–51]

He later becomes more specific about the treatment of the fermatas and cadences mentioned above:

> Great pains must be taken to achieve a uniform performance and prevent anyone's coming in before or after the others. This applies to fermate, cadences, etc., as well as caesurae. It is customary to drag a bit and depart somewhat from a strict observance of the bar, for the note before the rest as well as the rest itself is extended beyond its notated length. [p. 375]

In a manner that recalls Frescobaldi's earlier view, Bach attributes these procedures of rhythmic deviation not to an overt change of structure but rather to the expression of feeling: "On entering a fermata expressive of languidness, tenderness, or sadness, it is customary to broaden slightly" (p. 162).

It is in his discussion of closing trills, however, that Bach appears to take into account the relationship of rhythmic alteration to gesture and to pitch structure, and it is here that his treatise implies some principles well worth exploring. (The examples for the following excerpt are Bach's own.)

> Closing trills are often extended, regardless of tempo. . . . This kind of close, however, despite its good uses cannot be introduced into all contexts. Hence, some closing trills must be played strictly in tempo due to either the brilliant or the reflective character of a passage [ex. 5.1A]. It is understood, moreover, that the accompanist does not hold back when the trill appears over a moving bass [ex. 5.1B]. But if the last of these bass notes is the fifth of the key it should be held until it is observed that the principal part or the other executants are ready to conclude their trill [ex. 5.1C]. The same procedure is to be followed when solely the fifth of the key is repeated in the upper or lower octave after the entrance of a trill [ex. 5.1D]. [pp. 375–76]

Bach's explanation of his examples lacks one vital dimension here: he neglects to tell us why, in particular, it is dangerous to lengthen the trill and the bar in examples $5.1A^1$, A^2, and A^3, or what the precise nature of the ill effect might be should an accompanist "hold back" over the moving bass of example 5.1B, or why elongations of the bar are, on the contrary, permissible for examples 5.1C and 5.1D. It should be stressed that Bach's is a practical guide and that one must speculate to a certain extent in order to suggest music-theoretical principles that conform to his advice to the performer.

The best clue Bach provides is his concern for preserving the "character" of the examples in 5.1A. It is clear that a steady metrical pace leading to a close is the indispensable gestural content of each one— but what meters will be sustained should the trills be extended? Significantly, the first two of these examples have no bass motion under the trill that might divide the beat and clarify the maintenance of their respective meters; this can be absolutely assured only by a carefully measured trill in these two passages. In the third instance ($5.1A^3$), the dotted figure on the third beat answers the rhythmic motive of the first beat. Extending the trill here risks losing this orderly motivic procession by distorting the second appearance of the motive and, again, might threaten the identity of the meter. This same presence of an answering rhythmic motive on the third beat is also apparent in example 5.1B. Furthermore, the pitch structure itself of this example is endangered by an extended trill in that the

Example 5.1

extension would unduly prolong a weak $^6_4$ chord over the B-natural of the bass.

Where strictness of tempo may be relaxed in examples 5.1C and 5.1D with no jeopardy to metric identity, however, it is important to see that both examples allow such liberty only over a final V harmony in root position. In addition, the potentially adverse effect of a prolonged trill upon the meter is mitigated in both cases not only by the strength of the V harmony as a metrical underpinning but also by the subdividing rhythm of the bass tones. The four eighth notes of example 5.1C and the three-quarter notes of example 5.1D deliver their V harmonies in parcels of time that articulate the durations of the $\hat{2}$s under which they are played, and this articulation is in accordance with the particular meter of each passage. Hence tempo is more naturally retarded and meter more felicitously expanded here than in former examples because the process of extension can be observed in the context of temporal gradations in the bass.

Note then that the penultimate bars of examples $5.1A^1$ and $5.1A^2$ place only single notes on their V harmonies. The attack rhythm[5] of example 5.1D, on the other hand, divides its V metrically under the final trill, while example 5.1C contains, in addition to this kind of calibration of the bar, a structural ritard in its foreground rhythmic succession of first sixteenth and then eighth notes. Indeed, a prolonged trill in this last example constitutes merely an enhancement of the gesture already implicit in its rhythmic composition. Again, these temporal alterations would appear to be most acceptable when the harmonic function of the bass is clear and supportive of the meter, and when more articulated motion in some part allows them to be introduced somewhat gradually.

Interpretive change appears to be most admissible then when it is partial or gradual or both; a thing altered must be seen being altered in order for its essential character to survive the change. Bach's examples have been presented here mainly because they imply a differentiation between allowable and adverse change even in the context of what amounts to a rhythmic nuance—an extended trill. As such, they point the way towards a fuller discussion of the limits of rubato in that they imply the following general principle: a passage may be rhythmically altered only insofar as its characteristic accentual structure is not abused.

What precisely constitutes this characteristic structure? The answer can be found in Bach's presentation of a free fantasia that appears at the end of his treatise. This compositional genre formally invites a performer to improvise melodically and rhythmically; furthermore, the bar lines customary to music notation are omitted from the score lest their presence inhibit the imagination. The goal in performance is a unique and studied irregularity of motion—similar to a declamatory style for which, in Bach's words, "tempo and meter must be frequently changed in order to rouse and still the rapidly alternating affects. Hence the metric signature is in many such cases more a convention of notation than a binding factor in performance" (p. 153).

Yet an absence of regularity of metrical accent in such a composition does not imply an absence of structural accent itself. Presumably, two different performances of a fantasia will be recognizable as being based on the same score should the integrity of some fundamental configuration of pitch and rhythmic accent be maintained in both cases. On some level, certain underlying pitch events—and their rhythmic values—will be consistent, and this amounts to saying that any number of performances of the same fantasia must properly share the same middleground pitch structure and the same middleground rhythmic structure.

Bach's example is crystal clear on this point. He first presents an underlying harmonic and rhythmic plan (ex. 5.2) and then presents a sample realization of this plan (ex. 5.3). (Examples 5.2 and 5.3 are only the opening portions of Bach's examples, pp. 442–43.) Note that the rhythmic values of example 5.2 indicate the length of time these events are meant to be prolonged by whatever foreground motion a performer may choose. The implicit caution to the performer is apparent: freedom is allowed in the choice of foreground arpeggiation and rhythmic motive, but variances in tempo and long-span durational values must still more or less preserve the format of the underlying plan. It is this latter structure whose elasticity is the limit of a rubato treatment—not the foreground.

Example 5.2

The reason for this last observation calls forth the true rhythmic function of a middleground: it is the source of accents. This can be no more clearly seen than in the context of a fantasia. Here there is no functioning metric signature. There are no bar lines. There is no consistent tempo (indeed, this is to be avoided). There is little consistency of dynamic level. There is no prescription for measured pauses between harmonic areas of the composition. In short, there are none of the traditional guideposts by which the music may be characterized by metrical or any other kind of accent; and so, for its accentuation and segmentation, the foreground is thrust back upon the procession of middleground events, each one of which marks off its concomitant foreground moment as an accent when it appears in performance. In his essay on this fantasia, for example, Heinrich Schenker demonstrates how the opening flourish conceals an intervening middleground level that contains an arpeggiation of the tonic

Example 5.3

triad (ex. 5.4A) that is further subdivided (ex. 5.4B), and it is my opinion that the rhythm of these events suggests a rhythm of accents for the foreground.[6]

Turning now to the question of rubato with respect to meter, it should be observed that the same principles and processes that give rise to accent in the free fantasia also give rise to accent in more metrically rigorous compositions. That is, metrical pieces may be considered as if they are fantasias—as if they lack metric signatures and bar lines; in fact, this is done all the time when they are listened to without looking at a score. The crucial difference between the two cases is that metrical music requires more regularly recurring accents;

Example 5.4

it requires a more even procession of those middleground events that accentuate the foreground and sustain the meter. But, more importantly, metrical music requires some specific middleground conformation of pitch and rhythm, interacting with the foreground motion, which stamps the meter with its particular measure.

This process can be observed in example 5.5. The staff marked *A* in this example indicates arhythmically the vital middleground structure of the passage: an initial ascent from $\hat{1}$ to $\hat{3}$, with an intervening prolongation of $\hat{1}$ via a motion to, and a return from, its lower neigh-

Example 5.5 Bach, Brandenburg Concerto no. 5

bor. Note that certain subsidiary events are attached to this primary structure. An arpeggiation of the tonic triad carries $\hat{1}$ to its upper octave in two cases. The lower neighbor is itself prolonged first by a motion to its own upper neighbor (shown by the slurred noteheads in the sketch) and then by a passing descent to its consonant lower third A. This underlying A is prolonged by a foreground motion spanning a fourth down to E (also indicated by slurred noteheads).

The staff marked *B* in the example displays the actual rhythmic conformation of the middleground events, first shown on *A,* as a steady procession of half-note values. The staff marked *C* indicates a whole-note motion created by the recurrent statements of I that are separated by intervening, auxiliary V harmonies. The meter here is a function of the slower rhythmic procession of the middleground levels (*B* and *C*) whose events provide regularly recurring accents for the sixteenth-note, foreground rhythm of the passage. Note that both foreground and middleground rhythmic articulations are vital to the establishment of meter; the foreground provides faster events which are grouped by an interaction with slower middleground events.[7]

Example 5.5, together with example 5.6, can now be used to present a somewhat exaggerated demonstration of how the principles presented here apply to define the limits of rubato interpretation. The metrical character of example 5.5, based as it is upon a rigorous pitch-structural support, should survive any number of interpretive alterations. Accelerating the foreground, for instance, will accelerate levels *B* and *C* as well, and meter will remain locked into these interacting levels. Even an outrageous general pause at the point marked X in the example, although tasteless, would not destroy the clear metrical character of the passage—or the meaning of the middleground.

Introducing too abrupt a change into example 5.5, however, will likely warp the rhythmic conformation of the middleground and abuse the piece. There is room for the occasional foreground pause— but not for the wholesale transformation shown in example 5.6A. Here, rhythmic values are contracted so much that the rhythm of middleground events now defines a triple meter.

Similarly, examples 5.6B and 5.6C present a case of (somewhat amusing) unacceptable change. By no stretch of the imagination could 5.6C be considered as having resulted from a hyperemotional performer's rubato treatment of 5.6B.[8] As seen by comparing the

Example 5.6

Mozart, Piano Sonata K. 545

sketches above each of these examples, the rhythmic transformation of the middleground is so total that the most liberal guidelines for rubato can be said to have been exceeded. This would not be so, however, if the first three notes in bar 2 of example 5.6B were to be played as a quarter-note triplet. Again, though tasteless, the change would not occlude the particular metric character of the passage.

Thus, in the case of the older eighteenth-century sense of rubato, meter is rarely threatened, because one part retains strictness of tempo and consistency of metric division. In the case of rubato treatment of all parts simultaneously, however, it is clear that some rhythmic informality is permissible without affecting metric order or identity, while too much might create a wholly undesired effect. Whether the former or the latter holds true, the issue seems inextricably bound to the kind of change wrought by the rhythmic alteration upon the middleground of a composition. And far more essential to the sustaining of meter than strict adherence to foreground events is the preservation of that middleground's characteristic meaning.

NOTES

1. I cite the *Enciclopedia della musica* (G. Ricordi et al., eds. [Milan, 1964]), 4:71, for this early date, which is provided in an excellent short article on rubato.

2. Caccini: "*Sprezzatura* is that charm lent to a song by a few 'faulty' eighths or sixteenths on various tones, together with similar 'slips' made in the tempo; these relieve the song of a certain restricted narrowness and dryness and make it pleasant, free and airy, just as in common speech eloquence and variety make pleasant and sweet the matters being spoken of." This passage appears in Caccini's preface to *Nuove musiche e nuova maniera di scriverle* (1614); it is translated by H. Wiley Hitchcock on p. 45 of his edition of Caccini's *Le Nuove Musiche* (Madison: A–R Editions, 1970).

Frescobaldi: "This kind of playing, just as in modern madrigal practice, should not stress the beat. Although these madrigals are difficult, they will be made easier by taking the beat sometimes slowly, sometimes quickly, or even pausing, depending upon the expression or the sense of the words." From Frescobaldi's *First Book of Toccatas and Partitas* (1615); translated by L. Swinyard in Pierre Pidoux's 1948 edition.

3. Leopold Mozart, *Treatise on the Fundamentals of Violin Playing*, trans. Editha Knocker (New York: Oxford Univ. Press, 1948), pp. 223–24.

4. C. P. E. Bach, *Essay on the True Art of Playing Keyboard Instruments*, trans. and ed. by William Mitchell (New York: W. W. Norton, 1949) p. 162. Hereafter, in this chapter, page references will appear in the text at the end of quotations from this work.

5. "Attack rhythm" here refers to the total rhythm of attacks or new onsets of sound. Such a sequence of attacks will always define the extreme rhythmic foreground of compositions.

6. "Die Kunst der Improvisation" in *Das Meisterwerk in der Musik* (Munich: Universal Edition, 1925), 1:11–30. The sketch cited here appears on p. 27.

7. Further examples of this kind of analysis, together with a much more detailed theoretical explanation, are provided in chapters 3 and 4 of the author's *Stratification of Musical Rhythm* (New Haven: Yale Univ. Press, 1976).

8. Example 5.6A concurs with Schenker's reading of the opening of K. 545. Schenker's analysis includes actual rhythmic values and can be found on p. 82 of vol. 2 of *Der freie Satz* (Vienna, 1935); 2d ed., Oswald Jonas, ed. (Vienna, 1956).

PART 2

ANALYSIS SYMPOSIA

In part 2, four compositions are analyzed from a variety of analytic points of view in addition to that of Schenker's. Again, it must be stressed that this is in no sense a form of competition between the various approaches. We are fortunate not only to have Schenkerian technique viewed in a wider perspective but also to have the benefit of the alternate approaches for their own intrinsic value. —Ed.

Symposium I
Mozart, Menuetto K.V. 355

6. A Motivic-Harmonic Approach

Howard Boatwright

Mozart's remarkable little Menuetto (K. V. 355, revised by Einstein to 594a and dated 1790) is one of those works which demonstrate his special interest in chromaticism. It is a mate to (and is sometimes printed next to) the well-known chromatic Gigue K. V. 574 which Mozart wrote in the album of the Leipzig court organist Engel after his visit to Berlin and Leipzig in the spring of 1789. Perhaps it is not far-fetched to assume that contact with previously unknown works of J. S. Bach in Leipzig, as well as the tasks of orchestrating Handel's Messiah (1789), and Ode for St. Cecilia's Day and Alexander's Feast (1790), stimulated Mozart not only to intensified contrapuntal effort in his last works, but also to a style of harmony sometimes closer to baroque "affect" than to classical clarity. Looked at from another angle, Mozart's late chromaticism may appear to be an anticipation of romantic (or even later) harmonic practice—a manifestation of that clairvoyance which genius possesses.

There are remarkable chromatic passages in a number of the mature works of Mozart. The Menuetto in question, however, provides an especially good illustration because one can discuss not merely a section but a whole piece. Further, the nonfunctional character (no trio section; no place within a larger work) suggests that experiment as well as expression was perhaps Mozart's own objective. If so, all the more appropriate is analytical dissection, in itself a form of experiment.

There is no doubt that one is first struck by the prominence of chromatic sonorities in the Menuetto, especially since the mode is major. The first measure of the piece contains such a sonority, and there are six others (augmented triads), which are boldly emphasized by a forte accent and strong metrical position. Further, there are abrupt shifts of accidentals which change the mode or key or both in unexpected ways. Except for the last four bars of the A section (and the transposed repetition of these bars at the end of the piece), which seem deliberately calculated to contrast ingenuousness with

112

sophistication, nearly every measure contains some harmonic feature sufficiently complex to warrant discussion.

As challenging as the harmonic problems in the Menuetto are, I find even more interesting the high level of motivic development, all of which seems to be generated within the first four measures. I should like to discuss this aspect first, because a number of the surprising harmonic features may result, it seems to me, from compositional logic on the motivic level rather than from harmonic procedures as such.

The first important melodic motive in the piece is a chromatic sequence of three tones (ex. 6.1). This motive is developed in the sequences of bars 5–10 (ex. 6.2) and in the transposition of these bars, 33–38. The fact that the outer voices in bars 5–10, considered alone, reveal no unusual harmonic thinking, and that the augmented triads, of such striking effect, occur through the exposition of the three-note chromatic motive in the tenor would seem to bolster the appropriateness of a nonharmonic explanation of these sonorities.

Example 6.1

Example 6.2

Actually, the falling resolution in bar 2 is in itself germinal, whether or not three chromatic steps are involved. The first instance (bar 2) involves a chromatic passing tone; the second (bar 4) is a $^6_4$–$^5_3$ elaborated with a turn (ex. 6.3).

Example 6.3

Example 6.4

Having established that such a falling second occurs on the weak (thesis) bars, 2 and 4, it is not surprising that we find it again in bars 6, 8, and 10. Beginning with bar 5, the strong (arsis) bars have a dissonance, which enhances the effect of resolution in the weak bars. In bars 5, 7, and 9, this dissonance is the augmented triad, in which the crucial tone (always in the tenor) enters without simple melodic preparation, producing the maximum shock for such a sonority.

That the falling second after a strong dissonance on the accented bar functions as a genuine compositional element in this piece (and that it is not merely a commonplace of the style) becomes evident in the B section, after the double bar. This section introduces no new melodic phrase but consists entirely of a development of the falling second motive. The same conditions are present in each case: there is an unprepared dissonance on the first tone, and a resolution, albeit not a simple one, on the second. The first two statements are placed on alternate strong and weak bars, as before (ex. 6.5). But the meter is ignored after the third beat of bar 20, when the motive is treated sequentially in diminution, leading to a climax on the dominant, prior to dissolution into running figures and a return to the A strain (ex. 6.6).

Example 6.5

Example 6.6

So pregnant are the opening measures of the Menuetto that significant issue is brought forth even from the three eighth notes which serve as an upbeat link to bar 5. The same melodic figure occurs in the same metrical position in bars 6 and 8 (ex. 6.7) and in the return, at bars 34 and 36. One may also construe a rhythmic relationship between this melodic figure and the three staccato eighth-note upbeats in the closing phrase (ex. 6.8).

Example 6.7

Example 6.8

In spite of all the interesting features in the A section of the Menuetto and the B section "development," it is in the treatment of the return of the A strain that Mozart's thinking seems to reach the highest level of compositional sophistication within this piece. First of all, the tonic, D major, is not touched until the third bar of the return—a clear rejection of the common assumption in classical music that tonality is used to clarify and reinforce the formal structure, if not, in fact, to make it. Mozart's evasion of the tonic in this case is no mere deceptive cadence but a total negation of D major by a succession of tones implying other tonics before the dominant is reached on the second beat of bar 30 (ex. 6.9). Here, especially, it seems evident that motivic considerations have taken precedence over purely harmonic ones; and, in fact, that the complexity of the harmony results directly from such a shift in the order of priority.

The first move in this extraordinary *jeu* is not unharmonic in its implications: it consists merely in an inflection towards the subdominant, G, by the introduction of a minor seventh in what normally

Example 6.9

would have been the tonic, D. The next harmony is a secondary
dominant to the supertonic in D. Worked out in four voices, and resolved conventionally, the bar would be as it appears in example 6.10.

Example 6.10

But Mozart has treated the alto which expresses these harmonies in
the two-part version as though it were a structurally important motive, repeating it sequentially in the next measure (bar 30) and imitating it in the bass as well. The imitations are literal—half-step for
half-step and whole-step for whole-step—which means that a really
violent cross relation must occur between the soprano B (third beat
of bar 29) and the bass B-flat (first beat of bar 30). Further, the melody has an A over the B-flat, which may be construed as an accented
passing tone (or a suspension from the A of the previous bar 29,
ornamented by a returning tone). The A does not reach the G that
could form a sixth chord with the B-flat in the bass until that tone
itself has moved to A.[1]

By accounting for the A and G-sharp of bar 30 melodically (i.e., as
nonharmonic tones), and substituting the G, which is their goal, on
the first beat, we may postulate the completion of these two bars
(29–30) in four-part harmony as illustrated in example 6.11.

Example 6.11

The above harmonic sequence is not at all impossible within the
conventional limits of the style, because the grouping of the harmonic areas with the bars eliminates the incongruity of the cross
relation. In fact, if bar by bar grouping of the harmony were the
objective, the cross relation merely assists towards achieving it.

The point remains, however, that we have proved nothing at all by
showing that some sort of orthodox harmonic explanation can be

found for such a passage. Its very beauty is its flight into the harmonically improbable while in pursuit of motivic coherence in the lower voices. That such an event occurs at one of the most conspicuous intersections of the formal structure makes it all the more striking, giving the listener the maximum shock, or excitement, depending on how one looks at it.

While harmonic analysis alone may not approach very close to the core of musical thought as elegant as that of the mature Mozart, it would be begging the question not to examine any of the more unusual passages in the Menuetto from the harmonic point of view—especially those which involve the augmented triads.

If a sonority can function as a compositional element in the same way a melodic or rhythmic motive can, then the augmented triad is a "harmonic motive" in this piece. Once again, the genesis occurs in the opening bars. The second harmony in the piece (an augmented triad in 6/4 form, if regarded as an independent chord) serves warning to the listener that this is a context in which such sounds may be expected to occur.

It is not difficult to explain out of existence this first augmented chord: it results from a simple returning tone in the alto, which has its logic in being coupled in thirds to the melody. But to so dismiss this harmony is to lose sight of the significant fact that Mozart has given it deliberate prominence. Merely to demonstrate that its function is really that of a V^6 (secondary dominant) shows that Mozart was working within the bounds of functional harmony, but it does not even touch the more interesting question of why he utilized the freedom within that system to thrust this particular sonority at the listener in this particular spot. Nor does information about the harmonic function of this sonority relate it to the other similar ones, each of which has to be explained, functionally, in a different way. The number of augmented chords in this little piece, as well as their prominence, can only suggest that Mozart simply wanted those sounds, and that he was so much a master of the harmonic system of his time that he could bend it to his subjective musical desires. At the same time, in that remarkable fusion of aurally and intellectually motivated procedures characteristic of the greatest composers, there is present with the augmented chords in bars 5–9 the element of motivic development, discussed earlier.

But to continue a harmonic analytical approach, the augmented chords in bars 5–9 may also be explained as "nonessential" harmonies (although essential to this piece, they certainly are) resulting from the melodic tendencies of an inner part. However, the terms under which the crucial tone (always in the tenor) may be explained as a non-chord tone must be stretched to the limit. The following could be the explanations, in those terms:

1. The A in the bass at the end of bar 4 is carried by the ear to the beginning of bar 5, where it moves into an accented passing tone, A-sharp, on the way to B.
2. The G-sharp in bar 7 is an accented returning tone, coming from and returning to A.
3. The C-sharp in bar 9 is a suspension of the C-sharp in bar 8, transferred from the melody to the tenor and resolved to D.

Another possibility is to ignore the preparation of the crucial tones but to look at their resolutions. Each may then be regarded simply as a lower neighbor at the half-step of the tone which follows it. The basic harmony for each bar, according to this approach, is a sixth chord. Such an interpretation leads to resolutions of the preceding dominants as shown in example 6.12.

Example 6.12

To approach the problem in still another way, we may take the unfigured bass and melody as a starting point and assume that each augmented triad is a true altered chord, each having a raised fifth. If such were the case, the preceding dominants would then have the following resolutions shown in example 6.13, substituting unaltered chords for altered ones. If we consider the two sets of resolutions

Example 6.13

given in examples 6.12 and 6.13, the more convincing ones are examples 6.12c and 16.13a and b.

It now becomes clear that in spite of the sequential nature of the passage, bars 5–9, each augmented chord has a different melodic origin and a different harmonic function. Therefore, they could not have originated through a single melodic or a single harmonic-functional intention. The single intention of Mozart, then, seems to have been simply to have the same sonority, an augmented triad, on the first beat of every other bar in the passage. Or from the motivic point of view, to have the three-note chromatic motive in the tenor part in every other bar. Or perhaps Mozart may have had one of these intentions, and the other formation may have been one of those lucky accidents which Stravinsky admits to be so important in composition, if the composer is shrewd enough to know how to seize upon them and to weave them into the fabric so that the intentional and the accidental can no longer be distinguished from each other.[2]

The Menuetto contains a number of other features which are worthy of discussion in detail—the abrupt shift of mode and harsh double appogiaturas at the beginning of the B section (bars 17 and 19), the unconventional alignments of passing tones in the bass (bars 18 and 20), the vacillation between minor and major in the running figures which lead to the return of the A section (bars 24–28)—but the features already treated in some detail suffice to indicate main points about the piece which make it of particular interest, not only in itself, but in relation to later practice. In summary, these are:

1. Motivic development is sometimes carried to a level which places it in higher priority than functional harmony.
2. Delineation of the form is not always achieved by simultaneous delineation of the tonality.
3. Individual sonorities are sometimes treated for their sheer sound—their derivation through voice-leading or their position in the harmonic scheme being of secondary importance.
4. Modality (major or minor) is sometimes interchanged freely.
5. Musical thought of high density and multifaceted complexity is expressed within a very short form.

One cannot help speculating, after considering the implications inherent in this small but symptomatically important Menuetto, written when Mozart was 34, what course his music, and European music in general, might have taken had he lived as long as Haydn, to the age of 74. He would then have spanned the entire careers of Beethoven and Schubert and would have died in 1833, the year of the premiere of Schumann's First Symphony and five years after the composition of Berlioz's Symphonie *Fantastique.*

NOTES

1. This sort of occurrence is not uncommon in Bach. For example, in the following passage from the chorale "Puer natus in Bethlehem," the first chord of bar 15 has a suspension in the alto (G). But as the suspension resolves, the bass moves, forcing the alto to assume a new accidental (F-sharp).

2. Igor Stravinsky, *Poetics of Music in the Form of Six Lessons* (Cambridge: Harvard University Press, 1970), pp. 53–55.

7. A Schenkerian View

Ernst Oster

Nothing is known about the history of Mozart's Minuet in D Major. The autograph is lost, and it has been impossible to establish when it was composed. The piece was first published in 1801 under the title "Menuetto avec Trio pour le Piano-Forte par W. A. Mozart, et M. Stadler." Stadler added a trio in B minor, a second-rate composition, which was rightly omitted in later editions. The only modern edition which reprinted it is that published by Henle in 1951. In Henle's "improved edition" of 1955, however, the trio was again left out.

Köchel placed the piece in the year 1780 and assigned to it the number 355. Einstein (following Wyzewa and Saint-Foix) believed that it showed "all the characteristics of Mozart's most mature style" and gave it the number 594a (1790). In his appendix to Köchel 3, Einstein suggested that the piece might originally have been part of the Sonata in D Major K. 576 (1789); and, following this idea, the editors of Köchel 6 gave it still another number, 576b. But there is no real basis for Einstein's assumption, excepting the identity of key. And it appears highly unlikely that Mozart would have included a short minuet without a trio in a sonata of the length of the D Major K. 576.

Neither the Minuet's chromaticism, nor its sudden dissonances, nor certain contrapuntal devices would of necessity point to a late period in Mozart's work. All of these features appear in some of his much earlier compositions. And the strange diversity of texture seems to deny the possibility that the piece was written in the vicinity of masterworks such as the Sonata in D Major or the Quartet in D Major K. 575. At first glance, most of its middle section with the running sixteenths seems out of keeping with the rest of the composition. It may have been features of this kind which led Siegmund-Schultze to assume that the piece was written somewhat earlier than 1790.[1] Siegmund-Schultze also says that Mozart seems to have tried "special minuet studies" in K. 355 and mentions that Mozart, at that time (1790), "experimented" with other forms as well, for instance with the gigue (K. 574) and particularly the rondo.

At least as far as our Minuet is concerned, I think that Siegmund-Schultze hit the nail on the head when he spoke of "minuet studies" and Mozart's "experimenting." The piece is certainly a genuine Mozart, and in many ways it is of great beauty. But it also contains a few compositional weaknesses not usually to be found in Mozart. If the piece really is a "study," then we are provided with an explanation for its occasional imperfections and are able to see them in their proper light. It would also explain why Mozart did not complete the composition. I even wonder whether the last twelve measures of the main part were written by Mozart himself. I shall deal with this question later on.

In order to make clear what I mean by "weaknesses," I should like to discuss the beginning of the middle section, mm. 17–18. The g^1 on the first beat must be understood as a passing tone, either coming from a^1 in m. 16, or else from an a^1 implied on the first beat, as shown in example 7.6d. It then becomes apparent that the left hand repeats in smaller note values almost literally the lower part of the right hand (ex. 7.6e). One could almost call this a canon by diminution. Both statement and imitation come to simultaneous close on e, and the coinciding of the closures results in the rather "unpleasant" octaves f-sharp–e. (Clearly, d-sharp in the bass really represents a quarter note and thus weakens the effect of the parallel octaves to a certain degree. But since f-sharp in the left hand is melodically significant, the octaves undeniably exist and are heard.)

These consecutive octaves, coming about, as they do, unintentionally, show a certain awkwardness, a certain lack of routine or skill in contrapuntal and imitative writing which would never occur in Mozart's late compositions. A quick glance at the Rondo of the Quartet K. 575 or the corner movements of K. 576 makes us realize what incredible mastery, ease, and elegance in handling similar problems Mozart had arrived at in 1789. I wish to draw particular attention to the most beautiful open fifths in mm. 105–06 of the Rondo of K. 576: note how these fifths are motivically prepared in the preceding measures—"motivated" in this specific sense and thus made logical to the ear. (This is in addition to the basic explanation that the chromatic passing tone b-sharp^1 should really appear before the bar line but is, for motivic reasons, shifted to the first beat.) Even the most daring and most dissonant passages in Mozart's later works are in the same sense logical and convincing. (See, for example, the Minuet of the Quintet in G Minor; the famous dissonant "chords" in mm. 150ff.

of the Symphony in G Minor; the opening of the C Major Quartet, discussed in Schenker's *Harmony,* p. 346 in Appendix I by Oswald Jonas.)[2] In comparison with these late compositions, the Minuet in D Major appears somewhat labored. And, to this writer, the vehement dissonances in mm. 5ff. and mm. 17ff. sound willful and not fully convincing. Even Wyzewa and Saint-Foix call them harsh (*âpres*).

For a piece of such short duration, there are too many disparate melodic and contrapuntal devices. The texture changes too frequently and too suddenly. All of this is quite different from the late works, where Mozart's aim seems to have been to achieve the greatest possible unification and integration of the materials employed.

There is a whole group of compositions by Mozart which occasionally show a similar lack of skill and even some awkwardness in the handling of contrapuntal devices. I refer to those compositions which Mozart wrote after he had met Baron van Swieten and became more closely acquainted with the "old style" of Bach and Handel. For further study, I shall briefly mention the location of a few such unsuccessful passages:

1. Prelude (Phantasy) and Fugue in C Major K. 394 (383a): Fugue m. 4, first quarter; m. 5, first quarter; m. 13, second quarter.
2. Suite K. 399 (385i): Ouverture m. 48, second half; Allemande m. 3, third quarter and m. 19, last quarter; Courante—the two canonic passages mm. 9–13 and 36–41.

The canonic passages in the Courante especially show obviously that Mozart was at this time not skillful enough to cope successfully with the problem which he had posed for himself. Both the Suite and the Minuet remained fragments—possibly for the same reason.

It is my feeling, then, that the Minuet was written around 1782 and that it should be associated with Mozart's other "experimental" pieces of that period. Perhaps Mozart wanted to "see what happens" when he applied a variety of contrapuntal devices to a short piece of the type of a minuet. Perhaps the piece represents a first attempt at incorporating the "old" devices into his own, personal idiom, a first step towards their complete absorption and amalgamation in his music. If we accept this assumption, then Köchel, in 1862, was approximately right when he assigned the number 355 to the Minuet.

In view of the particular character of the piece, it might have been better if Köchel 3 and Köchel 6 had let it remain in its old familiar place.

OVERVIEW OF THE MINUET

The Minuet is written in the usual ternary form. The first section moves from I to V, the middle section prolongs the dominant, and the reprise rests mainly on I. The first two measures of the reprise, however, differ from mm. 1 and 2: they are based on the prolonged dominant of the preceding middle section. By embedding the initial melody in the still-prevailing dominant, Mozart binds the two sections closely together. At this point, the texture changes suddenly. Therefore, had Mozart started the reprise in the same way in which the composition began, a most noticeable gap would have resulted. The dominant is prolonged by means of the chromatically filled-in third-progression c-sharp^1–c-natural^1–b–B-flat–A. With the exception of c-sharp^1, these are exactly the same tones with which the top voice of the middle section began. Thus the beginning of the reprise relates back to the beginning of the middle section—truly a remarkable feat of achieving unity. And how beautiful it is that this reprise starts on c-natural^1 which, contrapuntally, is merely a chromatic passing tone! Note also the "dolce" at this point. Example 7.1 shows the basic progression of mm. 28–30. Beginning at m. 33, the passage following m. 5 appears simply transposed a fourth upward, with the result that we arrive on I in measures 39 and 40. The possible significance of this procedure shall be discussed later on.

Example 7.1

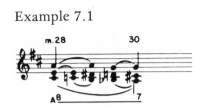

THE FIRST SECTION

Measures 1–4

The top voice shows a descending fourth-progression a^1–e^1. The bass supports the passing note g^1 by the neighboring note c-sharp, moves back to I and from there to V (ex. 7.2a). The fourth-progression falls into two groups of two tones: a^1-g^1, f-sharp^1-e^1. Before proceeding to g^1, a^1 moves to the (incomplete) neighboring note b^1. (The first two eighth notes in m. 2 are passing notes.) The melodic pattern a^1-b^1-g^1, marked by brackets in example 7.2b, forms a basic motive that recurs at various points in the composition.[3]

The f-sharp^1-e^1 is composed as an elaborated repetition of the same motive. (Again, f-sharp^1 and d^1 in the 6/4 chord m. 4 are accented passing tones.) Here we find repetitions within the repetition: a^1-b^1-g^1 in m. 3 repeats the contents of the first two measures, and f-sharp^1-g^1-e^1 in m. 4 repeats the contents of m. 3 and leads to the conclusion (ex. 7.2c). Together, these two repetitions in small note values represent a compressed repetition, a summing-up of the total contents of mm. 1–4. It is remarkable that, with the exception of a few passing tones and the turn, all the melody tones of mm. 1–4 are created by and are part of our motive. In example 7.2c the motives are indicated by brackets and asterisks.

Example 7.2

The bass supports the neighboring note g^1 in m. 3 by the cadential II, thus underlining the reappearance of motive *a* and the final intensification of the melody. In m. 2, before going to the neighboring note c-sharp, it moves chromatically to e. It is thus the bass that introduces the chromaticism of the piece and also the quarter-note rhythm of mm. 5ff. Much more importantly, d–e–c-sharp represents the basic motive of the top voice. One might even say that the motive appears in the form of a short canon at the fifth, with a quarter note's distance between the entries. This, and nothing else, is the reason why the bass starts on the second beat! Here, then, the groundwork is laid for the contrapuntal character of the piece. The very first two measures contain the germ of much that is to follow. They provide the artistic justification for many subsequent events, in particular for the canonic treatment of mm. 17–18 and also of mm. 29–30.

Let us look once more at mm. 28–30, the end of the middle section and the beginning of the reprise. Here we had found the chromatically descending third-progression c-sharp[1]–A which extends the dominant into the reprise, and which harks back to the beginning of the middle section. These features are astounding in themselves, but Mozart does even more: he adds the chordal thirds d-sharp[1] and c-sharp to the descending line. Thus, while the top voice again sounds a[1]–b[1]–g[1] in mm. 29–30, the two lower parts counterpoint this basic motive by inversions of the same motive in quarter notes. Indeed, mm. 29–30 again resemble a canon—this time a canon by inversion and diminution. We must marvel at the rhythmic variety of these canonic devices: in the first one, at the beginning of the piece, the *comes* enters at the distance of a quarter beat; in the second, which opens the middle section, it does so after two beats; and in the last one, in the first two bars of the third section, it begins simultaneously with the *dux.*

The basic voice-leading progression of mm. 28–30 was shown in example 7.1. We should like to leave it to the reader to find further harmonic, rhythmic, and tone similarities between mm. 29–30 and mm. 17–20. Even the imitative role which the bass plays in both cases contributes in bringing the two passages into the closest relationship to each other. At the same time, what a contrast in character between the harsh dissonances of mm. 17ff. and the *mancando* and *dolce* later on! Indeed, the beginning of the reprise is probably the most inspired, the most masterly, the most beautiful place in the Minuet.

Measures 5–11

It is most difficult to determine the inner meaning of mm. 5–10. The pattern of mm. 5–6 is repeated literally in mm. 7–8 and again in mm.

9–10. This is certainly an unusual thing to do, especially when the repeated pattern is as complex as it is here, and one wonders why Mozart chose this procedure. Some preliminary observations may be helpful. The repetitions are literal to the point that they reproduce the exact intervallic relationship set forth in mm. 5–6, without the slightest adjustment being made for the sake of harmony or for other considerations. This accounts for the strange bass tones c-natural and f-natural in mm. 7 and 9. Or, to express it differently, since m. 5 started with a B-minor-sixth chord, m. 7 had to begin with an A-minor, and m. 9 with a D-minor-sixth chord.

The augmented fifths at the beginning of each group are not part of "augmented triads." The nature of augmented fifths is always linear, contrapuntal; it is never vertical. When we keep this in mind and examine the three augmented fifths closely, we find a surprising thing. They each have a different contrapuntal function: a-sharp is an accented passing tone coming from a in m. 4; g-sharp is a neighboring note between the two a's of mm. 6 and 7; and c-sharp[1] takes over c-sharp[2] of the top voice and resolves it upward in the manner of a suspension. Similarly, with the sevenths B-a and A-g in mm. 6 and 8, g is an ordinary passing seventh between a and f-natural; the seventh a, however, cannot "resolve" to the augmented fifth g-sharp and instead acts in a very unusual, daring manner as anticipation of the sixth a in m. 7 (see the figures in ex. 7.4). Now we see that the "literal" repetitions are not so completely literal. The augmented fifths, which are so striking, and the sevenths "act" differently each time; that is, they actually sound differently. If it were otherwise, the bold, insistent repetitions of the two-measure groups would sound truly repetitious and annoying; they would not be worthy of a master of the rank of Mozart.[4]

In each of the two-measure groups 5–6, 7–8, and 9–10, the outer voices show descending third progressions moving in parallel major tenths. As a result, cross-relations arise between beginning and end of each group. D-d-sharp[2], and so forth. (The term *cross-relation* is not quite correct here: d-sharp[2] is really a passing tone in the passing motion D-d-sharp[2]-e[2], c-sharp[2] a passing tone in C-c-sharp[2]-d[2].) Basically, one and the same harmony is prolonged over two measures: B minor-major, A minor-major, D minor-major (see ex. 7.3).

The chromatic quarter notes of the left hand m. 5 show a certain resemblance to the bass of mm. 1–2. The chromatically descending broken thirds of m. 6 seem to be related to the right hand m. 2. And

Example 7.3

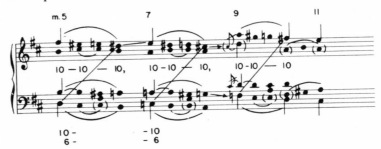

the right hand from m. 9 on to the e² in m. 11 shows a close similarity to certain features of mm. 1–4. The similarity becomes still closer when we realize that the inner voice reproduces almost exactly the bass of the beginning; even d–G–A of mm. 3–4 appears, now modified to d¹–g-sharp–a. And the bass moves in parallel tenths with the top voice, as if the intention were to reproduce even the parallel thirds of the beginning. Indeed, the whole passage seems to represent a free repetition of mm. 1–4 (without the embellishing eighths of m. 3), with bass and inner voice exchanged. Such a similarity cannot be accidental—not in Mozart.

But all the features we have discussed so far are only isolated details. The main question still remains: What is the inner meaning of mm. 5–10? what constitutes their guiding idea? The clue, in my opinion, lies not in the top voice but in the chromatic inner voice up to m. 9. The augmented fifth a-sharp and the subsequent chromatic quarter notes attract our attention and throw this part into focus. If we consider that a-sharp–b really comes from a in m. 4, we see that the inner voice represents an expanded, free repetition of the top voice of mm. 1–3 or 1–4 (see ex. 7.4). And b, then, is a neighboring note ("N" in the example) between a in m. 4 and a in m. 7. In

Example 7.4

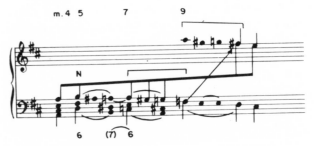

mm. 5–6, a-sharp–a-natural is not in itself significant; it serves as a preparation for the intended g-sharp–G-natural (m. 8), or as what one might call a "pre-figuration" of these tones. The g then leads to f-natural in the bass—that is, the inner voice "disappears" into the bass and the top voice takes over. By repeating the last tones of the inner voice a–g-sharp–g-natural–(f-natural) (see the brackets in ex. 7.4), the top voice virtually snatches the leading role away from the inner voice.

Since a–g-sharp–g-natural–(f-natural) of the inner voice represented an enlarged repetition of mm. 2–3, the repetition of the same tones in the top voice has the same meaning. Now we understand why mm. 9–10, in all three voices, refer back to the beginning. And it is clear why the top voice, having arrived at e^2 in m. 11, shows a design so similar to that of m. 4: it is as if m. 11 continued, an octave higher, where m. 4 left off. We are also able to explain the "lighter" character of the closing measures with their groups of sixteenths. All that happened in mm. 5–11 was a repetition; but it was a repetition of great complexity and seriousness. The complexities and difficulties have thus been explained, and the changed character of mm. 12–16 has been accounted for.

The charming chromatic passing tone e-sharp^2, added in m. 10, suggests the addition of still another tone, b^1, which is really a neighboring note to a^1. In this way the sixteenth notes are introduced, which soon after are to play such an important role. Also, the fifth f-sharp^2–b^1 now suggests the fifth e^2–a^1 in m. 11.

Two more details of mm. 5–10 require an explanation. If in mm. 5–6 the inner voice moves mainly from b through a–sharp to a, what is the purpose of the intervening c-sharp^1 (not shown in ex. 7.4)? The answer is that c-sharp^1 represents the second tone of the basic motive (mm. 1–2), which appears also here: b–c-sharp^1–a-sharp. In mm. 7–8 the motive reads a–b–g-sharp; and in mm. 9–10, where the inner voice repeats practically the entire bass of mm. 1–3, it again reads d^1–e^1–c-sharp^1 as in mm. 1–2. Further, with the inner voice playing the leading role, what is the function of the upper part in mm. 5–8? Because of the literal repetitions in mm. 5–10, each of the component parts had to appear each time. Yet as we pointed out before, their function, their significance, could not be and was not supposed to be the same in each repetition group. It seems to me that the top voice of mm. 5–8, aside from being musically "correct," has no special task to fulfill except to precede mm. 9–10 and to antic-

ipate the configuration of those measures, which are the final goal.
We must not forget that the threefold presentation of the same pattern in mm. 5–10 is a veritable tour-de-force: to achieve diversity of
meaning within sameness of appearance would seem an almost impossible undertaking. The right hand of mm. 5–8, although "on top"
and therefore apparently leading, does not contain the essential idea.
So we may perhaps be allowed to say that Mozart was not completely successful in achieving a high degree of clarity here.

Measures 11–16

In m. 11, the bass cadences in A, the dominant, the top voice skips
from e^2 to a^1. (This is an oversimplification but is sufficient for our
purposes.) The skip of a fifth, e^2–a^1, is first repeated an octave higher
in the form of a triad (m. 12). This repetition introduces the concluding fifth progression which fills in the triad: e^2–d^2–c-sharp^2–
b^1–a^1. Before e^2 proceeds to d^2 and c-sharp^2, a^2–e^2 in the first group
of sixteenths recalls diatonically the chromatic a^2–e^2 of mm. 9–11. In
the second sixteenths group, e^2, superimposed above c-sharp^2, harks
back to the primary tone e^2 (mm. 11 and 13) and goes on to d^2,
which in turn introduces c-natural^2 of the middle section.

Background and Middleground

Because of the abundance—one might almost say over-abundance—of
details in the first section, we have so far concerned ourselves mainly
with foreground features. For those readers who are familiar with
Schenker's concepts we present a middleground picture of the first
and middle sections (ex. 7.5a). The following brief remarks should be
added: The sixth a^1–f-sharp^2 (mm. 1–5) arises as an inversion of the
initial third (ex. 7.5b); this inversion is again in keeping with the
general character of the composition. When f-sharp^2 appears, a^1 has
already moved, or is in the process of moving, to b. Example 7.5a
shows the very beautiful interaction between background, middleground, and foreground. The background of course determines the
general course of the composition, specifically its form and the apparent keys in the foreground. On the other hand, it is the short
neighboring note b^1 in m. 1 that suggests the neighboring-note
motion a-b-a in the middleground of the first section. Indeed, the
same neighboring-note motion controls the entire middle section
(exs. 7.5 and 7.9). Here, then, the foreground determines, in part, the
middleground. Such interaction between middleground and fore-

ground is a phenomenon mostly overlooked by those who are only
superficially acquainted with Schenker's theory. In our Minuet, one
cannot even really understand the middleground of mm. 1–10 unless
one recognizes that it has its source in the foreground of mm. 1–2.

Example 7.5

THE MIDDLE SECTION

Measures 17–20

The top voice moves chromatically through the third c-natural^2–
a^1, which is subdivided into two two-measure groups, as was the
descending fourth of mm. 1–4. The two-measure groups give rise to
the accelerated two-tone groups in mm. 20ff.—c^2–b^1, d^2–c-sharp^2,
and so on.

We have already mentioned the "canon by diminution" in mm.
17–18 and 19–20. We also said that the first g^1 must be understood
as an (accented) passing tone. The first beat thus resembles the first
beats in mm. 5, 7, and 9 and those in mm. 29 and 30. Obviously,
these dissonant accented passing tones are a prominent characteristic
of the piece.

Example 7.6 shows the development of these measures, from the simple to the more complex. It would be wrong to understand the second beat of m. 17 as a diminished triad, to relate it to the initial harmony of m. 18, and, specifically, to hear the a^1 in the diminished triad as being tied over to a^1 in m. 18. In such an interpretation, e^1 in m. 17 would be a passing tone. But just at this point, the bass enters with A and gives added emphasis to e^1 as its true fifth, thus invalidating our hypothetical reading. Attention should be drawn to the bold juxtaposition of the last two thirds in m. 18 and the first two thirds in the following measure with their chromatically changed pitches.

The quarter-note motion of the inner voices bears a certain resem-

Example 7.6

blance to that of mm. 5ff. We would be going too far afield, in my opinion, if we tried to hear them as a very free, diatonic inversion of the chromatic inner voice of mm. 5–6. And it would be still more far-fetched to interpret the thirds of m. 18 as a retrograde version of the basic motive a^1–b^1–g^1 (mm. 1–2). The motion in thirds of course relates back to the thirds in mm. 1–4. But the specific melodic pattern which the thirds create in mm. 17–18 simply results from the voice-leading events demonstrated in example 7.6. Nevertheless, the three-tone motive of m. 18 plays an important role in the middle section (ex. 7.7), even in the middleground (see the upper bracket).

Example 7.7

Measures 21–28

The most striking feature of the middle section is the continuous use of the bass pattern of mm. 17–18. This pattern arises as an imitation of the lower inner voice, but because of its changed rhythmicization it comprises only four beats.[5] The next entry still imitates the inner voice; it appears two measures after the first entry and comprises five beats (four plus one), since d, which would have been its last tone, moves on to g. (In the following measures , d–g becomes a bass motive.) The third entry appears in the right hand after only one measure, slightly overlapping and with its ending adjusted to the subsequent harmony. Measures 21–22 show entries spaced at the distance of only two beats, each of them overlapping the last two beats of the previous entry. Thus the free canonic style of mm. 17–18 is continued through m. 22. The last entry, on g^2, is incomplete. It is noteworthy, however, that it continues further than one would assume at first glance; g^2–f-sharp^2 moves to e^2 and from there over d^2 (which relates to the bass g-sharp) to c-sharp^2. Example 7.8 shows this progression with most of the details omitted. We realize now that the

Example 7.8

descending line g^2–c-sharp^2 represents nothing less than an enlargement of the first five tones of the last entry—although this last entry is in the process of dissolution. And even the five sixteenths descending from b^2 (see the parentheses in ex. 7.8) sound as if they signified one more, still higher entry.

Notwithstanding these last faint imitations, the imitative texture of the middle section comes to an end here. It gradually changes into simpler passage work (still motivically related to the descending fifths of mm. 18ff. and those shown in ex. 7.8), and these passages, disappearing, as it were, into the low registers, make it possible for the initial idea to come in again.

The overlapping entries in mm. 21 and 22 result in groups of two beats. This rhythmic ordering continues through m. 23. Here the dotted rhythm of the bass gives added emphasis to the first beat of m. 24, the V, and thus permits the basic 3/4 meter to re-enter.

Background and Middleground of the Middle Section

The overall course of the middle section can be understood only through the background and middleground. In example 7.5 we presented a simple picture of the middleground. Example 7.9 shows the various structural levels in successive stages from the middleground level a to the foreground level e.

At level a we see the basic prolongation of V: a neighboring-note motion a^1–b^1–a^1 in the top voice, counterpointed by another neighboring-note motion a-g-a in the bass. The inner voice shows a 5–6–5 exchange, which produces the foreground effect of IV–II. The basic neighboring-note motion of the top voice has its origin in mm. 1–2 and in the same motion mm. 1–5–10 (ex. 7.5a). Simultaneously, it prepares for the reappearance of the same pattern in m. 29, the beginning of the reprise. And since the first a^1 appears at the end of the first section and the second a^1 is delayed until m. 29 (the beginning of the reprise), a^1–b^1–a^1 ties the three sections of the composition together into a structural whole.

Level b shows, as a first prolongation, the passing seventh f-sharp^1. This dissonance is transformed into a consonance by the bass-leap to d^1, which is the fifth of g (level c). Thus, the D-major triad in m. 23 does not represent a I in D major; it has nothing to do with the basic tonality of the composition. Its origin lies solely in the passing-tone motion g^1–f-sharp^1–e^1. The d^1 is introduced by its lower neighboring note c-sharp^1, and this, together with the tied-over g^1, gives the foreground effect of V–I in D major.

Example 7.9

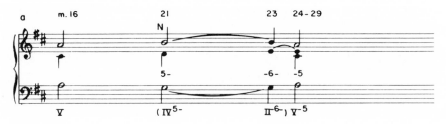

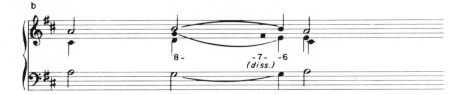

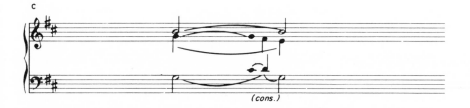

In level d, the same f-sharp[1] and e[1] appear transferred to the higher octave. The tied-over g[1] of level c is also transferred upward and sounds now almost like an upper neighboring note of f-sharp[2]. The neighboring note b[1] (m. 21) is introduced by its own neighboring note c-natural[2]. At the same time, the bass inserts d between a and g, producing the foreground effect of II–V–I in G major.

Example 7.6a presented the harmonies of mm. 17–20 as they appear in the actual composition. For this reason, we show at level e the contrapuntal (linear) basis of the same harmonies: a chromatic progression in tenths. The sixth b[1]–g[2] in mm. 21–22 now appears filled in by the third d[2], with the result that the top voice still outlines the G harmony of m. 21. The first step b[1]–d[2] is filled in by the passing c-sharp[2]; the bass follows in tenths. We must marvel at Mozart's ingenuity in carrying out this passage. We can virtually see the overlapping imitating entries stepping on each other's shoulders in order to reach higher and higher grounds and finally g[2], the goal indicated by the middleground level d. What consistency between the contents of the middleground and the technique used in the foreground! Clearly, the overlapping entries are not an aim in themselves, but they serve to express the middleground and are subordinate to it.

At level e, we show the descending passages of mm. 24–27 in their basic chordal shape. They express two third progressions e–d–c-sharp which stem from and repeat the same third progression first appearing in mm. 23–24. In m. 24 we may detect a foreshadowing of the reprise: a[1]–g-sharp[1]–g-natural[1]–f-sharp[1].

The whole middle section shows the following measure grouping: mm. 17 18 19 20, mm. 21 22 23, mm. 24 25 26 27, mm. 28 29 30 31 32. The three-measure partitioning at mm. 21–23 is due to the irregular two-beat groups, but it defies any further explanation. Obviously the metric equilibrium is restored by the five-measure group which begins in the last bar of the middle section. Here the dominant is extended to m. 30. But since its root A is suspended in m. 29, we hear this measure as an extension of the first measure of a basic four-measure grouping. Thus the reprise enters in a most subtle way over the extended dominant and within a metrically extended measure. What a marvelous overlap of events!

THE REPRISE

As I said previously, I seriously doubt that Mozart himself wrote the conclusion of the Minuet (mm. 33ff.). Even the transition from m.

32 to m. 33 is slightly awkward. Although contrapuntally correct, d-sharp[1] does not seem to come from anywhere and is weak in comparison to the powerful accented passing tone a-sharp in m. 5. The last three eighth notes in m. 4 have an obvious melodic-contrapuntal function; in contrast, the neighboring note a–g-sharp–a in m. 32 is merely a rhythmic "filler-in." One recalls Mozart's words, in his corrections of a pupil's counterpoint exercises: "just as the bad poets write some nonsense for the sake of a rhyme."[6]

The most persuasive argument against the authenticity of mm. 33ff. lies in their exact transposition, note for note, of mm. 5ff. Of course, nothing is musically "wrong" with the procedure: we arrive very conveniently at the closure in mm. 39–40. This solution to the recapitulation problem is very simple; in fact, it is so simple that any conservatory student could have found it. But when we examine Mozart's work, we recognize that he never resorts to this easy device of simple transposition.[7] (The same applies to Haydn and Beethoven.) Mozart would always modify the reprise by a variety of means, adding emphasis to the section, letting the previous material appear in a new light, establishing new relationships, or doing whatever else might appear necessary. Consider, for example, the reprise of the relatively short and simple Minuet of the Quartet in D Major K. 575. Clearly, Mozart could have modified mm. 53–56 in such a way that in m. 57 he would have arrived at the D-major version of mm. 13ff. Instead, mm. 56–58—and only these—differ melodically and harmonically from mm. 12–14. The remarkable thing is that mm. 56–58 relate to a previous passage of the piece and also to a later one. They are prepared, in a free manner, by the beginning of the middle section; and, at the same time, they themselves "prepare" mm. 66–71, which are nothing but a transposed restatement of the analogous measures in the first section. Thus Mozart creates entirely new relationships for the reprise—relationships which did not exist at all in the first section of this minuet and which replace those relationships which can be found there.

Not a trace of this masterly kind of writing exists in the reprise of the Minuet K. 355. Or if it exists, I fail to see it. Of course, it is always possible to discover repetitions of short-tone patterns anywhere. But if we find such repetitions, we shall have to ask: Are the tone patterns truly related? Do we really hear them as repetitions? What is the compositional purpose of the repetitions? Measures 35–36 are almost the same as mm. 9–10, but obviously, these measure groups have nothing to do with each other. In mm. 37–38, b-flat–a seems to reflect m. 30; but a in m. 38 is merely a passing tone, a "connective," and so the similarity exists only on paper. In mm. 33 and 35, b^2–a^2 does remind us of mm. 1–2, mm. 29–30, and the neighboring-note motion that spans the entire middle section (ex. 7.9). But b^2–a^2 is not continued in a manner that would correspond to its previous appearances. Instead, it is followed by what is practically the high point (in terms of register) of the entire piece. Measures 37–38 are crucial in our examination of the reprise, and we have to ask the following decisive questions: What does this d^3–c-sharp^3–c-natural^3–b^2 relate to? How is its appearance prepared, in the sense of the ingenious preparations in K. 575? What does this tone succession do? What is its compositional function?

In my opinion, these questions can be answered only in a negative way. The whole ending from m. 33 on is, in a deeper sense, not related to the rest of the composition; it is not an organic part of the whole, and it lacks any guiding idea within itself. Let us think back to the same group in the first section. Let us remember to what lengths Mozart went in order to make the three two-measure groups sound differently each time, and how miraculously the beginning of the piece re-emerged in the third group (mm. 9–10). Let us consider Mozart's artistic sensitivity, which suggested to him the subtle, profound beginning of the reprise. Compare such manifestations of highest artistry with this cliche—this perfunctory, mechanistic ending which any student could have found! At this point of the composition where the problem of the recapitulation had to be faced, would Mozart have settled for such a pseudo-solution as this, which only circumvents the real problem?

To me there is only one answer: Mozart did not finish even the main part of the Minuet, and Abbé Stadler completed it for publication. Of course we will never be entirely sure that this is what happened, unless, by some accident, the autograph should be discovered. But there is such a thing as internal evidence; and according to it, the ending is not well composed, not truly composed in the sense in which Mozart thought of and practiced composition.

We may well ask, Why did Mozart stop writing, just a few measures before the close? For many of his unfinished compositions, of course, an answer cannot be given. But in the case of our Minuet, one can very well imagine that Mozart stopped while searching for an ending that was musically logical and convincing. In particular, the answering, in a changed form, of what I called the tour-de-force of mm. 5–10 must have posed an almost insurmountable problem. Perhaps Mozart pondered the problem for quite a while—deliberated and rejected one solution after the other, and finally gave up the task. After all, the piece was just a study, an experiment in applying contrapuntal devices to minuet form.

It is almost a pity to have to end the analysis on this negative note. But from our negative finding we may gain a positive viewpoint. Musical analysis has of course various tasks; one of its most important tasks is that of evaluating a composition. It is not enough to furnish a purely descriptive analysis, that is, only to state that the composer did one thing or another. It is not even enough to discuss what may have motivated the composer to proceed along the particular paths which he chose to pursue in a given composition. Ideally, analysis should advance to the point where it can show to what degree the composer was able to realize the nature of his art, and to what degree he realized his own intentions through the material of that art. It will then be possible for analysis to distinguish between masterworks and compositions of lesser caliber, to distinguish between good and bad, and also, whenever necessary, to distinguish between authentic compositions and spurious ones.

NOTES

1. Walther Siegmund-Schultze, *Mozarts Melodik und Stil* (Leipzig, 1957), p. 139.

2. Heinrich Schenker, *Harmony*, ed. Oswald Jonas, trans. Elisabeth Mann Borgese (Chicago, 1954).

3. There is some doubt as to whether the second eighth note in m. 2 should read e-sharp[1] or e[1]. The first editions have e, most later editions e-sharp. The only modern editing showing e is that of Peters (Kurt Soldan, 1935). Einstein advocates e in the appendix of Köchel 3; the incipit in K. 6 has e. I am nevertheless convinced that e-sharp is the only possible reading. An e-natural would have to be understood as an anticipation; g-sharp above it is a chromatic passing tone. But the combining of a chromatic passing tone and an anticipation would be an odd thing to do; it would be too complicated for this beginning, where the lower voice simply follows the melody in thirds. The "stumbling" e–e would also be at variance with Mozart's "dolce." Furthermore, mm. 2–4 of the Minuet are almost identical with 3 bars of Leporello's aria in Don Giovanni; of course, Mozart writes e-sharp in the second violins and the violas. And the words are: "nella bianca la dolcezza." Dolce, dolcezza: this might be only a curious coincidence. Yet the "gliding" character of both compositions makes the apparent coincidence meaningful.

4. Only the neighboring note g-sharp in m. 7 does not have any real "task" to fulfill and may not be entirely convincing.

5. Even the rhythm of the bass imitates that of the lower inner voice. In m. 16, the starting point of the inner-voice line, a^1 represents a dotted half note; it is followed by quarter notes. This rhythmic pattern of a long note followed by shorter ones reappears, contracted, in the bass line. But we must go still further: a^1 occupies the last measure within the four-bar group 13–16. Since a in m. 17 is the starting point of the repetition-in-contraction, it occupies an analogous metrical position within a single bar, namely, the last beat. This is why the bass, in such seemingly unprepared fashion, enters on the upbeat. (Compare what was said about the entry of the bass in m. 1.) Subsequently, the upbeat pattern continues through mm. 21 and 22, creating a hemiola. Only at g in m. 23, which is a decisive point in the middleground (exs. 7.5a and 7.9), does the pattern weak-strong reverse into strong-weak. The dotted rhythm of m. 4 comes about in a similar way to that of mm. 17–18. It mirrors, in smaller note values, the basic rhythm of the three-tone motive discussed previously (see exs. 7.2b and 7.2c, especially the rhythm at bracket *a* in ex. 7.2c). We see in these two instances that specific rhythms may be brought about by tonal events. Rhythm, here, is not something existing per se, an element that is in some fashion combined with the rest of the tonal events. It is rather that the tonal events themselves create specific rhythms—a phenomenon which is rarely recognized. Of course it is true that the dotted rhythm of m. 4 is in keeping with the character of a minuet. Still, in this particular instance, the rhythm comes about through the contraction of the basic motive mm. 1–2 and mm. 3–4, together with the contraction of the fundamental rhythm of that motive.

6. Köchel 453b, published in its entirety in Robert Lach, *Mozart als Theoretiker* (Vienna, 1918).

7. The only exceptions are to be found in the recapitulations of a few early piano sonatas. It would go beyond the scope of this discussion to show in what respects the situation in these recapitulations differs from that in the Minuet.

Symposium II
Schubert, Op. 94 no.1

8. A Quantitative Analysis

Matt Hughes

Through the creative thoughts of various musicians and mathematicians, the quantitative approach in analysis has cultivated the premise to an area in musicological thought which has yet to be either exposed or expressed in its entirety. In this new area of "quantitative musicology," the wise researcher is one who recognizes its many limitations in some respects and, at the same time, realizes its almost boundless possibilities in other respects. As the technique is conceived in mathematics, an area often frightening to musicians, many reactions are to label it as being beyond the comprehension or interest of a musicologist and to discard the technique and results as uninformative. This procedure was ameliorated for the benefit of the musician; and, therefore, it foregoes the complexities of mathematics to find its foundation in simple mathematics. Because the nature of this type of analysis appears to be perplexing to many musicians, a necessary portion of this paper will have to be devoted to the analytical procedure, in addition to discussing the results of this technique.

The objectives of this procedure may be stated quite simply: (1) After counting the notes with their duration, some notes prove to be more significant than others. When viewing these important tone elements in terms of the circle of fifths, the wider the distance in steps of the circle of fifths and the greater the number of statistically important notes, the more complex is the tonal orientation of the composition. What is advantageous is that tonality may be expressed in terms other than functional; this mathematical precision can be invaluable.[1] (2) The other result is called tonal orientation, a term adopted to differentiate between it and tonal organization. Analysis of organization is an analysis of chords, progressions, measures, and

The author wishes to express his gratitude to Hans Heinz Draeger, Professor in the Music Department of the University of Texas at Austin, for his encouragement and many helpful suggestions in the preparation of this article.

144

periods in their mutual relationships. Orientation is at no time a chord-by-chord analysis but is a result of the total occurrence of each note and its durational value. This phenomenon is expressed in the statistically important notes discussed in the first result and is understood to be the overall tonality or tonal orientation of a composition. This condensation of important notes or tonal orientation could reveal that a composition in C major, for example, was in reality tonally oriented toward G major, a consequence of semantic salience.[2]

This technique is no more than a tool for the researcher. At no time is it meant to be a substitute for critical intellectualization. Rather, it is a tool for organizing data so that one may more discernibly view tendencies and interassociations. Analyzing the piano preludes of Skriabin, this tool proved to be successful.[3]

Turning to the music, Schubert has divided this composition into five parts (mm. 1–8, 9–29, 30–37, 38–58, and 59–65). The tempo of the composition is marked moderato and the meter signature is $\frac{3}{4}$.

The division of the beat is basically simple, but Schubert chooses to enhance the playful character of the melody in the first two sections of the composition by the utilization of a triplet figure. Adding to this character, the triplet figure is juxtaposed with the simple beat and developed upon with relative frequency. The texture in these two sections is either basically melody heard alone or doubled, or it is harmonized in a pianistic fashion in which the chords and a melody line reverse hands at the end of the second section. It is important in this analysis to note that the first two sections (which are repeated after the last three sections) are given the key signature of C major. In the last three sections, the key signature is changed to G major. Here, the texture remains basically the same as in the first twenty-nine measures although the beat becomes primarily compound. In the fourth section, simple-beat chords are placed above an ostinato-like triplet figure. Also in this section, this rhythmic activity is continued, whereas the ostinato becomes a pedal point on G. Although the parts are not equally divided, a sectional analysis by this tool is easily accessible.

MEASURES 1–8

Step 1a: Closely related to Wilhelm Fucks' approach, the first step is to count every note of the composition according to its duration value.[4] Counting duration can not be overemphasized as every note would be of equal value if duration were ignored. Alike note-name frequencies are then added together forming a scale pattern of an octave span. Step 1a, in itself, does not give a complete answer, and hasty interpretations should be warned against. This, then, would establish that occurrence does not necessarily determine the tonality of the composition. Although the results are not available, it is to be expected that, for example, in Bach's Prelude no. 1 in book 1 of *The Well-Tempered Clavier*, the tonal orientation would be identical with the tonality of the piece; however, it might be questionable with regard to Bach's Chromatic Fantasia and Fugue in D Minor.[5] Thus, the series which contains all notes with duration used in this composition is:

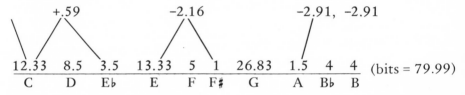

+.59				−2.16			−2.91, −2.91			
12.33	8.5	3.5	13.33	5	1	26.83	1.5	4	4	(bits = 79.99)
C	D	E♭	E	F	F♯	G	A	B♭	B	

This may also be shown in the form of a graph (see fig. 8.1). Above the series of numbers another row of digits is listed. This additional row is the result of an analysis of the complexity of the peaks. The digits are preceded by a plus (+) or minus (−) sign, indicating the peak's relationship to its theoretical extreme, 100-percent information or 100-percent redundancy. This complexity of the peak is seen graphically when the peak affects either a convex or concave shape. The minus sign or concave shape indicates a tendency towards 100-percent information; and the tendency toward its opposite extreme, 100-percent redundancy, is represented by the plus sign or convex shape. This result is derived from the series by a sequence of three

Figure 8.1

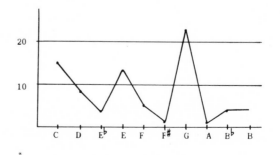

steps or more in either an increasing or decreasing direction. The two numbers at the poles of the complexity are then added together and the arithmetic mean is found. Then the number between the poles is subtracted from the mean. If this number is smaller, the result is closer to 100-percent information; thus, a minus sign is placed before the result. If the number is larger than the mean, the result is given a plus sign to indicate its tendency towards 100-percent redundancy.

Step 1b: In this, the second part of step 1, the arithmetic mean is found and the letters are sorted, as they compare, above or below the line.

$$7.99 = \frac{\text{C} \quad \text{D} \qquad \text{E} \quad \text{(F)} \qquad \text{G} \quad \text{(A)} \quad \text{(B}\flat\text{)} \quad \text{(B)}}{\text{E}\flat \qquad \text{F} \quad \text{F}\sharp \qquad \text{A} \quad \text{B}\flat \quad \text{B}}$$

It should be noted that all letter names are listed; hence, F, B-flat, B, and A are found in parentheses to indicate that their actual value is below the mean.

Step 2a: Here, the letters are arranged as to their order of importance.

$$\frac{1 \quad 2 \quad 3 \quad 4 \quad 5 \qquad 6 \qquad 7 \qquad 8}{\text{G} \quad \text{E} \quad \text{C} \quad \text{D} \quad \text{(F)} \quad \text{(B}\flat\text{)} \quad \text{(B)} \quad \text{(A)}}$$

Step 2b (C-major tonal orientation): This step is designed as an attempt to perceive a tonal orientation. In this instance, the notes form a C-major scale, B-flat excepting. In other compositions, a comparison with different types of scales, patterns, tone rows, or chords is valuable.

Step 3a: Barring the correct computation of notes, the following steps in this series of consequential events are perhaps the most important. First, the notes above the arithmetic mean are given their corresponding numbers in the circle of fifths.[6] This approach is achieved by a numbering of the letters in the circle of fifths from d-double-flat to b-sharp. The notes are counted in the following manner:

dbb	abb	ebb	bbb	fb	cb	gb	db	ab	eb	bb	f	c
1	2	3	4	5	6	7	8	9	10	11	12	13

g	d	a	e	b	f♯	c♯	g♯	d♯	a♯	e♯	b♯
14	15	16	17	18	19	20	21	22	23	24	25

Perhaps it will be thought that the connection between the circle of fifths and the important peaks appears remote, and that it is unusual for it to be used at all for further analysis. Because we are dealing entirely with underlying tonal orientation and have the problem of reducing it to as simple a structure as possible, it is quite logical to contend that further insight might be achieved when given an equally simple structure. The circle of fifths, as a basic tool, fulfills this essential requirement for simplicity and this procedure offers a possible solution. Therefore in op. 94 no. 1, the notes and numbers are:

G	E	C	D	F	B♭	B	A
14	17	13	15	12	11	18	16

Step 3b: Immediately, the numbers are arranged in an ascending consecutive order if possible. From measures 1–8, we discover a conjunct series of eight numbers with no interruption in the consecutive arrangement: 11, 12, 13, 14, 15, 16, 17, 18.

Step 3c: In this portion of step 3, we count numerical distances between 11 and 18. Breaking the preceding example into more detail, there are: seven 1-distance relationships (11–12, 12–13, 13–14, 14–15, 15–16, 16–17, 17–18); six 2-distance relationships (11–13, 12–14, 13–15, 14–16, 15–17, 16–18); five 3-distance relationships (11–14, 12–15, 13–16, 14–17, 15–18); four 4-distance relationships (11–15, 12–16, 13–17, 14–18); three 5-distance relationships (11–16, 12–17, 13–18); two 6-distance relationships (11–17, 12–18); and one 7-distance relationship (11–18). This situation is unchangeably true in every case offering a consecutive series. There are no exceptions and it does not matter what size the numbers are. The reason for forming this arrangement is that it facilitates counting all possible relationships with regard to the circle of fifths. In other words, by counting numerical distance between the numbers, we are also counting distance relationships in the circle of fifths. The following trend is seen:

$$\begin{array}{l} \text{Distance Relationships} \quad 1\ 2\ 3\ 4\ 5\ 6\ 7 = 28 = 1 \\ \text{Occurrence} \qquad\qquad\quad\ 7\ 6\ 5\ 4\ 3\ 2\ 1 = 28 \end{array}$$

The distance relationships are then added separately as are the number of distances. Both equal 28 in this case as in all other identical situations. The distance relationships are then divided by the number of distances. Again in this composition, as in all exact situations, the quotient is 1. Thus, the underlying orientation is reduced to its simplest base, also giving the means for determining the degree of tonality. From the preceding, the following formula may be stated:

$$\sum \frac{a}{b} = x$$

Hence, the sum of the distance relationships (a) is divided by the sum of the number of distances (b) and equals the degree of tonal complexity (x). In every case in which the pattern is not consecutive, the result varies. Nonconsecutive arrangement may then be understood to mean a more complex tonal orientation.

Step 4: The note numbers are added together and the arithmetic average is found: $11 + 12 + 13 + 14 + 15 + 16 + 17 + 18 = 116 \div 8 = 14.5$. This last number (14.5), when referred back to the numerical circle of fifths, pinpoints the location of the composition as shown by the circle.

Step 5: Another type of interpretive question is raised by the meaning of the peaks. The peak is singled out as the most important factor in this analysis. All other notes falling around the peaks are of environmental importance and therefore are of secondary value in matters of interpretation. In this step, the peaks and only the peaks are listed, and the note's number according to the circle of fifths is added. This step differs from step 3 in that peaks are used exclusively. Step 3 used both peaks and other statistically important notes above or below the median. Because step 5 is more restrictive than step 3, the result of step 5 might be considered less comprehensive, but not less conclusive. In fact both steps are necessary to gain the final result.

Before understanding this result, several points should be made clear. First, because of its less restrictive character, step 3 is more detailed than step 5; and therefore step 3 shows a more complex picture than step 5. And second, if step 5, which is less comprehensive than step 3, is larger than step 3, the tonality is more complex. In step 5, which is restricted to peaks only, the smallest and largest distance relationships are usually the same as step 3, but the occurrence of all possible distance relationships is usually smaller. Therefore, when the number of occurrences (abbreviated Occ.) is divided into the number of distance relationships (abbreviated D.R.), the result is larger than step 3.

C	E	G	Bb	B
13	17	14	11	18

11, 13, 14, 17, 18

D.R. 1 2 3 4 5 6 7 = 28 = 2.8
Occ. 2 1 2 2 1 1 1 = 10

Step 6: The final step in this procedure shows the difference between the resulting number of step 3 and step 5. First, in order to gain a correct basis for comparison, the result of step 3 is multiplied by the largest distance relationship in that step. Then the same is applied to step 5, after which step 3 is subtracted from step 5.

$$(2.8 \times 7) - (1 \times 6) = +13.6$$

If the result of step 3 is larger than step 5, a minus sign is placed before the final conclusions. A plus sign, on the other hand, is placed before the final conclusion if step 5 is larger than step 3. The greater the distance from the 0 axis in either direction, the more complex is the tonality.

This analytical tool is best utilized when viewing groups of compositions or sections of a composition rather than a single work. With this in mind, the results of the other sections are given as well as the results of an analysis of the composition as a whole.

MEASURES 9–29

Step 1: See figure 8.2 for the corresponding graph.

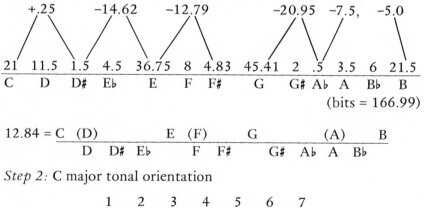

+.25   −14.62   −12.79   −20.95   −7.5,   −5.0

21	11.5	1.5	4.5	36.75	8	4.83	45.41	2	.5	3.5	6	21.5
C	D	D#	Eb	E	F	F#	G	G#	Ab	A	Bb	B

(bits = 166.99)

12.84 = C	(D)			E	(F)		G		(A)		B
	D	D#	Eb		F	F#		G#	Ab	A Bb	

Step 2: C major tonal orientation

1	2	3	4	5	6	7
G	E	B	C	(D)	(F)	(A)

Step 3:

G	E	B	C	D	F	A
14	17	18	13	15	12	16

12, 13, 14, 15, 16, 17, 18

D.R.	1	2	3	4	5	6	= 21	= 1
Occ.	6	5	4	3	2	1	= 21	

Step 4: Total steps in the circle of fifths = 105
Arithmetic mean of total steps = 15

Step 5:

C	E	G	B
13	17	14	18

13, 14, 17, 18

D.R.	1	2	3	4	5	= 15	= 2.5
Occ.	2	0	1	2	1	= 6	

Step 6: $(2.5 \times 5) - (1 \times 6) = +6.5$

Figure 8.2

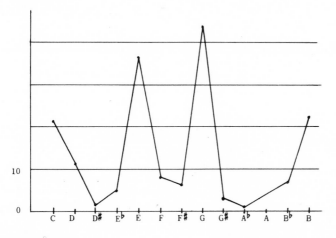

MEASURES 30–37

Step 1: This short section is interesting for two reasons. First, this is the section in which Schubert changes to another key signature. It should be noted that the tonal orientation shifts to G major as well.

Second, this is the only section of the composition that is entirely diatonic. For this reason, all tone elements are considered statistically important; therefore, step 5 is regarded as redundant and the results of step 3 are repeated in its place. Compare the following with figure 8.3.

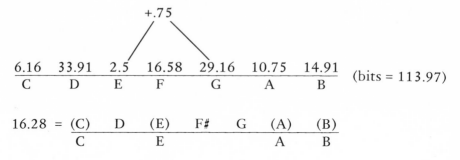

6.16	33.91	2.5	16.58	29.16	10.75	14.91	
C	D	E	F	G	A	B	(bits = 113.97)

16.28 =	(C)	D	(E)	F♯	G	(A)	(B)
	C		E			A	B

Figure 8.3

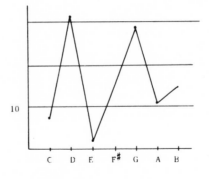

Step 2: G-major tonal orientation

1	2	3	4	5	6	7
D	G	F♯	(B)	(A)	(C)	(E)

Step 3:

D	G	F♯	B	A	C	E
15	14	19	18	16	13	17

13, 14, 15, 16, 17, 18, 19

D.R. 1 2 3 4 5 6 = 21 = 1
Occ. 6 5 4 3 2 1 = 21

Step 4: Total steps in the circle of fifths = 112
Arithmetic mean of total steps = 14.58

Step 5: See step 3.

Step 6: $(1 \times 6) - (1 \times 6) = 0$

MEASURES 38–58

Step 1: See figure 8.4 for the corresponding graph.

$$-3.79, +2.46 \qquad\qquad +2.67$$

19	4.5	70.25	11.33	29.33	35.58	54.91	6.16	15.25	(bits = 246.31)
C	C♯	D	E	F♯	G	A	B♭	B	

27.36 =	(C)			D	(E)	F♯	G	A		(B)
	C	C♯			E				B♭	B

Step 2: G major tonal orientation

1	2	3	4	5	6	7
D	A	G	F♯	(C)	(B)	(E)

Step 3:

D	A	G	F♯	C	B	E
15	16	14	19	13	18	17

13, 14, 15, 16, 17, 18, 19

D.R. 1 2 3 4 5 6 = 21 = 1
Occ. 6 5 4 3 2 1 = 21

Step 4: Total steps in the circle of fifths = 112
Arithmetic mean of total steps = 14.58

Step 5:

C	D	A	B
13	15	16	18

D.R. 1 2 3 4 5 = 15 = 2.5
Occ. 1 2 2 0 1 = 6

Step 6: $(2.5 \times 5) - (1 \times 6) = +6.5$

Figure 8.4

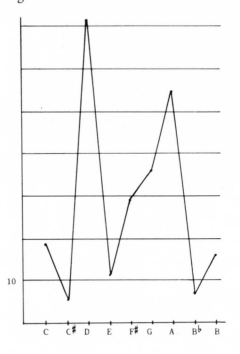

MEASURES 59–65

Step 1: See figure 8.5 for the corresponding graph.

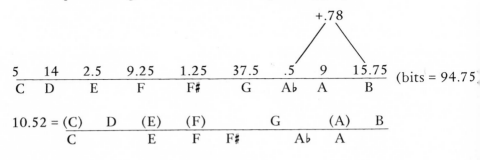

						+.78		
5	14	2.5	9.25	1.25	37.5	.5	9	15.75
C	D	E	F	F♯	G	A♭	A	B

(bits = 94.75)

10.52 =	(C)	D	(E)	(F)		G		(A)	B
	C		E	F	F♯		A♭	A	

Step 2: G-major tonal orientation

1	2	3	4	5	6	7
G	B	D	(F)	(A)	(C)	(E)

Step 3:

G	B	D	F	A	C	E
14	18	15	12	16	13	17

12, 13, 14, 15, 16, 17, 18

D.R. 1 2 3 4 5 6 = 21 = 1
Occ. 6 5 4 3 2 1 = 21

Step 4: Total steps in the circle of fifths = 105
Arithmetic mean of total steps = 15

Step 5:

D	F	G	B
15	12	14	18

12, 14, 15, 18

D.R. 1 2 3 4 5 6 = 21 = 3.5
Occ. 1 1 2 1 0 1 = 6

Step 6: $(3.5 \times 6) - (1 \times 6) = 15.0$

Figure 8.5

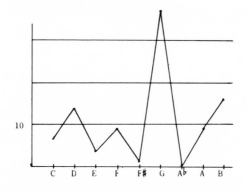

THE PIECE AS A WHOLE

Step 1: See figure 8.6 for the corresponding graph. Bits = 1556.25.

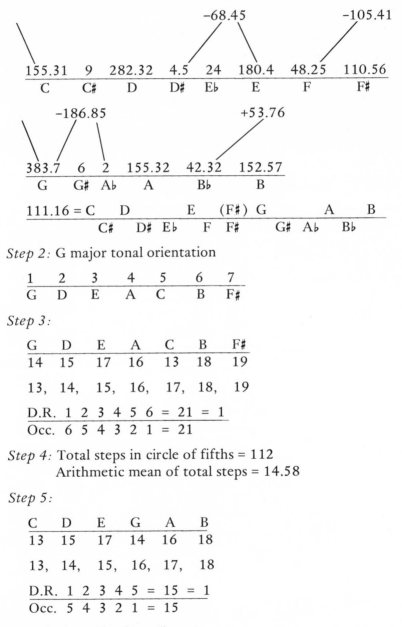

Step 2: G major tonal orientation

1	2	3	4	5	6	7
G	D	E	A	C	B	F♯

Step 3:

G	D	E	A	C	B	F♯
14	15	17	16	13	18	19

13, 14, 15, 16, 17, 18, 19

D.R. 1 2 3 4 5 6 = 21 = 1
Occ. 6 5 4 3 2 1 = 21

Step 4: Total steps in circle of fifths = 112
Arithmetic mean of total steps = 14.58

Step 5:

C	D	E	G	A	B
13	15	17	14	16	18

13, 14, 15, 16, 17, 18

D.R. 1 2 3 4 5 = 15 = 1
Occ. 5 4 3 2 1 = 15

Step 6: $(1 \times 5) - (1 \times 6) = -1$

Figure 8.6

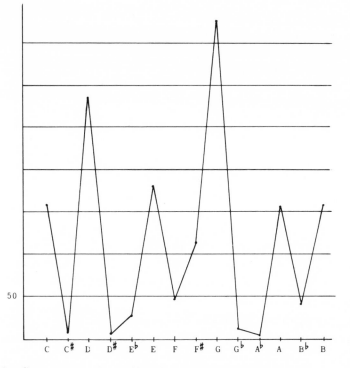

50

C C# D D# E♭ E F F# G G♭ A♭ A B♭ B

Since, in figure 8.7, the 0 line is a result of a subtraction of step 3 from step 5, 0 indicates the axis of tonal orientation, above or below which every tonally notated composition could be placed. This graph shows the development of tonal orientation in this regard. It is important to note that mm. 30–37, an entirely diatonic section, is the only section placed on the 0 axis. Considered as a whole, the results of op. 94 no. 1, located very close to the 0 axis, indicate a rather simple tonal complexity much closer to the key of G major than to the key of C major as presented by Schubert.

Utilizing an approach developed by Draeger, a discussion of the cadence at the end of each section is warranted. Using the numbering system for the circle of fifths previously given, the basic idea, as outlined in "An Attempt Towards a Semantics of Chordal Progressions,"[7] is that a chord is defined by the sum of its numbers. For example, G major is defined as 14 + 18 + 15 = 47. Also each step upwards in the circle of fifths is described as a tendency towards an open, nonfinal effect; likewise, each step downwards in the circle of

Figure 8.7

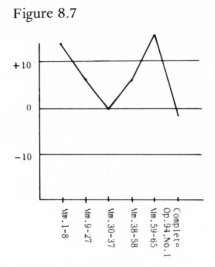

fifths results in a tendency towards a close, final effect. In the case of a change from major to minor and vice versa, the following have to be considered:

1. Major–Minor in the circle down increases the final effect.
2. Major–Minor in the circle up decreases the nonfinal effect.
3. Minor–Major in the circle down decreases the final effect.
4. Minor–Major in the circle up increases the nonfinal effect.

The terminology remains a problem as the terms *final* and *nonfinal* are not to be confused with satisfying and unsatisfying musical endings. From a psychological point of view, a legitimate description seems to be *up* and *down*. It is valid, therefore, to distinguish two attributes of melodic and chordal movement: an external direction and an internal direction. Following Handschin,[8] the external means the spatial distance between two tones, and the internal meaning is the tonal distance.

Concerning the open and closed effects, the cadence shown in figure 8.8 (mm. 7–8 and 28–29) illustrates both. Shown in a chart, the vertical lines represent the chord. The dotted lines depict the open and closed effects by connecting roots with roots, thirds with thirds, and fifths with fifths. From G minor to G_7 major, a change from minor to major upwards in the circle, increases the nonfinal effects. And G_7 major to C major, results in a tendency towards a final effect. This is also true in mm. 36–37, 57–58, and 64–65. How-

Figure 8.8

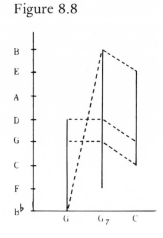

ever, the cadence in mm. 64–65 is much more static than the others. Mathematically, mm. 7–8 and 28–29 may be represented as:

$$\begin{array}{ccc} & f & \\ d & d & g \\ b\flat & b & e \\ g & g & c \\ 40 + 59 & +44 & = 143 \div 3 = 47.66 \end{array}$$

Finding the arithmetic mean, the final number indicates how well balanced this cadence is when referred to the circle of fifths. A balanced cadence, such as

$$\begin{array}{cccc} g & c & d & g \\ e & a & b & e \\ c & f & g & c \\ 44 + 41 & + 47 & + 44 & = 176 \div 4 = 44 \end{array}$$

would equal its final chord. The following tabulation pinpoints the result.

A♭	E♭	B♭	F	C	G	D	A	E	B	F♯	etc.
32	35	38	41	44	47	50	53	56	59	62	

f	c	g	d	a	e	b	f♯	c♯	g♯	d♯	etc.
34	37	40	43	46	49	52	55	58	61	64	

a♭	e♭	b♭	f	c	g	d	a	e	b	f♯	etc.
25	28	31	34	37	40	43	46	49	52	55	

Measures 36–37 and 57–58:

				c	
d	g	g	d	a	d
b	e	a	b	f♯	b
g	c	f♯	g	d	g

$$47 + 44 + 49 + 47 + 63 + 47 = 297 \div 6 = 49.5$$

Measures 64–65:

a	a♭	a	f
f	f	f	d
b	b	b	b
g	g	g	g

$$60 + 53 + 60 + 59 = 232 \div 4 = 58$$

The result of mm. 7–8 and 28–29 reveals an almost perfectly balanced cadence. This is not true of mm. 36–37 and 57–58 and even less true of the result of mm. 64–65.

The definition of a chord by number may often be misleading. The number 47 can portray either a G-major triad (g–b–d) or the notes g + a + e. Because of this, the individual voices must be considered. The remaining examples are of the last two measures of each section; however, in order to be brief, only the results of the last two chords will be given or discussed. The tonal structure in mm. 7–8 and 28–29 is the same although the voices are rearranged. Basically it consists of a cadence from G_7 to C major. Comparison proves the cadence in mm. 28–29 to be the more balanced.

Measures 7–8 (see fig. 8.9): This cadence is characterized by the downward tonal movement. Although the balance of the downward tonal movement toward the final chord is good, a slight imbalance is indicated by the numerical definition of chordal movement. Also the tonal orientation (+13.5) is slightly more complex than is indicated by the final result. In terms of the circle of fifths, the first voice

Figure 8.9

a

Figure 8.9 (*continued*)

b

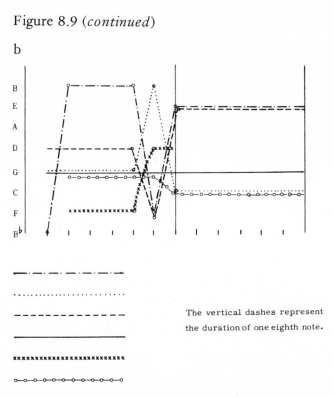

The vertical dashes represent
the duration of one eighth note.

ascends 5 steps; the second voice descends 5, the third voice ascends, the fourth voice remains the same, the fifth voice disappears, and the sixth voice descends 1 step.

Measures 28–29 (see fig. 8.10): Chordally and mathematically the

Figure 8.10

a   b

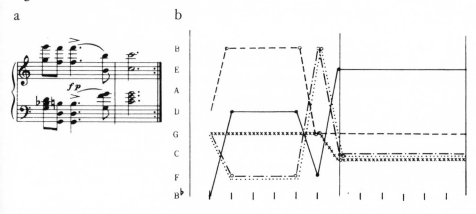

characterization of this cadence is identical with that of mm. 7–8. What is different is the tonal orientation and the rearrangement of chord tones. By analysis of tonal orientation, the results signify a simpler orientation much closer statistically to diatonicism. As illustrated by the diagram, the arrangement of the voices allows tonic to be more strongly emphasized. Both of these qualities increase the balance and stability of the cadence to a point that intensifies the effectiveness of this cadence when compared to mm. 7–8. Again, in terms of the circle of fifths, the first and second voices descend 5 steps, the third voice remains constant, the fourth voice ascends 5 steps, and the sixth voice descends one.

Measures 36–37 and 57–58 (see fig. 8.11): More active rhythmically, the cadence in mm. 36–37 and mm. 57–58 is based upon D_7 major to G major. In this instance, the depiction at both points is exact. Significantly, the tonal orientation of mm. 30–37 denotes a section diatonically oriented to G major. Measures 38–58 are slightly more complex; however, this cadence does not result in as balanced a construction as the cadence in mm. 28–29. A characterization of this cadence compares favorably with that of mm. 7–8. Anew in terms of the circle of fifths, the first and fourth voices ascend 5

Figure 8.11

a

b

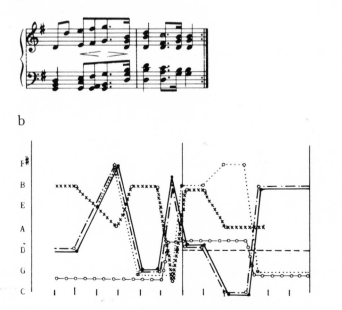

steps, the second voice descends 5 steps while the third voice remains static, and the fifth voice descends 1 step.

Measures 64–65 (see figure 8.12): The cadence with the simplest melodic construction and least rhythmical activity is most vividly described by its static nature.

Figure 8.12

a

b

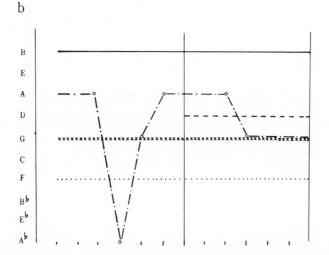

One might think of mathematics and music as having engaged in a rather sporadic conversation. Once in a while, a mathematician asks a question which the musician is able to answer or reshape; or an idea in mathematics strikes the musician as relevant to his field. This paper has attempted a contribution in that direction.

NOTES

1. Hans Heinz Draeger, "A Quantitative Analysis of Music as Exemplified by Beethoven's Sketches for his Opus 131," in *Festschrift Walter Wiora* (Hamburg: Bärenreiter, 1967).

2. Kuhnau must have been aware of this significance in his discussion of the tonal orientation of the Gigue in the Suite *La Medica*, in the introduction to his *Biblical Sonatas*.

3. M. C. Hughes, "Tonal Orientation in Skriabin's Preludes: An Analysis on the basis of Information Theory," Master's Thesis, University of Texas at Austin, 1965.

4. F. Winkel, "Die informationstheoretische Analyse musikalicher Strukturen," *Die Musikforschung* 17, no. 1 (January/March 1964):1–14.

5. Here the difference between tonal orientation and tonal organization should be absolutely clear.

6. H. H. Draeger, "An Attempt Towards a Semantics of Chordal Progressions," in Kongressbericht Salzburg 1964, Kassel, 1966, pp. 261–68.

7. Ibid.

8. J. Handschin, *Der Toncharakter* (Zürich, 1948).

9. A Compositional Analysis

Lawrence Moss

The first of the *Moments musicaux* (op. 94 no. 1) does not seem, at first, particularly momentous. What could be simpler than the collection of pitches in the first phrase? And yet the piece exerts an undeniable charm, not to mention power, within its self-imposed limits. What these limits are, and how they are overcome will be the subject of the next few paragraphs.

To begin with, there is the limitation of the piece's overall symmetricality. The opening section, *A,* is the same length as the Trio (I am excluding the last eight measures, which serve as a retransition to the da capo). Not only this, but the internal subdivision of each is exactly the same: eight measures to the double bar, thirteen for the middle section immediately following (one could cavil at this for the opening section, but more on that later), and finally eight measures to complete each section, or twenty-nine in all.

Further, this formal symmetry is married to an extremely clear overall harmonic scheme. The tonic chord is stated forcefully at the outset and conclusion of the opening section. The Trio moves to the dominant and, after the double bar, to the dominant of the dominant (m. 38). Measure 45 begins the leisurely return to the opening, with D major finally resolving to G (the minor key at m. 51 is a temporary delay), and G in the last eight measures becoming the dominant of C. It is interesting to note that the new tonics in this harmonic ascent (G and then D) are each introduced without preparation (i.e., without being preceded by their dominants). They are simply stated and become "tonicized" (to use Sessions's term)* through repetition. On the way down however, to continue the metaphor, these tonics are carefully transformed into dominants through the addition of sevenths (mm. 45 and 63), thus giving a firm—if somewhat overly direct—push back to the home key of C major.

---

*Here is a good example of the indirect absorption of Schenker's ideas into the mainstream of musical thought, as described by Allen Forte in his introductory essay. The English term *tonicization* may be Sessions's, but the music-theoretical origin of the concept is one of Schenker's main contributions.—*Ed.*

Let us now turn to the opening eight measures. First of all, the theme is an articulated tonic chord: each beat in mm. 1–4 reiterates this chord. At first there is almost no dilution of this sound; the appoggiatura in m. 1 is simply the added sixth. Gradually the dominant is brought in to create tension, first through the appoggiatura in m. 3, then on the offbeat chords in m. 4 (note the accompanying V–I motive in the left hand). A chromatic change, E-natural–E-flat, in m. 5 gives us the favorite Schubertian shift from major to minor and serves to throw us briefly to the flat side of things. In rapid order, c minor leads to E-flat major, which then leads as VI to g minor in mm. 6–7. Here an answering chromatic shift, B-flat–B-natural, rights matters, leading to the climactic F-E in mm. 7–8, which returns us to the opening motive's high point. The first arch I to I has been completed. Note how the ascending fourth motive in the left hand furthers the drive to the cadence by outlining V (G-g in mm. 4–7) and how this buildup finally spills over to the right hand with the tritone of m. 7 resolving finally to the climactic fourth B-E. Of course dynamic indications help this, beginning with the dramatic *pp* of m. 5, which makes the following crescendo more telling. But Schubert seems afraid of overdoing things; the dynamic climax is staggered with the melodic climax, as the cautionary *p* in the last beat of m. 7 indicates (ex. 9.1a). Here is a case where Schubert's dynamics and phrasing are revealing. The transfer of the left hand ascending fourths to the right hand in m. 7 comes out clearly in the original phrasing as shown in example 9.1a. (I am assuming Gieseking's version[1] to be correct; the manuscript has been lost.[2]) Later "edited" versions, an example of which is shown in example 9.1b, obscure this.

Example 9.1

a   b

Speaking of Schubert's intentions vis-à-vis those of later editors, it is interesting to compare the first two measures as well in this respect (see ex. 9.2). Probably no great harm is done by the added crescendo

Example 9.2

a   b

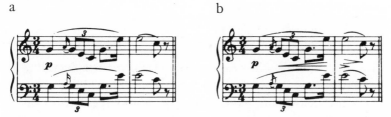

(ex. 9.2b). It is simply unnecessary, the necessary impetus to the downbeat of m. 2 having already been supplied by Schubert's increase in rhythmic tension during the course of m. 1. Overemphasis of this through an added crescendo would possibly obscure the later much more important crescendo to the cadence. Like Mozart, Schubert knew better than his later editors when to quit.

Turning now to the measures following the double bar, we find an obvious reference in mm. 9–10 to the events of mm. 1–4; the opening E heard as appoggiatured fifth of the chord A-C-E recalls m. 1, while the rhythm of the right hand of course repeats m. 4. Then comes a surprising cancellation of G-sharp in m. 11, bringing us up again on a tonic chord and incidentally recalling previous chromatic shifts. As if to reinforce this allusion, m. 13 moves (after the brief I–V interruption of mm. 11–12) to the minor dominant of A minor, in a move analogous to mm. 7–8. From here on the developmental character of this section is emphasized by progressively shorter phrases. Repeated two-beat phrases in mm. 15–16 are followed by one-beat phrases in m. 16, with the last of these reinforced by a simultaneous extension of register in both hands—the first so far.

Note how the harmonies of this section (mm. 9–16) have mirrored in the small the overall harmonic scheme sketched out in the opening paragraphs. Assuming that vi is our "tonic" in m. 9, we move first to the related dominant key, e minor, in m. 13, and then to its dominant a measure later. A measure's rest dramatically follows, and then what appears to be its resolution. The one-beat *fz* phrases in m. 16 have become a *p* ostinato pulsing on the beat in mm. 18–20. But the missing B of this e-minor triad never materializes, and we are given instead our opening motive in the left hand in m. 20, completing the chord with an almost Haydnesque wit. Example 9.3 shows how our C-major chord has been exploited so far for its potential as a pivot chord. Circled notes are the common tones held over. It is important to remember that these pivot-chord modulations articulate the three major subdivisions of the opening section. The symmetries empha-

Example 9.3

sized by this example thus further the clarity of the overall design.

One other point, before proceeding to the Trio. While the entrance
of the theme in the left hand in m. 20 would seem to begin the expected return to the opening, it does begin in fact two measures later
(though this point could be debated). For me the matter of texture is
crucial. Measures 20–21 continue the previous little ostinato as
accompaniment, creating the expectation that the entire recapitulation of mm. 1–8 will be so embroidered. This in fact does not happen.
Instead, we shift to a new solo texture in m. 22 which then is elaborated in a consistently canonical manner and spun out to the
requisite eight measures of the opening. Measures 20–21 can thus in
retrospect be likened to a false recapitulation—something like a brief
echo of the famous big bang in the recapitulation of the first movement of the *Eroica.*

Now, to the Trio. If anything, it is even simpler than the opening.
The relatively dynamic form of the piece's first eight measures gives
way in mm. 30–37 to a simple period marked by continuous reference to the new "tonic," G major. Example 9.4 gives the Trio up
to the first double bar and also shows relationships with the opening.

Example 9.4

The circled G-A-G in mm. 30–31 recall the opening three notes of m. 1. The notes under the first bracket are an augmentation of the left hand in m. 4. Those under a slur are a rhythmically distorted recall of the right hand in that measure. Note that although the left hand motive in m. 4 came to be developed in a progressively more dynamic fashion up to m. 7, the basic confines of that progression— G to G—are preserved in the octave skip g^1 to g^2 in mm. 32–36. The second bracket in m. 36 emphasizes Schubert's division of this octave into skips of the ascending fourth—again, a reference to the opening.

Measure 38 moves abruptly to a new key, analogously to m. 9. The regularity of the previous eight measures is preserved, though there is an increase in pacing with $4+4$ measures being replaced by $2+2$ (mm. 38–41). Measures 42–43 bring an interesting rhythmic shift through accents, giving us in fact a 3/2 measure followed by one in 3/4. The hemiola effect thus produced has been heard before (cf. mm. 15–16, first three *fz*). Just one more reason, perhaps, for Brahms's well-known admiration of Schubert.

The dotted rhythm of the Trio (borrowed of course from m. 1) becomes progressively more pronounced as we prepare for its return in mm. 45–51. Here comes the first "surprise" of the Trio—g minor instead of the expected G major. The linkup with mm. 4–5 is obvious. After four measures of this Schubert goes on blithely to the Trio's consequent phrase, and in so doing reinforces his switch of mode with a cross-relation (B-flat–B-natural in mm. 54–55) recalling the analogous spot in the first section (mm. 25–26).

The retransition to the da capo (mm. 59–66) is fairly routine, de-tonicizing (if one may use such a word) G major, just as was done with D major previously. In fact, these eight measures are so much less interesting than the others, one is tempted to picture Schubert already thinking of the next piece. That would explain the mechanical recapitulation of the opening section which follows.

Concluding, I would like to go back to the symmetrical arrangement of subsections mentioned earlier. The following diagram brings this out:

    (A) ‖ : 8 meas. :‖ : 13 meas., 8 meas. :‖
Trio (B) ‖ : 8 meas. :‖ : 13 meas., 8 meas. :‖ (retransition 8 meas.)
      (a)   (b)   (a')

Of course, one could think of the second section of the *A* part as being divided eleven and ten measures. However, as I tried to show,

compositional as well as notational details reinforce the above interpretation. Schubert could have used a fermata in place of the one
measure rest in m. 17, or even a rest plus fermata, as he does in
op. 94 no. 4, right before the Trio. That he didn't makes me wonder
whether in fact he was aware not only of the symmetries in the overall structure but even of the relative proportions of the subsections.
The reader will have noticed by now, of course, that I am referring to
the Fibonacci series, each of whose numbers is the sum of the preceding two. This is evidenced not only by the eight and thirteen
measure durations, but by the overall length of twenty-one measures
for each second section (b + a'): $\frac{21}{13} \approx \frac{13}{8}$.

One usually associates the Fibonacci series with post–World War II
music, though Bartok's reliance on it has been strongly documented
by Lendvai.[4] In this connection I can offer a personal memento.
While looking over manuscripts in the Bartok archives in New York, I
was struck by a series, 21 13 8, etc., in the margin of the manuscript
of the Sonata for Two Pianos and Percussion. The series of numbers,
in Bartok's handwriting, had gone unnoticed by the curator.

If the Fibonacci series has been used as an organizational principle
in nineteenth century Western music, this has certainly gone unnoticed by scholars and historians. It would be tempting to think of
op. 94 no. 1 as a link in the use of the Golden Section (which any
three numbers of the series approximates) from the Middle Ages to
the present.

NOTES

1. Franz Schubert, *Impromptus–Moments Musicaux*, ed. Walter Gieseking (Munich and
Duisburg: G. Henle Verlag, 1966).

2. O. E. Deutsch, ed., *Schubert Thematic Catalogue* (London: Dent, 1951) pp. 360–61.

3. Deutsch says that the title was "probably . . . an invention of the publishers" (*Schubert
Thematic Catalogue*, p. 361).

4. Ernö Lendvai, *Béla Bartók—An Analysis of His Music* (London: Kahn & Averill, 1971).

10. A Schenkerian Analysis

Carl Schachter

Schubert's opus 94 no. 1 is so unpretentious and apparently simple that a collection of analyses of it might seem to be a kind of musical "Pooh Perplex." Actually the piece contains a number of unusual and irregular features and is rather more elusive than it appears to be at first. The difficulties it presents result neither from complexity nor from obscurity; they are due, rather, to the wayward, unpredictable character from which the piece—or at least the A part[1]—derives so much of its charm.

THE *A* PART

Measures 1–8

The unison statement of the opening measures sounds like a motto; we expect its elements, presented in such clear focus, to recur significantly. Which are the most important of these elements? The first thing we hear is the neighboring figure g^1-a^1-g^1 caused by the grace note; the significance of this fleeting idea will become evident only later in the piece. We are more forcibly struck by the broken triad g^1-e^1-c^1; the evolutions of this pattern begin at once. The leap of a sixth from g^1 to e^2 in the second broken triad is the first and most important of these evolutions (see ex. 10.1). The juxtaposition of g and e—both tones occurring in various registers—is to pervade much of the A part. In addition e^2 functions as the initial tone of the embracing melodic progression $\hat{3}$ $\hat{2}$ $\hat{1}$.

As example 10.1 indicates, the development of the broken triad continues in the right-hand part of mm. 3–8. Measures 3–4 "reinvert" the ascending sixth to a descending third, g^1-e^1. This third is filled in; the grace note of m. 3 hints at the more explicit passing tone of the next measure. (The passing tone progression g^1-f^1-e^1 finds its simplest rhythmic embodiment in binary division, as in second-species counterpoint. The broken-chord pattern of m. 1, on the other hand, fits most naturally into a triplet division. Thus melodic

171

Example 10.1

elements give rise to the rhythmic figures whose alternation and combination permeate the design of the piece.) In m. 5 the change of mode brings about the inflection of e^1 to e-flat^1. As example 10.1 shows, the filled in third g^1–f^1–e-flat^1 is followed by a stepwise ascent to c^2 producing another transformation of the broken-chord figure.

Example 10.2 shows the context in which the motivic transformations described above take shape. It indicates that the initial phrase (it is best to hear it as a single eight-measure phrase) expresses a broadly unfolded tonic harmony supporting e^2 as top-voice tone.

Example 10.2

The right-hand part contains two linear continuities. The upper one centers on e^2 decorated by its upper neighbor f^2; the lower passes from g^1 to e^1 and e-flat^1 and thence up to c^2. The bass shows the imprint of the pervasive broken-chord figure, but in ascending direction and in minor. In mm. 5–7 the bass extends the tonic minor and leads to the cadential dominant by means of the arpeggiated progression c–e-flat–g, each tone preceded by its own dominant. The filled-in fourths of mm. 4–5 prepare the disjunct ones of the following measure and become a motivic element of some importance.

Measures 9–19

The eleven measures comprising the *b* section of the *A* part present some of the most challenging problems of the entire piece. Especially the first phrase (mm. 9–12), with its rapid changes in tonal focus and vacillating top-voice line, requires careful study before it reveals its meaning.

The suggestion of a-minor in mm. 9–10 is too brief and inconclusive to be considered a decisive departure from tonic harmony. In order to understand the contents of these measures we must remember that they follow the extensive tonic elaboration of mm. 1–8. Viewed in this context the a^1 of m. 9 reveals itself to be the upper neighbor of the persistent inner-voice tone g^1 of the opening phrase. The g-sharp^1 (in the foreground part of the V of a-minor) functions as a chromatic passing tone leading again to g^1 in m. 11 (see ex. 10.3). The origin of this inner-voice motion lies in the fleeting neighboring progression caused by the grace note of m. 1. This connection may seem forced, and it would be if this were the only instance of similarity. But the use of a^1 as neighbor to g^1 becomes a most significant motivic event in the *B* part and occurs both at the beginning (mm. 30–31) and retransition (mm. 64–66) to form a link with the *A* part.[2]

Example 10.3

We can now examine as a whole the phrase of mm. 9–12 (see ex. 10.4, a graph of the entire *b* section). The bass, like that of mm. 5–6 grows out of the broken-chord figure of the opening measure. The c of m. 8 vibrates in our memory through m. 9. In m. 10 e enters, to be prolonged through the beginning of m. 12 (briefly displaced by c^1 through an interchange with the top voice). The arpeggiation finds its goal in the g of m. 12. In a more conventional piece this g might well function as a dominant of high structural order paving the way for the tonic of the *a'* section. Here, however, the g constitutes a brief departure to the upper fifth, pointing back to the initial tonic but not fated to usher in the recapitulatory one.

Example 10.4

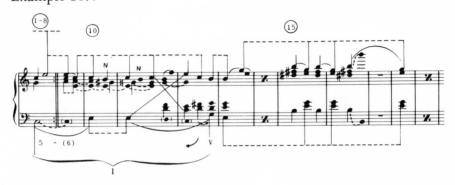

The melody of mm. 9–10 begins with the structural top-voice tone
e^2, the grace note echoing the f^2 of m. 7. However the change of
chordal position at the third beat of m. 9 brings to the fore the inner-
voice tone c^2. For the rest of the phrase the right-hand part exploits
the inner-voice region (note, however, the recollection of e^2 in m. 12,
preceded by the diminished fifth b^1–f^2 as in the cadence of mm. 7–8).
The melody wavers between c^2 and b^1 as if uncertain about the
course it should take. In so doing it resembles somewhat the shifting
figure-ground patterns of the psychology textbooks; which is the
main tone and which is neighbor? The problem for the analyst is
greatest in m. 11 where the playful alternation makes it difficult to
judge whether the underlying chord is a C^6 or an E^5_3.

Only reference to a broader context provides us with an anchorage
by means of which we can stabilize and order our perceptions. Heard
in context rather than as a succession of autonomous chords the
measure takes on a definite C-major physiognomy. Analysis of the
first two beats as an E chord would require us to disregard the C
arpeggio of the left-hand part, the interchange

and the framing tonic before and after (mm. 1–8 and m. 12).

In mm. 9–12 the competition between b^1 and c^2 has mainly fa-
vored the c^2; only at the end of m. 12 does b^1 begin to prevail (as
top-voice tone of the G chord). At the E minor of mm. 13ff. (with
c^2 reduced to a neighboring grace note), b^1 comes into its own,

asserting itself ever more strongly until after the dynamic and registral climax of m. 16. However assertive, b^2 and its registral variants
represent a manipulated inner-voice tone. The top-voice region comes
into play again with the g^2 of m. 13. (The events of m. 13, incidentally, compress into a single bar the essential contents of mm. 1–2;
even the sixteenth rest derives from the eighth rest of m. 2.)

After b exhausts itself in the climax of mm. 15–16 only e and g are
left to represent the E chord. As the memory of b—already weakened
by the rest of m. 17—grows fainter, the implication of E minor becomes attenuated; e and g as third and fifth of tonic harmony provide a bridge into the *a'* section. Example 10.5, which presents a
synoptic view of the entire *b* section in relation to context, should
now be consulted in connection with the more detailed graph of
example 10.4. The symbol EM, originated by Felix Salzer, indicates
a non-stepwise decoration; here the embellishing E-minor chord
allows a further development of the pervasive relationship between
the tones e and g. Note that the melodic outline of mm. 12–23, as
shown in example 10.5b, constitutes an expansion of the idea of
mm. 1–2.

Example 10.5

Measures 20–29

Almost every tone in the *a'* section (mm. 20–29) can be traced back
to the first eight measures and functions as a direct repetition, registral variant, or contrapuntal inversion of its "original." However the
structural meaning of the *a'* section differs greatly from that of the
opening one. For here the melody, instead of centering on the third
step of the scale, progresses to its goal, the tonic. The simplicity with
which this is accomplished constitutes—for me at least—one of the
most beautiful and admirable features of the piece.[3]

As example 10.6 indicates, g^2, the top-voice tone of mm. 13–19, continues into the beginning of the *a'* section, effecting an overlap with the preceding section and permitting the hesitant entrance of the theme in the left-hand part. The right-hand part of mm. 24–25 lies an octave above the corresponding idea of mm. 3–4. This change of register stabilizes e^2 in preparation for the forthcoming structural descent. In addition it fulfills the expectations created by the falling thirds g^2–e^2 of mm. 13–19. Note the parallelism between the g^2–f-sharp^2–e^2 of mm. 15–16 (where g^2 predominates) and the g^2–f-natural^2–e^2 of m. 25 (which gravitates to e^2).

Example 10.6

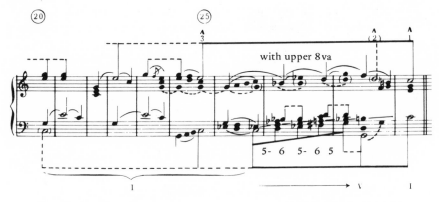

As indicated by the above, I read the contents of mm. 26–27 quite differently from those of mm. 5–6, of which they form a contrapuntal inversion. As in many other pieces, changes in the contrapuntal organization require us to hear one—and sometimes more than one—of the constituent melodic lines in a changed manner. In the left-hand part of mm. 5–6 the harmonic implication of the sequential fourths (the lower tones are dominants of the upper ones) creates an emphasis on the upper tones. The harmonic implication is removed now that the fourths occur in the top voice. In addition the upper tones of the fourths now constitute octave doublings of the bass, whereas the lower tones produce a satisfactory counterpoint (the bass of mm. 26–27, incidentally, is a slight variation of the alto part of mm. 5–6). For these reasons I hear the lower tones of the fourths as forming the main direction-giving element. While the bass is still in transit to the V, the melody begins a "premature" arpeggiation of the G^7 chord with minor third; the b-flat gives way to the required leading tone in m. 28. By starting in the middle register (m. 26) and adding the upper octave at the end of the measure, Schubert strongly indicates that the lower tones of the octaves are fundamental and the upper ones are doublings. The structural resolution of the melody, therefore, occurs on c^2, in the same register as the initial e^2, but reinforced by its upper octave. The doubling is required to balance the rather heavy left-hand part of three tones in close position.

The cadential V–I of mm. 28–29 supports a melodic progression which is the inversion of the one found in mm. 7–8. Here, however, the descending diminished fifth has a different meaning from the ascending one of m. 7; it substitutes for the melodic supertonic ($\hat{2}$) as connection between $\hat{3}$ and $\hat{1}$. Schenker remarks that such substitutions for the $\hat{2}$ frequently occur in short compositions.[4] This one is particularly appropriate in view of the motivic reference it provides. The d^2 in parentheses in example 10.6 represents the underlying melodic tone substituted for and bypassed in the actual piece.

THE *B* PART

If the reader will play through the first part of the piece he will discover that it stands on its own and makes musical sense apart from the piece as a whole. If he tries the same experiment with the second part (mm. 30–58) he will find that it cannot stand alone; its meaning becomes clear only in the context of the whole piece. The reason is the following: The first part expresses a complete musical thought leading, both in the melody and harmony, to a stable conclusion on the tonic. The G-major section, on the other hand, never reaches a definitive conclusion in the melody; the top voice, as we shall see, remains centered on d^2. (Middle sections of three-part song forms, incidentally, often express complete harmonic-melodic progressions; the Trio of op. 94 no. 6 offers a convenient comparison with our present piece.)

Measures 30–37

These eight measures form the *a* section of the middle part. In mm. 30–31 g^1 is prolonged by a sequential two-note pattern featuring its lower and upper neighbors. As example 10.7 indicates, the upper neighbor, a^1, should be considered the primary one. The origin of this neighboring progression lies in the grace-note figure of m. 1; the melodic succession g^1–a^1–g^1 is to play an important role throughout this middle part.

Example 10.7

Example 10.8 presents a graph of the entire eight measures. The reader will note that I consider the V, the harmonic goal of the first phase, to "arrive" at the $\frac{6}{4}$ on the downbeat of m. 33 rather than at the D chord of the preceding measure. The reasons for this admittedly odd reading are the following: The sustained G drops out of the left-hand part at the beginning of m. 32 and the lowest tone of the broken chord (verticalized from the second beat on) takes over as bass. As I hear it this fact does not become manifest until the down-beat of m. 33 where the impression of a melodic and rhythmic goal clearly obtains. The d of m. 32, on the other hand, seems to function mainly as consonant support for the passing a^1 of the melody.

In m. 34 d^2 appears; it will be intermittently present throughout the B part and functions as the central top-voice tone. The contents of mm. 34–37 are pretty straightforward and my analysis should be clear from example 10.8.

Example 10.8

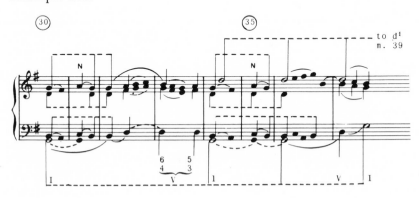

Measures 38–50

Example 10.9 explains the *b* section with its extended prolongation of the V of G. Note the persistent use of A^1 as fifth of the D chord

Example 10.9

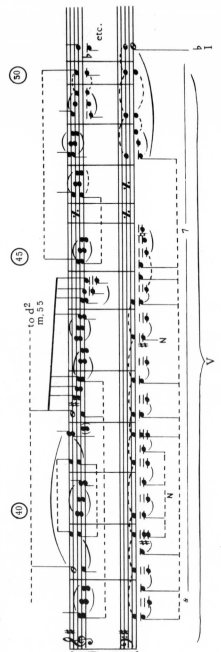

below the functional bass; in m. 45 the rising third A^1–B^1–C adds the seventh to the chord (cf. the right-hand part of m. 32). A passing motion within the V leads to the G of m. 51; the bass progression echoes, in a differing harmonic context, in low register, and in broadened time values, the right hand part of m. 36 and can possibly be traced back to the filled-in fourths of mm. 4 and 5. Example 10.10 concerns a detail, the contrapuntal background of the melodic dialogue of mm. 38–41.

Example 10.10

Measures 51–58

The *a′* section (mm. 51–58) is the same as mm. 30–37 except for the minor coloration of the first phrase. This, of course, is in marked contrast to the C-major part where the recapitulatory section shows a structural function very different from that of the opening one. We can therefore dispense with a graph of mm. 51–58. Example 10.11 offers two reductions of the entire *B* part and indicates that the neighboring figure g^1–a^1–g^1 underlies the entire middle voice; d^2, of course, acts as the sustained top-voice tone.

Measures 59–66

These measures contain the retransition to the reprise of the *A* part. This section has a number of compositional tasks to perform. It must accomplish a harmonic reorientation through which G ceases to be a stable center and becomes an active element pointing to and demanding the reappearance of C. This is accomplished here in the most usual fashion, by means of the seventh, f-natural^1 (mm. 63–66). In addition the melody must prepare the lower register of the beginning of the *A′* part; this is brought about by the descending progression d^2–c^2–b^1–a^1–g^1 (mm. 58–62). The tones leading down to the g^1 are prolonged by progressions filling in descending thirds; melodic thirds, descending and ascending, have dominated the entire middle part. Schubert solves the structural problems, but in a somewhat perfunc-

Example 10.11

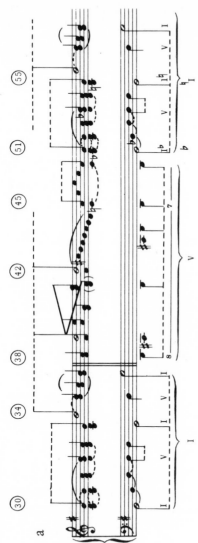

tory and unimaginative way; I, for one, find the obvious sequential elaboration of the descending fifth (and the persistent rhythmic repetition) rather hard to take. The one saving touch is the beautiful introduction of a^1 (mm. 64–66) with its reference to the important g^1–a^1–g^1 figure of the *B* part and its preparation for the final statement of the innocent grace-note motive that has led to such unforseen consequences. Example 10.12 explains.

Example 10.12

THE PIECE AS A WHOLE

The key to understanding the structure of the piece as a whole lies in the recognition of the rather peculiar relationship subsisting between the *A* and *B* parts. This relationship can be characterized as combining a high degree of contrast with a binding harmonic and melodic connectedness. The G major of the middle part, in relation to the whole piece, represents a broadly expanded and tonicized V. This V supports d^2 as principal top-voice tone; in relation to the C major of the whole piece, d^2 represents the second degree of the scale ($\hat{2}$). The *B* part therefore, is grounded in a $\frac{\hat{2}}{V}$ sonority. Now the V, although it

appeared as a structural element at the final cadence of the *A* part
(and as a prolonging chord earlier), was never the basis of a large-scale
prolongation. Indeed mm. 1–29 use the V just about as unobtrusively
as is possible in major-minor tonality. The $\hat{2}$, also a fundamental
component of the tonal system, is circumvented by the melodic
substitution of m. 28. The *B* part, therefore, is related to the *A* part
by means of elements underplayed or bypassed in the earlier part.
This fundamental contrast is accompanied by others: the rhythms
are repetitive and symmetrical in contrast to the fluid prose rhythms
of the *A* part; the character is more given, more real than that of the
searching, mysterious opening section.

Example 10.13 shows a synoptic reduction of the whole piece;
having already presented two reductions of the middle part in example 10.11, I have represented it here by its governing chord and
top-voice tone. The graph indicates that the *A* and *B* parts together
form the first segment of an interrupted linear-harmonic structure.
The tension always generated by the technique of interruption,
together with that caused by the contrast between the *A* and *B*
parts, requires the reprise of *A* with its effect of completion and
repose. Note that the first *A* part, in relation to the whole, constitutes a large-scale descent into the inner-voice region; the e^2 functions as a retained tone eventually connecting with the d^2 of mm.
34ff. The *B* part represents the expansion of the interrupting V
(divider). The reprise of *A* brings the second segment of the interrupted progression.[5]

Example 10.13

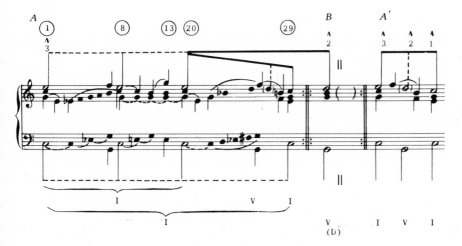

NOTES

1. I use the capital letters *A B A'* to refer to the three main parts of the piece. Each of these shows a tripartite interior organization; I indicate the sections within each part by means of small letters *a b a'.*

2. As I see it a group of tones becomes a significant compositional element if (1) it forms part of a pervasive foreground pattern through literal or disguised repetition, or if (2) it penetrates to deeper levels of structure.

3. I write this bearing in mind Joseph Addison's remark: "When we say a woman has a handsome neck we reckon into it many of the adjacent parts."

4. Heinrich Schenker *Der freie Satz* (Vienna, 1935); 2d ed., Oswald Jonas, ed. (Vienna, 1956), 1:89.

5. Interruption frequently underlies this sort of tripartite organization either of whole pieces or of sections. See, for example, Schenker, *Der freie Satz*, example for fig. 43a (2:180), and Felix Salzer, *Structural Hearing* (2d ed., New York, 1962), example 500 (2:290–92).

11. Another View on Schubert's Op. 94 no. 1

John Rothgeb

Schubert's op. 94 no. 1 contains many interesting compositional features that were not mentioned by any of the participants in the preceding Analysis Symposium, and some others that appear to me to have been inaccurately described. I should like to discuss only a few of these, beginning with the theme of the first part (mm. 1–8).

Mr. Schachter refers in his discussion of the opening measures to the use of triadic arpeggiation as a primary motive. In tracing the evolutions of this triadic idea, which is stated in its most compact form in the first two beats of the theme, he cites an immediately following arpeggiation, g^1–e^2–c^2, from the last beat of m. 1 through m. 2. I would question the assumption that this tone sequence derives, in any significant sense, from the initial g^1–e^1–c^1. The motive as a whole is formed in such a way as to project e^2 as the goal of the entire unit, giving the e^2 a meaning radically different from that of the e^1. Schachter himself shows this very well in his example 10.2, where he correctly identifies e^2 as the principal tone, $\hat{3}$. Measures 1 and 2 are so forcefully and economically directed to their purpose of yielding a C-major triad headed by e^2 (see ex. 11.1) that it seems arbitrary to segment them into the two constituent arpeggiations shown by Schachter in his first example. A more natural segmentation would be simply g^1–c^1/e^2–c^2, which has three advantages: (1) it conforms to the meter, (2) it does not contradict e^2 as the principal tone, and (3) it is supported by the similarity of directional thrust of the two defined groups.

A further question is raised by Schachter's representation of mm.

Example 11.1

185

3-4 in example 10.1. These two measures are shown as presenting essentially the same motion, a third g^1-e^1 filled by a passing tone. It is curious enough that in m. 4 the e^1 is given in Schachter's sketch as the third eighth note of the measure; surely e^1 does not really arrive in the deeper sense until the figure is completed at the fifth eighth note. But there is still more to the problem: g^1 of m. 4, indeed, should not be equated with g^1 of m. 3. Where m. 3 presented g^1-e^1 as a triadic third within the tonic harmony, m. 4 is based on the dominant, giving the simultaneous e^1-g^1 on the downbeat the character of a "nonharmonic" configuration. (The e^1 is literally "nonharmonic" and the g^1 takes on a similar quality by virtue of its parallel-thirds relation to the lower voice; such patterns abound in the tonal literature.) In other words, I maintain that e^1-g^1 on the downbeat of m. 4 should be heard as an appoggiatura to d^1-f^1 on the second eighth. Accordingly, the first two beats of m. 4 answer the third g^1-e^1 of m. 3 not with a repetition of this same third, but rather with f^1-e^1-d^1, as a small prolongation of the higher-order passing tone f^1. Example 11.2a shows the resulting interpretation of m. 4, and 11.2b places this measure in context.

It is true, as Schachter remarks (p. 171), that "the grace note of

Example 11.2

m. 3 hints at the more explicit passing tone of the next measure";
but the passing tone f^1 of m. 4 basically occupies the first two beats
of m. 4 (thus giving a rhythmic analogue of m. 2 and forming, together with m. 3, a repetition of the rhythmic content and, roughly,
the contour of mm. 1–2 as shown in ex. 11.2c), and it relates, in a
larger sense, to g^1 of m. 3 rather than to g^1 of m. 4.

Measure 5 begins the concluding phrase of the first eight measures.
As a point of departure, an initial impetus, so to speak, this closing
phrase "detaches" the final part (merely a fragment!) of the preceding motion and repeats it almost in the manner of an echo, jus-
tifying most poetically the change of mode and the *pp*. This way of
composing, of ensuring continuity by combining an advancement of
content with a reference to a past event, will be encountered again in
the middle section, mm. 9–29.

Moss and Schachter apparently agree that the initial harmony in
m. 11 is a sixth chord above the bass tone e, or a first inversion of a
C-major triad. Moss speaks of a return of the tonic chord, and
Schachter cites an exchange of voices between the bass and soprano
of mm. 11 and 12:

While I agree with Schachter that m. 11 would present an ambiguity
if considered in isolation from its context, an evaluation of the relevant context leads me to a conclusion different from the one that
he reached. First let us consider the evidence presented in favor of
reading m. 11 as a C-major harmony. The "exchange of voices"
described by Schachter cannot of itself constitute a proof of a harmonic prolongation; for as soon as we speak of an exchange, it is
already assumed that a single harmony is prolonged.[1] To argue the
contrary is to reason from conclusions to premises. The mere appearance of a soprano tone in the bass and vice versa does not necessarily
define a true exchange: an analogy of function must always be
presupposed. Observe in example 11.3 that the soprano and bass
superficially satisfy the conditions for an exchange, in that F over D
is followed by D over F; but the exchange arrows as shown are
nevertheless erroneous. The initial D in the bass is the stable third of
an inverted B-flat triad. When it appears in the soprano, however, the
D has a different meaning: it is now an accented passing tone be-

Example 11.3

$(= \text{I}^6 \quad \text{II}^6 \quad \text{V}^{6\text{-}5}_{4\text{-}3} \;)$

tween E-flat (of II⁶) and C (of V). Thus, D in the soprano exists solely by the favor of the third E-flat–C and is by no means to be equated with D in the bass. The underlying structure, accordingly, is as given in example 11.3b, which, being "de-rhythmicized," restores the soprano's D and the accompanying B-flat to their conceptually original "unaccented" position.

Regarding Schachter's supporting evidence for a C-major harmony in m. 11, it may be admitted that the left-hand arpeggiation on the second beat presents a sixth above the bass that has a full beat's duration; but this sixth can be explained in contrapuntal rather than harmonic terms, as I will show later on. And the "framing tonic before and after (mm. 1–8 and m. 12)" that Schachter mentions is problematic in that the relation of the C-major harmony in m. 12 to the tonic of mm. 1–8 has not been demonstrated. In fact, the scope of the C major at m. 12 does not extend outside its immediate context, and, as will be shown presently, it must be regarded as "framed" rather than "framing."

To understand the meaning of m. 11, I think we must consider very carefully its parallelism to m. 10: the tone-pair c^2–b^1 is established there as a motivic feature that will be repeated with delicate inflections of significance in this section of the work. And here, above all, I find Schachter's analysis especially puzzling. Whatever the long-span function of the tone b^1 might be, it surely is not locally a lower neighbor to c^2 of the $^6_4$ chord in m. 10 (see Schachter's ex. 10.4). Six-fours are rarely embellished by $^5_3$s! The root tone E could hardly be more clearly expressed than it is in m. 10 with its left-hand arpeggiation through the fifth of the E triad. Thus, we are presented with a c^2 as a suspension from the previous measure, resolving over the same bass to b^1: $^{6\text{-}5}_{4\text{-}\sharp}$. In a most beautifully improvisatory fashion, Schubert now moves forward, coupling a repetition of c^2–b^1— and in the same relationship, that of an embellishing tone to its resolution—with the replacement of the major third G-sharp by the minor third G-natural required for the forthcoming G major (see ex. 11.4). Even the repeated grace note f in the left hand underscores the parallelism. Thus there is no change of root from m. 10 to m. 11; there is merely a change of mode from an E-major triad to an E minor. It is precisely the melodic parallelism between m. 10 and m. 11—the preserved and repeated relationship of c^2 and b^1 as auxiliary and tone of resolution—that saves the right hand in m. 11 from ambiguity and gives priority to b^1 as the main melodic tone. More-over, I agree with Moss that the "surprising cancellation of G-sharp" recalls "previous chromatic shifts"—most especially, the shift from C major to C minor at mm. 4–5. In fact, the whole compositional procedure here harks back to the *A* section. Again, we have an example of advancement (signalled in m. 11 not only by the change of mode but also by the altered articulation) combined with a reference to the tail of an immediately preceding event. The unmis-takable analogy of mm. 10–11 to mm. 4–5 is further confirmed by their respective rhythmic contexts, as the reader can easily verify by noting the preserved succession of the triplet arpeggiated figure and the pattern .

Example 11.4

Understood in this way, the melodic events of mm. 10–11 already begin to take on a deeper significance than would be indicated by Schachter's remark that "the melody wavers between c^2 and b^1 as if uncertain about the course it should take" (p. 174). But there is still more to observe about the content of these measures: the motivic feature involving the tone pair c^2–b^1 is only part of a larger repetition pattern discernible in mm. 9–12. It is true that, following the estab-lishment in mm. 1–8 of e^2 as the composition's principal tone, the inner voice b^1 takes over; and, concurrently, the bass begins an ar-peggiation from c through e to g, as correctly shown by Schachter (ex. 10.4). Associated with this arpeggiation is the significant melodic pattern $e^2-(d^2)-c^2-b^1$, which is presented first in mm. 9–10 and is immediately elevated to the status of a motive by being repeated in a compressed form in m. 12. Example 11.5 shows the elements of the repeated pattern. The parallalism is reinforced by the coincidence of the final tone, b^1, with first the e and secondly the g of the bass, the primary structural points in the bass arpeggiation. Finally, if any

Example 11.5

doubts remain about the presence of this repetition, they should vanish with the recognition that Schubert introduces the e^2 of m. 12 in just the same way that the former e^2 was brought in: by the diminished fifth b^1-f^2 (see ex. 11.6). This correspondence between m. 8 and mm. 11–12, then, strengthens the resemblance of mm. 9–12 to m. 1–8 already noted in connection with the analogous changes of mode (mm. 4–5 and mm. 10–11). If we add to these features the observation that e^2-c^2 of m. 9 recalls e^2-c^2 of m. 2, the similarity of the whole of mm. 9–12 to mm. 1–8 becomes apparent.

Example 11.6

Now let us consider the techniques applied in negotiating the final stage of the large bass arpeggiation, the motion from the E-minor harmony of m. 11 to the G major of m. 12. In so doing, we will discover the true meaning of the small left-hand arpeggiation (a feature of the diminution) on the second beat of m. 11, referred to by Schachter in support of his reading of a C-major harmony throughout m. 11. In example 11.7a the total progression from the E-minor triad to the G major is reduced to the simplest contrapuntal prototype: (1) a seventh chord on D is inserted as an auxiliary dominant to the G and (2) above the bass tone E there occurs a 5–6 motion which brings in c^2 as a consonant sixth preparing the dissonant seventh of the auxiliary dominant. Thus the C-major triad on the first beat of m. 12 fundamentally represents a sixth chord that appears for purely contrapuntal reasons and has nothing to do with the main C-major tonic. But for several reasons the C harmony is compositionally expressed in the stronger form of a root-position chord. Examples 11.7a and 11.7b have the corresponding elements vertically aligned; but example 11.7b contains additional detail to

Example 11.7

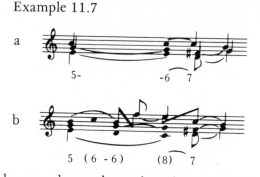

represent the lower-order prolongation that carries out the motion from E-minor triad to the C major on the first beat of m. 12. The space of a third between the root of the E minor and that of the C major is filled by a passing tone d (which at the same time provides a counterpoint for the upper neighbor f^2 in the soprano). As often happens when a fifth moves to a sixth by stepwise descent in the bass, an additional sixth—in this case c^2 above e—is inserted to form a 6–6 counterpoint with the bass. That is the configuration shown by the upper voice in m. 11: b^1–c^2–b^1, with, of course, f^2 superimposed at the end. It happens that here an additional diminution appears, to connect the bass and tenor registers, as a consequence of the expression of the descending second e–d in the bass as an ascending seventh e–d^1; and it is this diminution that gives rise to the arpeggiation in the left hand on the second beat of m. 11. Example 11.8 gives a reconstruction of the passage in three stages. The c^1 of the left hand is shown as basically a passing tone.

Example 11.8

To conclude, I would like to comment briefly on the first eight measures of the Trio. Schachter shows the d^2 that appears on top in m. 34 as the principal tone of the Trio (see ex. 10.8). I would argue that it is merely a covering tone superimposed over the true melodic content. As such, it adds a rather orchestral element to the otherwise pianistic character of the passage. Now, regarding the motion that takes place beneath it (mm. 34–37), I must ask whether it is, as Schachter's sketch indicates, merely a repetition of the first four measures—that is, a neighboring tone embellishment centering on g^1. Such an explanation appears to me to disregard the fact that the motion b–a–c^1–b, formerly an inner voice, is now placed an octave higher to form an elaboration of b^1. (The fact that there is a pianistic reason for changing the position of the right-hand chord does not in any sense give us license to disregard the presence of the b^1.) This would account for the sense of progression between the first and second phrases. Taken as a whole, these eight measures manifest strongly the quality of an ascending third, g^1–a^1–b^1, and certain parallelisms support such a conclusion; they are illustrated in example 11.9.

Example 11.9

I offer these remarks in a spirit of constructive debate, for I believe that the Analysis Symposium performs an important service in providing a forum for the exchange of ideas about specific musical problems. Such a forum is particularly welcome at a time when so much musicological literature is devoted to questions of a metatheoretic nature.

NOTE

1. I am simplifying the question slightly by leaving out of consideration those instances in which exchange of voices and progression are simultaneously expressed, so that, e.g., a soprano tone is resolved by the bass without being explicitly stated there, and vice versa. Such cases are not relevant to the present discussion.

12. More about Schubert's Op. 94 no. 1

Carl Schachter

In the preceding essay, John Rothgeb raises questions about some of the readings contained in my earlier article about Schubert's op. 94 no. 1. I believe that some of his interesting and valuable observations call for further discussion and clarification, and I would like to address myself to these.

Concerning mm. 1–2 Mr. Rothgeb questions whether the melodic progression g^1–e^2–c^2 "derives, in any significant sense, from the initial g^1–e^1–c^1" (m. 1, second quarter). He does so on the grounds that e^2 (m. 2) has a radically different function from that of e^1 (m. 1). I certainly agree that the two tones function differently; e^2 is a primary melodic element, e^1 part of a fleeting figuration. But does the significance of a motivic or thematic connection depend upon the unchanged function of all the constituent elements of the repeated group? Certainly not; indeed changes in melodic or harmonic function often form a large part of the "significance" of a repetition. Before turning to the Schubert, I should like to comment briefly upon excerpts from two other works. In the Air from Bach's Third Suite for Orchestra (see ex. 12.1), a two-note figure occurs three times in immediate succession. The first two statements contain a chord tone preceded by an appoggiatura; in the third, however, the chord tone is presented first and followed by an anticipation. Surely one hears this last two-note group as an outgrowth of the preceding ones, not as a "new" element. And it is from the changed contrapuntal relationship and the delicate shadings it produces that the passage

Example 12.1

193

derives a part of its beauty. Similar instances could be found, I daresay, in almost any tonal composition.

The beginning measures of Mozart's Piano Sonata K. 332, offer a more challenging example; here, the repetition is not literal but disguised. As example 12.2 indicates, mm. 13–16 summarize the melodic contents of mm. 1–9 so closely that we might well call them a variation of the opening measures. In mm. 1–9 the melodic line falls from c^1; in mm. 13–16, however, c^2 functions as an embellishing upbeat to a^2, which forms the real point of departure for the motion (and, as I hear it, for the fundamental melodic structure of the movement). Are we to disregard the beautiful connection between these melodic ideas because one moves from the fifth of the underlying triad and the other from the third? Were we to do so, we should lose sight of the real significance of this opening with its two different but inwardly related "themes."

Example 12.2

Now the broken-chord figure in the Schubert piece is a neutral configuration of tones which might appear in any composition; this marks a difference from, say, the Mozart sonata. But the whole piece is permeated with arpeggiated progressions; they occur in the top voice and in the bass, over both small and large spans. If a composition shows so pervasive a use of a broken-chord figure, I should consider it perfectly logical to regard the figure as a "primary motive." And if the motive appears "in its most compact form in the first two beats of the theme," I should consider it equally logical to hear later arpeggiations as outgrowths of the first one despite changes in the function of tones contained within them.

The opening two measures of the Schubert show a motion ascending from g^1 to e^2 (as principal tone) and falling from e^2 to c^2. This is surely an arpeggio and, in my view, develops and transforms the figure first heard at the beginning of m. 1. Mr. Rothgeb, however, is correct in stating that the two measures should be heard as a unit rather than separated into two segments. And I must agree that my explanation, especially example 10.1, was misleading in this regard. In trying to demonstrate as clearly as possible the development of the triadic motive, I separated the second and third beats of m. 1. The correct grouping could, I believe, be inferred from my example 10.2 in which the contents of m. 1 are represented by a single g^1, which connects with e^2 of m. 2. The triadic figure on the second beat of m. 1, then, is an offshoot of the sustained g^1—an arpeggio within an arpeggio, so to speak, rather than one of the two consecutive arpeggios of my original explanation.

Mr. Rothgeb raises two questions about my reading of the right-hand part of m. 4. In the first place he maintains that the melody reaches e^1 as temporary goal at the fifth eighth note of the measure rather than at the third as in my reading. In my analysis of this measure, as it happens, I was led to a large extent by the configuration of the bass line. For it is here that the bass first enters as a real voice part; this entrance, for me, constitutes the crucial event of the measure. Now the bass expresses two motions of a fourth from G to c. The first of these is filled in with passing tones in a rhythm of eighth-sixteenth-sixteenth. The driving force of this rhythm emphasizes the c of the third eighth and makes it sound like a goal. The second fourth, presented without passing tones in a more neutral rhythm, sounds like an echo of the first. Now if c "arrives" in the bass at the third eighth note, it follows logically that e^2 arrives in the melody at the same point. Rothgeb's example 11.2 does not indicate the bass in full (neither did mine, I must admit). But it clearly suggests that the c on the third eighth represents merely a support for passing tones of the right-hand part rather than a goal of motion. For me this reading contradicts the flow of the music's rhythm (see ex. 12.3).

Example 12.3

Rothgeb's second observation about m. 4 concerns the meaning of the g^1 on the downbeat. In my examples 10.1 and 10.2 it was shown as a principal tone; Rothgeb believes that g^1 and its lower third e^1 function as appoggiaturas to the seventh and fifth of a V^7 chord. Here our disagreement centers on a small detail; however it touches upon a general consideration which it is impossible to deal with fully within the framework of this reply. The question, briefly put, is the following. If, in the course of a melodic line, elements of tonic harmony are projected over a prolongation of V, which is the more significant: their function as dependent "nonharmonic" tones in their immediate context or their power to represent displaced principal tones in a broader context? Although a general question can be posed, no generally valid answer can be given; each case must be decided individually.

In this connection let us consider the opening of the first movement of Brahms's Symphony no. 2. In m. 2 the f-sharp^1 of the first horn sounds against the A of the cellos and basses and moves to the fifth of the V chord in m. 4. In relation to the V, f-sharp^1 functions as a "nonharmonic" element. Yet ought we to hear it merely as an appoggiatura to e^1? Not at all! For the V of mm. 2–4 forms part of a longer prolongation of the tonic; the f-sharp^1 is heard in relation to this more inclusive context as well as to the immediate environment provided by the V. And here its significance as a displaced third of tonic harmony far outweighs in importance its local dependency on the fifth of the dominant. For the melodic progression f-sharp^1–e^1–d^1 (mm. 2–4) constitutes a motivic event of prime importance; moreover f-sharp^1 begins the fundamental melodic structure of the entire movement. To hear the opening phrase as expressing a melodic second decorated by an appoggiatura would be to misconstrue it completely (see ex. 12.4).

To show the problem in a somewhat different perspective I would like to discuss briefly mm. 18–23 of the Adagio movement of Beethoven's String Quartet op. 18 no. 2. In m. 18, the first violin brings in f^3 as the seventh over the dominant harmony. The resolution of f^3 to e^3 (an upward transfer of the principal melodic tone, e^2, of mm. 7–10) constitutes the crucial melodic event of mm. 18–22. The e^3 would normally appear over I; however it is shifted so that it forms the sixth of a cadential $^6_4$ over the V of m. 22. The delay of e^3 permits Beethoven to create several parallelisms to the melodic contents of mm. 1–7. Here again the e^3, although part of a $^6_4$, functions

Example 12.4

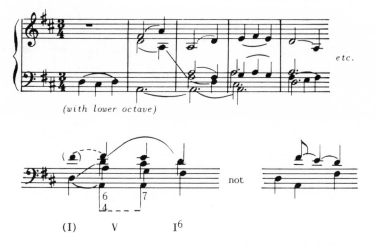

as a principal tone, not merely as an appoggiatura to d³ (ex. 12.5).

Both of the preceding examples demonstrate, I think, that a "nonharmonic" tone over the V can sometimes function as a principal tone representing a displaced member of the tonic. To be sure m. 4 of the Schubert piece differs from the Brahms and Beethoven citations in several important respects. The "appoggiatura" chord is an ⁸₆ rather than a ⁶₄; the V is unobtrusive enough to cause little more than a ripple on the surface of the prolonged I; g¹ has already sounded within the tonic harmony of the preceding measures. Of these considerations only the last, I think, might speak against my reading. However the motivic parallelism between mm. 3 and 4 (referred to in my original article) and the repetition in minor (m. 5) of the contents of m. 4 support our hearing the third g¹–f¹–e¹ as an integral melodic unit rather than as a second embellished by an appoggiatura. Incidentally, if I adopt this reading primarily because of motivic relationships, I am in good company. In his analysis of m. 37—where the configuration of voice leading is very similar to that of m. 4—Rothgeb presents a reading very much like mine of m. 4 and for the same reason—a presumed motivic connection (see his example 11.9).

In the measures immediately following the double bar (mm. 9–12), Rothgeb's reading and mine diverge in several details. The central difference concerns the chord on the first beat of m. 11. I hear it as

Example 12.5

a C-major sixth chord connected with the prolonged tonic of mm. 1–8 and, by part interchange, with the C chord on the downbeat of m. 12. Rothgeb reads m. 11 as expressing an E-minor chord which moves to the G chord at the end of m. 12; he maintains that the two C chords are contrapuntal details within this larger progression and connects them neither with one another nor with the tonic expressed in mm. 1–8. To support his reading, Rothgeb adduces the following pieces of evidence: (1) Measure 10 contains a $\begin{smallmatrix}6\\4\end{smallmatrix}\begin{smallmatrix}5\\\#\end{smallmatrix}$ succession over a sustained e in the bass; the top voice moves from c^2 (sixth) to b^1 (fifth). (2) "Six-fours are rarely embellished by $\begin{smallmatrix}5\\3\end{smallmatrix}$s!" In m. 10, therefore, b^1 functions as the essential melodic tone and c^2 as its embellishment. (3) Because of the close parallelism between m. 10

and m. 11, the tone pair c^2–b^1 must be read in the same measures; that is as decoration moving to tone of resolution. If b^1 rather than c^2 is the main melody tone, the underlying chord of m. 11 is obviously an E-minor one.

The crux of Rothgeb's argument occurs in the second of the above statements. Now it is certainly true that "$^6_4$s are rarely embellished by $^5_3$s" but "rarely" does not mean "never." (Nor, as we shall see, is his statement precisely applicable to my analysis.) To be sure, an essential characteristic of the $^6_4$ is its dependency upon more stable sonorities; but the resolution $^{6-5}_{4-3}$ is only one instance (though perhaps the most typical one) of this dependency. My analysis shows the $^6_4$ resolving to a $^6_3$ on the downbeat of the following measure; it shows the $^5_3$ of m. 11 not as an embellishment of the $^6_4$ (as implied by Rothgeb's statement) but as a decoration of the resolution $^{6--}_{4-3}$. Now the progression $^{6--}_{4-3}$ over a stationary bass constitutes a logical and valid voice leading and one that can very well serve as the basis for compositional elaboration. In its most abstract form it occurs frequently in the fourth species of Fuxian counterpoint. Example 12.6 shows a voice leading abstracted from my reading of mm. 8–11 of the Schubert piece and expressed in the form of fourth-species, three-part counterpoint.

If one can accept the premise that a voice leading like that of example 12.6 underlies these measures, then the remainder of my original reading follows quite naturally. The g-sharp^1 of m. 10 would be heard as a chromatic passing tone rather than as a tone of resolution; the b^1 of the top voice would function as lower neighbor to c^2. The close parallelism between measures 10 and 11—correctly cited by Rothgeb—would require us to hear c^2 as main tone in m. 11 as well thus producing the C sixth chord to which Rothgeb takes exception. (Both Rothgeb and I respect this parallelism though our different premises lead us to different readings.) Rothgeb correctly maintains that my original article did not really substantiate the presence of an interchange between the top voice and bass of mm. 11–12; but such an interchange would also emerge as a logical consequence of the voice leading of example 12.6.

But are we in fact justified in hearing such a voice leading as the basis of the passage rather than the $^{6-5}_{4-3}$ suggested by Rothgeb? One

Example 12.6

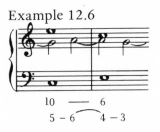

important consideration certainly supports Rothgeb's reading. The fifth is a far more stable consonance than the sixth; the progression $\frac{6-5}{4-3}$ therefore constitutes a more "satisfactory" resolution than the progression $\frac{6--}{4-3}$. Other things being equal, then, the ear will more readily accept a $\frac{5}{3}$ than a $\frac{6}{3}$ (or presumed $\frac{6}{3}$) as the chord of resolution especially if, as here, the $\frac{5}{3}$ occurs immediately after the $\frac{6}{4}$. In the present case, however, I wonder whether other things are really equal. In m. 9 the tones e^2 and c^2 carry over from the preceding measure; the only new tone is a^1, which moves from the persistently reiterated g^1 of the opening phrase. In m. 10 a^1 is restruck as a suspended fourth. At first, certainly, the ear accepts the g-sharp^1 of m. 10 as a resolution of the fourth. But it does not, I think, accept it as the goal of a motion. For the g-sharp^1, as a chromatically altered tone with strong leading-tone implications, demands to be continued; we expect a further progression that will integrate the tone into a larger context. Our expectation, of course, is primarily directed to a^1 as part of a tonicized submediant. Instead, and most beautifully, Schubert moves the g-sharp^1 down to g-natural^1. The progression g-sharp^1–g-natural^1, in contrast to the chromatic inflection of mm. 4–5, is from an unstable to a stable tone. The ear, therefore, can reinterpret the g-sharp^1 as a chromatic passing tone instead of a leading tone and can hear it as forming part of a broad inner-voice progression g^1–a^1–g-sharp^1–g-natural^1. In this process of reinterpretation—a process, incidentally, that occurs in our listening to many tonal compositions—g-natural^1 is revealed as the true resolution of the a^1 of m. 10.

As I mentioned in my original article, the neighboring progression g^1–a^1–g^1 constitutes a motive of fundamental importance in this piece. (It is the most significant link between the C-major part and the Trio, for example.) Now the inner-voice progression cited in my last paragraph expands and develops this basic idea. In Rothgeb's reading, on the other hand, the a^1 is heard as an embellishment of g-sharp[1] and this motivic connection is lost. I believe, therefore, that my analysis, without in any way contradicting normative voice-leading considerations, is more faithful to the individual design of the piece than his. In my view none of the motivic parallelisms cited by him possesses the importance of the neighboring figure which I conceive to underlie the passage. And one of them (the echoing in mm. 11-12 of the melodic diminished fifth at the cadence of mm. 7-8) is, I think, a support for hearing the C chord of m. 12 as a continuation of the initial tonic.

Rothgeb's final observations concern the first eight measures of the Trio. He reads the top voice as expressing an ascent to b^1, stated initially in m. 34 and confirmed as the melodic goal at the cadence of m. 37. I hear d^2 as principal melodic tone of the Trio as a whole, and the motion around b^1 (mm. 34-35) as a figuration embellishing the inner-voice tone g^1 at the upper third. There are two questions here. The first is whether or not b^1 acts as the main tone of the melody in mm. 34-35. Rothgeb's reading of these measures is a possible one and one I would readily agree to if Schubert had supported it by rhythmic emphasis (placing b^1 on the strong part of the beat) or by notational clues (double stems, for example). In the absence of such evidence I still prefer to read a return to the idea of m. 30 paralleled at the upper third instead of the lower sixth and coinciding with the entrance of d^2 in the highest part.

The second question is whether, as Rothgeb maintains, d^2 is "merely a covering tone" employed to give an orchestral quality to the passage. In my opinion, the melodic events of the retransition (mm. 59-66) make it clear that it is the d^2 which relates the melodic line of the Trio to the fundamental melodic structure of the piece as a whole. Therefore even if I were to accept Rothgeb's interpretation of mm. 34-35, I should still consider d^2 to be the central melodic tone of the Trio. In that case I should place the b^1 within the framework of a more inclusive ascent from g^1 to d^2; in such a reading, d^2 would arrive as principal tone two measures later than was shown in my original analysis (see ex. 12.7).

Example 12.7

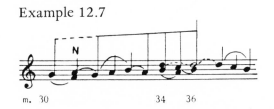

m. 30   34   36

Symposium III
Beethoven, Piano Sonata Op. 53
Introduzione

Attacca subito il Rondo

13. A Schenkerian Analysis

David Beach

Beethoven's Piano Sonata in C (op. 53), dedicated to Count Ferdinand von Waldstein, was composed in 1803–04 and first published in May of the following year by the Bureau des arts et d'industrie in Vienna. According to Nottebohm, Thayer, and others,[1] the sonata originally had three separate movements, the two existing ones in C, plus a long middle movement (an andante) in F major. As the story goes, Beethoven then decided not to include the Andante movement and in its place he inserted an introduction (Introduzione) to the Rondo.[2] (An examination of the autograph reveals that the Introduzione was written with a different colored ink than the rest of the sonata.[3] However this is not conclusive evidence that it was inserted sometime later.) If Beethoven did indeed make this last minute change, it could be reasonable to assume that length was an important consideration behind that decision. Inclusion of the Andante movement would have made the sonata exceptionally long, particularly for that time, and the effect and stature of the other movements would certainly have been diminished. However, further investigation reveals that the Andante has little structural relationship to the other movements and, in my opinion, is of inferior quality. The Introduzione on the other hand, plays a significant role in the overall scheme of the sonata. Its existence not only depends upon but gives added meaning to the Rondo which follows.

From a pedagogic point of view, the Introduzione is a particularly good subject for analysis. It is compact—only 28 measures long—yet it contains many interesting and even unusual features which require careful consideration. One's attention is immediately drawn to the more striking characteristics of the foreground—the use of chromaticism, the rhythmic-motivic organization, and the registral organization, to name a few. As one progresses in the investigation of the harmonic-contrapuntal organization at the middleground and background levels, the significance of certain compositional details— Beethoven's dynamic markings, for example—becomes increasingly apparent. In fact, careful evaluation of Beethoven's markings is necessary for a proper interpretation of the larger-scale structure. (This, of course, points to the absolute necessity of consulting original sources—in this case the autograph—whenever possible.) And although it is possible and even advantageous to isolate the Introduzione for the purpose of analysis, it is necessary to keep in mind that its real significance lies in its relationship to the rest of the sonata.

The Introduzione is composed of three phrases, the last two of which overlap. The following analysis corresponds to this division, as follows: phrase 1, mm. 1–9; phrase 2, upbeat to m. 10 to the downbeat of m. 17; and phrase 3, mm. 17–28.

PHRASE I

The opening phrase can be divided into two parts, the first of which is controlled by the chromatic descent from F to C in the bass (mm. 1–6); the second is the ensuing cadential pattern which leads to a full close on the tonic (F) in m. 9. The material of the first part and its organization into two-measure units is based on the harmonic-motivic structure of the first two measures. The opening melodic interval of a sixth (c to a) is articulated by a three-note rhythmic figure

♪.♫ . The dotted character of this figure directs one's attention to the second note (a) of the interval which is given further emphasis by the marking tenuto. The repetition of this figure introduces a d-sharp, forming an interval of an augmented sixth with the stationary bass note F. The instability caused by this interval forces the outer voices to resolve stepwise in contrary motion to the e's in m. 2.[4] The E-major chord in m. 2 is articulated by the rhythmic

pattern ♪ ♫ ♩♪ , characterized by its avoidance of the downbeat. The rhythmic organization of mm. 3–4 is exactly the same as that of mm. 1–2. This time the opening interval is a minor sixth (b-natural–g^1), the g-natural being an alteration of the g-sharp from the previous measure. The repetition of the rhythmic figure introduces an a-sharp, forming an interval of an augmented fourth with the bass note e. The implied $\frac{4}{2}$ chord then resolves to a B-major chord in the sixth position in m. 4. (An exact harmonic-melodic sequence would have resulted in a D-sharp (or E-flat) major chord at this point, thus altering the course of the composition considerably). This suggests that the progression is contrapuntal, not harmonic. In m. 5

the bass voice begins on d-natural rather than continuing the bass note of the previous measure (d-sharp) as had been done before (m. 3). This acceleration of the chromatic descent in the bass is continued through d-flat to C (the immediate goal of this motion), emphasized by its placement on the downbeat of m. 6. The opening melodic interval in m. 5 is an augmented fourth (f^1–b^1), not a sixth as in mm. 1 and 3. This interval is inverted and restated over the change of bass, thus preparing the suspension of f^2 in m. 6. The resolution of f^2 to e^2 over the bass note C is covered by g^2, marked *sf* in the autograph. This dynamic marking shifts the emphasis away from the following b-flat^1, which would normally be accented because of its metric, rhythmic, and melodic placement.[5] Arrival at the dominant seventh chord in m. 6 completes the harmonization of the chromatic descent in the bass which began with the tonic harmony in m. 1.

The voice-leading of mm. 1–6 is shown in example 13.1a.[6] The ascent of the upper voices over a descending bass is accomplished by a process of superimposing one voice on the other through registral transfer. In this manner the inner-voice note c of m. 1 is led to

Example 13.1

b-flat^1 in m. 6 through the passing note b. Likewise the a of m. 1 is led to the f^2 of m. 5, which then resolves to e^2 in the following measure over the bass note C. This represents a motion from a to an inner voice. As shown in the second part of example 13.1a, the resolution of the sixth a–f^2 to another sixth (g)–e^2 appears in the detail of the composition as the third g^2–e^2. The superimposition of g^2 over the inner-voice resolution of f^2 to e^2 is the result of registral transfer. Thus the larger-scale resolution of a (*ten.*!) is to g^2 (*sf*!), the high-note of the phrase. A simplification of the contents of example 13.1a is given in example 13.1b. This registral condensation of the voice-leading reveals that the motion from a to an inner voice moves in parallel tenths with the chromatic descent in the bass. The larger-scale motion of the upper voices is stepwise over a change in the bass from f to c.

The cadential pattern which follows is relatively straightforward in contrast to the chromatic motion of the opening measures. The rhythmic structure of mm. 6–9 (with the important exception of m. 8) is based on the rhythmic pattern first stated in m. 2. Interpretation of the contrapuntal structure of these measures is slightly more difficult. At first glance the harmonic progression V^7 VI II^6 V^7 I would seem to support the stepwise descent of the inner voice from b-flat^1 in m. 6 to f^2 in m. 9. However, more careful examination reveals that the g^1–f^1 motion of mm. 8–9, which is supported by the harmonic progression II^6 V^7 I, is a continuation of the upper-voice motion of mm. 6–7 transferred down an octave. The inconclusive harmonization of the resolution of g^2 to f^2 in m. 7 forces the phrase to continue until the harmonization of this motion is complete. The resolution of the inner voice from b-flat^1 to a^1 in mm. 6–7 is also transferred down an octave; it does not continue to the g^1–f^1 motion of mm. 8–9. This change of register between m. 7 and m. 8 is articulated by a change in the rhythmic pattern.

The larger-scale structure of the entire phrase is shown in example 13.2. The registral condensation of the voice-leading at the background level shows the main melodic motion as a descending third, marked $\hat{3}$ $\hat{2}$ $\hat{1}$ in the sketch. In the detail of the composition these pitches appear in different octaves: $\hat{3}$ = a in m. 1; $\hat{2}$ = g^1 in m. 8 (the g^2 of m. 6 is a passing note); $\hat{1}$ = f^1 in m. 9. This descent of a third is summarized by the melodic leap of a third (f^1–a^1–f^1) in m. 9. The b-flat^1 in m. 6 is a passing note belonging to the inner voice; it is not the upper neighbor note of a^1 as shown by Salzer.[7] One's inter-

Example 13.2

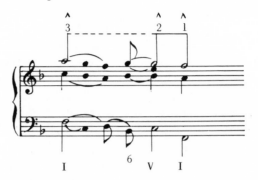

pretation of the function of the dominant seventh chord in m. 6 is crucial to the interpretation of the larger-scale motion of the phrase. If that chord is considered as the dominant harmony which supports $\hat{2}$, it is necessary to consider the following chords as neighboring chords which prolong that harmony until its resolution in m. 9. However the impetus of this chord seems to force it on to the d-minor chord in the following measure. Although the bass note C in m. 6 is the goal of the chromatic descending motion, it supports a passing chord which finds its immediate resolution in m. 7. This bass motion supports a preliminary descent of a third (a to f) as shown in example 13.2. Within the larger-scale structure of the bass, an arpeggiation is formed which begins on f in m. 1, moves to d in m. 7 (prepared by the c of m. 6), and finally moves to B-flat (which supports a g-minor chord in sixth position) in m. 8. This motion prepares for the dominant harmony in m. 8 and its resolution in m. 9, which support the background descent of $\hat{2}$ $\hat{1}$.

PHRASE 2

The second phrase can also be divided into two parts. The first of these, mm. 10–13, offers a certain degree of contrast—in fact the only contrast in the entire Introduzione—to the material of the first phrase. The most obvious point of difference is the use of chromaticism: In the second phrase, chromatic notes are used only as a means of embellishing diatonic motion at the foreground level, whereas in the first they participate in a middleground motion. The primary unifying device (foreground) is the dotted rhythmic figure from the opening measure. But here the figure always begins on the last eighth of the measure so that the rhythmic emphasis on the third note of the figure coincides with the metric accent of the downbeat. It is first used as the upbeat to m. 10 with the sixth c-a (the opening melodic interval of m. 1!) and later as the upbeat to m. 12 with the seventh c–b-flat (an expansion of the earlier sixth). Both are marked *rinforzando.* The use of this figure helps to articulate the motivic division of this part into two 2-measure units supported by the harmonic motion I–V, V–I.

The voice-leading of mm. 10–13 is shown in example 13.3. The main melodic note a and its supporting bass note F are prolonged, at least at one level of the composition, by their upper and lower neighbor notes (N). This motion is indicated by half notes in the sketch. Unlike the first phrase, the important pitches are stated in the same register and all are either metrically or rhythmically accented. At a more detailed level each of these notes is prolonged by an ascending motion of a third. In m. 10, c^1—as the third above a—and its upper neighbor note d^1 are given special emphasis by being marked *sf*. These same pitches, stated in reverse order, are also marked *sf* in m. 12. (The significance of this emphasis on c will be discussed later when we consider the larger-scale structure of the entire phrase.) The c^1 of m. 12 then returns to a in m. 13 through the passing note b-flat. The motion of an ascending third is also the basis for the material in mm. 11 and 13. In m. 11 the g is prolonged by overlapping statements of a figure which moves up to b-flat, and in m. 13 this motion is a step higher. The registral expansion which results from these overlapping statements offers a contrast to the restricted range of the more significant events of the alternating measures. The use of the upper registers in particular prepares for the important registral change in m. 14. At a detailed level the transition to m. 14 is accomplished by a third statement of the dotted rhythmic figure (this time on c^2) over an implied dominant $\frac{4}{2}$ chord.

Example 13.3

The remainder of the phrase, m. 14 to the downbeat of m. 17, is clearly based on the contents of mm. 6–9. Measure 14 is both a condensation and an elaboration of the main features of mm. 6–7. Here the outer-voice motion f^2–e^2–g^2 and the following b-flat^1–a^1 are both articulated by the dotted rhythmic figure from the opening measure. These two "voices" are connected by a slur between g^2 and b-flat^1. On the last eighth of the measure, the a^1 is embellished by a new rhythmic figure of four thirty-second notes which is used again in the third phrase. The marking *sf*(!) on the last of these thirty-second notes reinforces the important inner-voice note c^2 in preparation for its descent to a^1 (through b-flat^1) in the following measure. The bass voice in m. 14 which supports this motion is also more elaborate than in mm. 6–7. It begins on A, the third of the tonic harmony, and returns to a tonic chord at the end of the measure through various positions of the dominant. The tenor and alto voices are particularly important here because of their rhythmic organization (hemiola). The first three notes of the alto are a tonal inversion of the pitches f^2–e^2–g^2 in the top voice, which are derived from the same motion in m. 6. The rhythmic emphasis is on the g^1, and the marking *sf* at this point probably refers to it (to be consistent with the emphasis on g^2 in m. 6) rather than to the e^2 in the top voice. This suggests that the alto, as well as the top voice, should be articulated as clearly as possible in performance. The following measure repeats the contents of m. 14 with a few minor changes. The bass note A on the downbeat is left out and this time the harmonic movement at the end of the measure is "deceptive" (a reference to mm. 6–7). The thirty-second note figure on the last eighth note in the top voice is also left out in preparation for the following cadential pattern. Measure 16, which is exactly the same as m. 8, leads to the tonic harmony on the downbeat of m. 17. Although the bass voice reaches its destination here, melodic closure is avoided (the f^1 is left out) and the end of phrase 2 becomes the beginning of phrase 3.

Interpretation of the larger-scale structure of the second phrase requires careful consideration of the connection between its two parts. As was mentioned previously, a and its supporting bass note F are prolonged by their upper and lower neighbor notes—at least at the foreground level—in mm. 10–13. However the larger-scale functions of the b-flat and its bass note G in m. 12 are passing notes (not neighbor notes) leading to c^1 and A respectively. (This is not a contradiction but a reinterpretation of function at a higher level of structure.) The melodic motion from a to c^1 is prepared in m. 10 and stated again in m. 13. This interpretation of the larger-scale motion explains the emphasis (*sf*) given to c^1 and its upper neighbor note d^2 in mm. 10 and 12. The c^2 on the last beat of m. 13 (articulated by the dotted rhythmic figure) confirms the significance of that pitch and also prepares for the registral change in m. 14. (The meaning of the curious *sf* marking under c^2 in m. 14 also becomes clearer.) The bass motion from F to A in m. 10 prepares for its equivalent larger-scale motion which reaches its goal on the downbeat of m. 14. As shown in example 13.4, the outer voices in this larger-scale motion from m. 10 to m. 14 move in parallel tenths. The remainder of the sketch requires only brief commentary. The f^2–e^2–g^2 motive stated in mm. 14 and 15 is superimposed on c^2 by octave transfer; the return of g^2 to f^2 (shown in parentheses) actually occurs in the tenor voice (g to f) in m. 15. Meanwhile c^2 is returned to a^1 through the passing note b-flat^1 and, as in phrase 1, this motion is then transferred down an octave (shown by the dotted line). The larger-scale motion in the bass is stepwise from F in m. 10 (which supports $\hat{3}$) to c in m. 16 (which supports $\hat{2}$). The background descent of a third is interrupted at this point (shown as two parallel perpendicular lines) and $\hat{3}$ (a) is reinstated in m. 17 as the third phrase begins.

Example 13.4

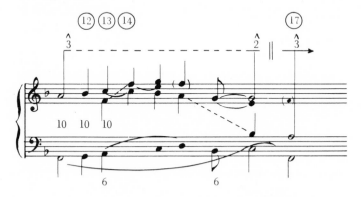

PHRASE 3

The beginning of the third phrase is the same as mm. 1–5 except for a few minor changes. These changes are important, however, because they make the rhythmic motion more continuous than in the first phrase. Use of the thirty-second note figure (from m. 14) on the up-beats to mm. 18 and 20 necessitates their rhythmic resolutions on the downbeats of those measures (as opposed to the eighth-note rests on the downbeats of mm. 2 and 4). The chromatic motions in m. 18 (g-sharp to g-natural) and m. 20 (f-sharp^1 to f-natural), which antic-ipate the following downbeats, also effect the rhythmic continuity. The motion generated by these changes becomes the basis for the in-crease in rhythmic activity which follows.

The most significant changes occur in mm. 21–28. In m. 21 the f^2 is arrived at in the same way as the f^2 in m. 5 and one might ex-pect the resolution of that note to e^2 in the following measure, as had happened previously. Instead f^2 is prolonged until its resolution to e^2 in m. 27. (The primary reason for this change is harmonic: These measures function as a transition to the Rondo by preparing for the establishment of C major as the new tonality.) The prolonga-tion of f^2 is accompanied by a change in texture and an increase in rhythmic activity (based on the thirty-second note figure) which begins in m. 21 and continues through m. 25. These changes coincide with the registral climax and dynamic emphasis (*sf*) given to f^3 (and the bass note A-flat) in mm. 24–25. The voice-leading involved in this process is shown in example 13.5. The f^2 is first prolonged by an arpeggiation (articulated by the repetition of the dotted rhythmic figure on f^2) up to f^3 in mm. 23–24, and then by a second arpeggia-tion down to f in m. 26 (shown by the dotted line). The resolution of f to e in m. 27 is accompanied by the corresponding motion of those pitches in the original register two octaves above. The bass mo-tion beginning in m. 21 is shown as a descent from d to g. However, the dynamic and metric accents are given to the A-flat in mm. 23–24,

Example 13.5

and the resolution to G in m. 25 is only momentary. Introduction of the G-sharp in m. 26 forces the bass up to A, thus harmonizing the e^2 in m. 27 by an a-minor chord (VI in the new tonality). This progression corresponds to the similar motion in mm. 6–7.

In the autograph there is a seven measure segment which is crossed out. This segment, which corresponds to mm. 17–23 in the final version, is shown in example 13.6. Most of the changes made by Beethoven are minor and can easily be seen by comparing example 13.6 with the corresponding measures in the final version. The most significant change occurs in m. 21: In the original version the f^2 is not reached in the same way as in the first phrase. This feature is changed in the final version and the prolongation of f^2 is then extended until its resolution in m. 27. Beethoven obviously wanted to preserve the connection between the f^2–e^2–g^2 motive in m. 6 and the extension of that motive in mm. 21–28. The resolution of f^2 to e^2 in m. 27 is then extended down to d^2 in m. 28 before g^2 is superimposed on that motion. The reason for this expansion of the motive is harmonic: The d^2 and g^2 are supported by the progression II^6–V in the key of C, thus completing the transition to the Rondo.

The larger-scale structure of mm. 17–28 is shown in example 13.7. The main melodic motion at the background level is a descent from $\hat{3}$ (a in m. 17) to $[\hat{2}]$ (g^2 in m. 28). This motion is summarized in its original register by the a to g motion in the left hand part in m. 28. The $\hat{2}$ (*sf*!) is shown in brackets because g^2 no longer functions in the key of F at that point; it prepares for the main melodic note ($\hat{5}$) of the Rondo. The inner-voice motion from f^2 to d^2 also leads directly into the Rondo and is continued down to c^2 in m. 4 of that movement. The bass voice, particularly in mm. 21–28, also contains a number of features worth mentioning. Although the immediate goal of the descending bass motion is the G in mm. 25–26, the dominant seventh chord it supports has only a passing function. It leads on to the A in m. 27 through the chromatic passing note G-sharp and, as was mentioned previously, this motion corresponds to the similar one in mm. 6–7. The overall motion in the bass from m. 17 to m. 27 is shown in example 13.7 as an ascending third from F to A through the passing note G. (One might also consider this motion as a descending sixth from f down to A.) Associated with the larger-scale connection of f (F) in m. 17 to the F in m. 28 is the voice-leading change from 5 to 6. The function of F is thus transformed from its role of supporting a stable triad (the tonic harmony in F) to

Example 13.6

Example 13.7

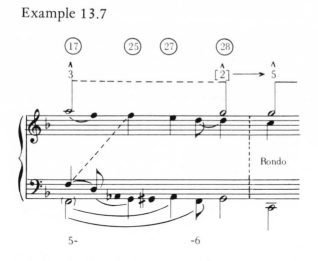

its role of preparing for the following G (which supports the dominant harmony in the key of C).

The Introduzione thus prepares for the Rondo at many different levels. The function of the F-major triad, which is established and prolonged as the tonic harmony in the first seventeen measures, is transformed to function as IV in the key of C. At the macrocosmic level, the harmony can be heard as a motion from IV to V which finds its harmonic fulfillment in the Rondo. This progression supports a large-scale melodic motion of a (3̂) to g², which becomes 5̂ in C major. It is interesting to note that this registral change is anticipated by the motion from a to g² in the first six measures of the Introduzione. These structural preparations are accompanied by an equally important dramatic one: The high level of tension generated in the Introduzione finds its release in the relative simplicity of the Rondo. In the most complete sense, the Introduzione functions as a transition between the two main movements. It borrows material from the first (e.g., the chromatic descending bass motion) while preparing for the second.

NOTES

1. See Georg Kinsky, comp., *Das Werk Beethovens* (Munich: G. Henle, 1955).

2. The alleged middle movement was published separately under the title *Andante favori* (Kinsky Wo O 57).

3. A facsimile edition of the autograph was published in limited quantity by the Beethovenhaus in Bonn: *Dritte Reihe: Beethoven*, vol. 2.

4. The resolution of the bass voice is displaced to the upper octave. The reason for this is that F, two octaves and a fifth below middle c, was the lowest note on the piano at the time this piece was written.

5. Literal interpretation and execution of the sforzando would seem musically inappropriate here. As is the case with many of the dynamic markings in this piece, the intention seems to be to bring one's attention to notes which should be emphasized because of their structural significance.

6. A similar voice-leading sketch of these measures is given by Oswald Jonas in *Das Wesen des musikalischen Kunstwerks: Eine Einführung in die Lehre Heinrich Schenkers* (Vienna: Im Saturn Verlag, 1934), example 205, p. 172.

7. An analysis of this phrase is given by Felix Salzer in *Structural Hearing: Tonal Coherence in Music* (New York: Dover Publications, 1962), vol. 2, ex. 430. Salzer incorrectly shows the b-flat[1] of m. 6 as the upper neighbor note of a (m. 1) which returns to a[1] in m. 7. As was mentioned previously, that b-flat[1] comes from the c of m. 1 through the chromatic passing note b. Its resolution is to a[1] in m. 7 (and a in m. 9 through octave transfer), not down to f[1] in m. 9, as shown in Salzer's diagrams.

14. An Original Analytic Technique

Robert Palmer

The following analysis of the Introduzione from Beethoven's Sonata in C op. 53 is based on a method of analysis for tonal music which I developed some years ago. The graphic representation of this analysis appears in the form of an analytic chart (ex. 14.1). Since the method of analysis represented in this chart has not yet been published in any form, a brief explanation of concepts and symbolism is essential. The analytic chart has the following elements from top to bottom:

1. Phrase structure.
2. A reduction to the linear framework and some basic harmonies.
3. Melodic vectors, here in the bass voice.
4. The functional micro-level giving the relationships and distance numbers of the diatonic harmonic functions. The positive functions are from weakest to strongest: III (+4), VI (+3), II (+2), V (+1). The subprimary function IV lies below the tonic and is the only negative function: IV (–1).
5. The tonal or key functions, the macro-level, symmetrically arranged on either side of the tonic, each with its relative key. The six diatonic keys with their distance numbers are: Tonic (O), Rel. (R), Dom. (+1), S. Dom. (–1), Dom. Rel. (+1R), and S. Dom. Rel. (–1R). The remaining keys lie outside the diatonic area and are termed transdiatonic. They proceed +2, +2R, –2, –2R, and so on. A modulation from lower to higher is negative, from larger to smaller positive. Movements to the negative domain –2, –4, and so on, are rapidly destructive of tonal sense and must be highly controlled by the composer. The symbols for harmonic functions are presented on page 220.

Example 14.1   Analytic Chart

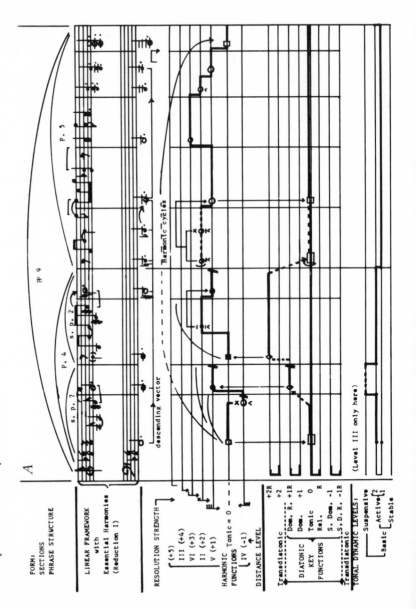

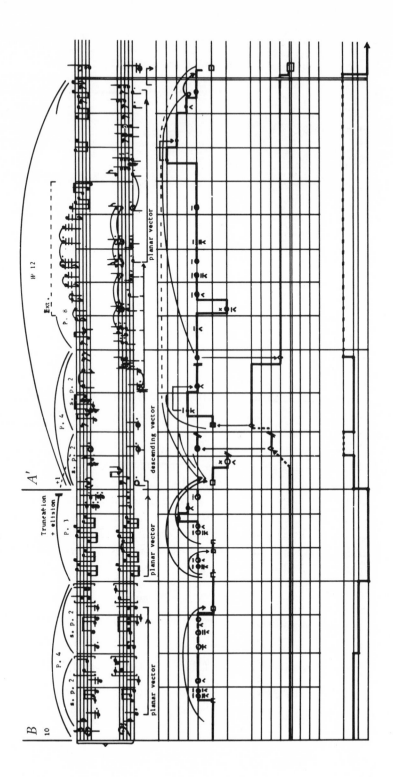

Harmonic Functions

	Tonic Key	Non-Tonic Key
+2 or above		
Dom. (+1)		
Tonic T		
V of IV		
(Tonic Line)		

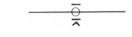

Inversion symbols: 1st   2nd   3rd   Combined

Chord type: triad   7th   9th   2nd inv., 7th chord

Key Functions

Tonic Key: All Other:

The richer the chord and the higher its inversion the more active and intense it is. It thus increases the instability and consequent forward momentum at whatever functional level it may exist.

6. Tonal intensity/stability levels. I will now define the concept of tonal dynamic levels (intensity-stability levels) of any essential structural unit of the length of a phrase or less. In attempting to deal with tonal dynamics in a more meaningful way I have come to distinguish between units with regard to whether the beginning and/or ending is closed (I) or open (V and all other functions). These have to be worked out completely, but the chief types are:

I. Basic Tonality

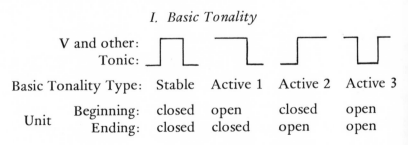

		Stable	Active 1	Active 2	Active 3
Basic Tonality Type:					
Unit	Beginning:	closed	open	closed	open
	Ending:	closed	closed	open	open

The dynamic level increases from right to left—from stable to active 3. In all cases the tonic is in root position.

It is well known that stability is decreased and tension and momentum are increased if any chord is in inversion. It increases considerably in the first inversion and very greatly in the second, which becomes virtually a dominant and is so considered by some theorists. The next step is to consider progressions which contain only I in its inversions, the V, and higher functions. These levels I call suspensive tonality.

II. Suspensive Tonality

Suspensive I   I in 1st inv. only
Suspensive II   I in 2nd inv. only
Suspensive III   V only (no I present)

Obviously the tension can vary greatly depending on how much a given function dominates. These categories assume an average distribution.

These more active and suspensive types play an increasingly important structural role in music from Beethoven through the end of the century. A study of this as an aspect of the tonality of Brahms has proved to be of considerable interest and tends to confirm Schoenberg's notion of "Brahms the Radical."

With these theoretical formulations we can now proceed to the analysis.

Beethoven radicalized the Sonata Principle in his outer movements of the middle period, particularly from opus 31 on. We know that in the Waldstein there exists the original slow movement in F major for which this one was substituted. The second theme group in the first movement employs transdiatonic key functions by using E major and A major, lying on either side of the tonic by thirds. The long areas in C and in V of C, as well as the large time spans of C in the finale, demand a balance. The F major of the Introduzione provides this as does some IV function and Sub. Dom. key within the movements.

A further reduction of the linear framework is given in Reduction II as shown in examples 14.2–14.4. These examples correspond to the division of the Introduzione into three sections. The form is *A B A'* with the last an extension and modulation to the key of the finale. One suspects that Beethoven may have begun with the idea at

Example 14.2

Example 14.3

m. 9 as most closely related to the original movement. The importance of $\frac{6}{8}$ ♪. , the initial rhythmic motive, and its subsequent transformation in the finale to $\frac{2}{4}$ ♪ would make
this at least problematic. At m. 9 a subtle connection is seen between the three parts though they are much contrasted in texture
and general intent. Examples 14.2 and 14.3 show a connection in
which the stepwise bass and fifth with upper semitone resolution are
replaced by simple step motion which is carried out in the contrapuntal detail of the motive structure. The upward semitone of mm.
1–2 is recalled in m. 10 and takes over completely in m. 13 (ex. 14.5).
The short brackets indicate the degree to which the semitone has a
structural use in the pitch syntax, and the arrows designate when it
has a leading tone function as well. With the complete linear framework and reduction in mind, we can discuss the form and tonality
dynamics.

Legend for Examples 14.2–14.5

Half step = [

Whole step = ⫦

Fifth = {

Leading tones =

Example 14.4

Example 14.5

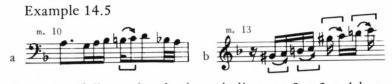

Each section follows the classic periodic type 2 + 2 + 4 but with Beethoven's characteristic extensions and truncations of the basic 8 bar norm. We have a declarative binary phrase articulating its subphrases followed by a responsive unitary phrase.

Periods	:	9(Unified)	7(Binary)	12(Unified)
Phrases	: 4 + 5	4 + 3	4 + 8
Subphrases:	2 + 2 —	2 + 2 —	2 + 2 —

The first period is under a single profile arc (unified period) as is the last. It unfolds a rich closed harmonic cycle to be discussed later. The climactic area is mm. 5–6, subsiding in mid-register to the tonic as a drop in the bass confirms the cadence. The second section truncates its responsive unitary phrase, eliding for closure to the opening of section three. The registral structure is of great interest. While this section is stable in its tonal dynamic level (see the Analytic Chart) there are important contrasts of register.

Subphrase 1 (mm. 10–11):   low-high
Subphrase 2 (mm. 12–13):   low-high
Phrase 1 (mm. 10–13)   :   relatively low
Phrase 2 (mm. 14–17)   :   relatively high then subsiding

Thus the subphrases echo the registral profile of the period as a whole. Asymmetries occur within the harmonic cycles.

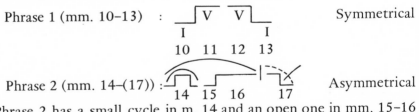

Phrase 1 (mm. 10–13)   :   Symmetrical

Phrase 2 (mm. 14–(17)) :   Asymmetrical

Phrase 2 has a small cycle in m. 14 and an open one in mm. 15–16 which is completed by elision as the new phrase begins in m. 17. *A'* is an amplification of the responsive phrase of *A* from 5 to 8 + (1) bars eliding to the last movement. We can proceed now to a fuller discussion of harmonic and key function and tonal dynamic levels.

In harmonic progression, a movement away from the tonic is negative directionally as a ball thrown in the air. A pull toward the tonic is positive. Each level nearer the tonic increases "tonic attraction" with the maximum on V. The IV lying below and rising to the tonic is a negative function. The attraction is not as great as V but it does relate directly to I as a primary function. The proximity of its root to that of V makes IV V I a powerful key generating progression. We see the relationship of diatonic functions as:

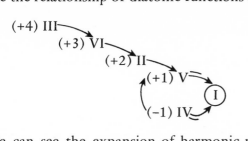

We can see the expansion of harmonic progression cycles from primary to those with secondary enrichment to those with secondary dominants (with or without other functions) to those involving modulation (developed during the 18th and 19th centuries). The opening of *A* and *A'* illustrates the latter type.

Primary: I⌒V⌝I   or   I⟍IV⌿I

Secondary enrichment: I⌒(III, VI, II)⟍IV⌿V—I

Secondary dominants: I⌒V/V—V—I

We begin with a move from F major (I) to V in a-minor. This is a negative key function movement to the Dom. Rel. (distance status = +1 Rel.). Furthermore there is no tonic in a-minor so its tonal dynamic level is Suspensive III. Measures 3–4 continue both negative harmonic and key movements to e minor, which is already outside the diatonic key area (status = +2 Rel.). Then by chromatic syntax, at the outermost part of this key circle, level +2 Rel. is connected with V/V (harmonic level = +2). The key distance of O (Tonic) at this point closes the key cycle. The remainder of the harmonic cycle is a rich progression V–VI–II–V–I. Thus the beautifully molded melodic arc has been supported, and its distance from the tonic has been paralleled by the harmonic and key function distances. We reach harmonic level +2 just as the climax is approached in m. 5. The dominant is asserted at the climactic point with a suspension for added structural tension. From there the harmonic gravity supports the melodic fall to the tonic.

The remarks regarding section *B* above need little amplification. Its role is to strengthen and confirm the strong arrival at F in m. 9. It provides the area of stability in the tonal scheme needed to balance the outer sections as well as the "subdominant balance" for the sonata as a whole.

The *A'* section modulates to its dominant and the key of the finale is skillfully managed by repeating the opening to the beginning of bar 5. Here what was V of V becomes V of I in C. The entire expanded last phrase is at level Suspensive III in a rich progression of secondaries focusing on V. The key distance and tonal dynamic levels relate as shown below. Both levels are open cycles linking to the finale.

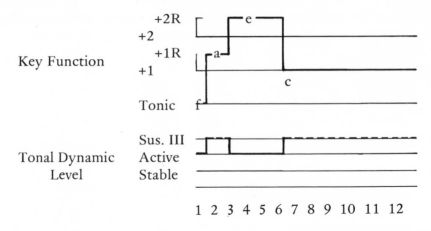

The movement thus is both an introduction to the finale and a link between the two monumental Allegros in C. For all its sense of fantasy and freedom, it is a marvel of balance and formal symmetry.

Symposium IV
Brahms, Song Op. 105 no. 1

Wie Melodien zieht es mir

fasst es und führt es vor das Aug, wie Ne - bel-grau er-

blasst es und schwin - det wie ein Hauch, und

schwin - det wie ein Hauch.

Und den-noch ruht im Rei - me ver - bor - gen wohl ein

Duft, den mild aus stil — lem Kei — me ein feuch — tes Au — ge

ruft, den mild aus stil — lem

Kei — me ein feuch — tes, ein feuch — tes ___ Au — ge

ruft

15. A Literary-Historical Approach

Austin Clarkson

Brahms's "Wie Melodien zieht es" has aroused much less interest than one might expect of so fine a product of the composer's maturity. Perhaps it is because, as Frau Elisabet von Herzogenberg acutely observed in a letter to the composer, the poem is unusually abstract.[1] Whereas most of Brahms's texts are in the more concrete, narrative and descriptive vein of the Romantic lyric, "Wie Melodien" deals with the aesthetic of the lyric in an almost symbolist manner. If the tune did not reappear in the first movement of the Violin Sonata in A Major op. 100, it would have been noticed even less. In the fourth volume of his redoubtable biography, Max Kalbeck discusses the relationship between the song and the sonata at some length and then treats Brahms's attitude to the connection between music and poetry.[2] He returns to "Wie Melodien," when describing the late song collections op. 105, 106, and 107, to draw an interesting parallel between it and "Meine Lieder" (op. 106 no. 4), another song on the nature of the lyric.[3]

After Kalbeck, the song receives little comment as studies of the Brahms lieder seem to focus on dimensions and issues that leave "Wie Melodien" out of account. Walther Hammermann's metric and harmonic analysis in the Riemann manner (1912) passes over it very lightly, and Max Friedländer's handbook (1922) does little more than quote Frau Liesel's response and note the connection with the violin sonata.[4] Rudolf Gerber's study of the form of Brahms's songs (1932) fails even to cite op. 105 no. 1 as an example.[5] The author is intent on demonstrating that the gross form of the songs is controlled by the explicit content of the text, and accordingly he concentrates on songs whose poems have broad and obvious contrasts of imagery, thought, or mood that can be clearly compared to the musical setting, Klaus Groth's poem is bypassed probably because the development of its thought is subtle, the imagery is of essences, and the mood is introspective. Had Gerber cited "Wie Melodien," he would have classed it as a variation type of strophic song along with

230

"Mit vierzig Jahren" (op. 94 no. 1), a song with a similar structure. In op. 94 no. 1 Gerber sees the musical variations of each strophe corresponding to the changing thought and imagery of the poem and, on the basis of such songs, concludes that in Brahms's songs the tonal structures are dominated by the thought and feeling of the poem. Nevertheless, in some purely strophic songs, Gerber is unable to discover any connection between the structure of the music and the meaning of the text.

Konrad Giebeler's more recent dissertation (1959) is the first to study seriously the declamation patterns of the songs, but he too tests the word-tone relation by searching for "purely musical" responses to the content of the text. Regarding op. 105 no. 1 he observes that the form of the song (including the declamation) is strongly determined by the musical structure and contains no particular references to the text.[6]

Students of song are likely to fall into two large categories depending on their fundamental notion of the nature of song. On the one hand are the separatists who say that song is a compound of language and absolute music and that the history of vocal music is a contest for supremacy between the two media in which an equilibrium is seldom attained. When the separatist describes a song, he compares the verbal and purely tonal components in an effort to discover the properties of the "music-language relation." He notes whether the composer embodies the prosody, verse structure, literary imagery, and affective content in the musical setting and then concludes whether or not he has achieved a "good" relation. Separatists appear to assume that "good" music-language relation is a universal ideal unrestricted by local differences in the form and function of song. On the other hand are the assimilationists who see song essentially as absolute music in which the words are for the most part transformed into purely musical elements. The description of a song from this vantage point is in some ways unproblematic. The composition is treated as though it were virtually an instrumental piece throughout, and the text plays a very small, even negligible, part in the description.

I hope to avoid the pitfalls of both the separatist and assimilationist approaches in the following discussion of "Wie Melodien." I wish, instead, to construe the song as an instance of a medium which is quite distinct from absolute music on the one hand and from speech on the other. I would prefer to express the imagery of the song in terms of features of the whole signal rather than in terms either of relations between the verbal and tonal components of the signal, or of the purely tonal dimension alone. I shall therefore attempt to constitute the song as a structure of what Walter Wiora refers to as *Ganzheitseigenschaften*—features of song that are lost when the words and tones are examined separately.[7]

My first step will be to offer a reading of the poem, not to disavow the principles stated above but to simplify the description of a complex phenomenon. I do not set up the text as a given, against which to judge the composer's tonal setting, but as a poem which we shall observe Brahms singing. Describing the poem simplifies the task of description, but it also identifies those poetic values and structures which play important roles in the song. In effect, this reading of the poem is guided by the hindsight gained from knowing Brahms's setting.

THE POEM

Wie Melodien

Wie Melodien zieht es	Like melodies it steals
mir leise durch den Sinn,	gently through my mind,
wie Frühlingsblumen blüht es	like spring flowers it blooms
und schwebt wie Duft dahin.	and drifts thither like fragrance.
Doch kommt das Wort und fasst es	But if the word comes and grasps it
und führt es vor das Aug,	and brings it before my eye,
wie Nebelgrau erblasst es	it fades like a gray mist
und schwindet wie ein Hauch.	and vanishes like a breath.
Und dennoch ruht im Reime	And yet, there resides in verse
verborgen wohl ein Duft,	an essence well hidden,
den mild aus stillem Keime	which softly from the still core
ein feuchtes Auge ruft.	calls forth a moistened eye.

Klaus Groth (1819–99), from *Hundert Blätter* (1854), "Klänge"

If Groth's poem seemed abstract to Frau Liesel in 1886, it must have seemed even less concrete in 1854 on first printing. At a time when authors sought to arouse thought and feeling by assaulting the reader with explicit narration and depiction, Groth stimulates responses through the allusive power of a set of symbols. For example, although the poem is about sound, one of the principal symbols is the eye. In the second stanza the eye stands for the reason which reads the word but is unmoved by emotion, and in the third stanza the eye, moistened by a tear, represents the feelings aroused by the lyric. Throughout the poem, effects are obtained by a series of metaphors dressed up as similes that mark the poem as an early essay in the symbolist manner.

The poem treats the aesthetics of the lyric by comparing the ability of the various sonic media—absolute music, speech, and lyric poetry—to arouse feeling. Of the three, pure tone (*Melodien*) arouses mood but fleetingly; it fades like spring flowers and the clouds of their fragrance. The spoken word (*Wort*) tries to grasp emotion and even to display it to the eye in script, but mood eludes speech too, fades like a mist, and disappears like a breath of air. Of the three, it is only the lyric (*Reime*) that fully arouses emotion. Hidden within the lyric's blend of tone and word lies the power to bring tears to the eye. The strongest appeal to emotion is made by a combination of the explicit meanings of language with the evocative power of absolute music.

Joined to the strong and logical progression of the poem's argument is a marvelously wrought structure of language sounds themselves. Groth was not only one of Germany's foremost philologists, linguists, and folklorists, he was also an accomplished amateur musician. That "Wie Melodien" appears among a group of poems entitled "Klänge" suggests that he was sensitive to the phonological structure of his poetry.

The first couplet contrasts the front, spread vowels of *Wie, Melodien, zieht, mir, Sinn,* with the back, rounded, high vowels of the second couplet: *Frühlingsblumen, blüht, Duft.* But the two couplets are united by the soft *l*s, *v*s, *m*s, and *d*s which help evoke the evanescent play of melodies and the hovering scent of spring blossoms. The hard, rough consonants *k, g, f, s,* and χ contrast the next stanza strongly with the first. They suggest the rough treatment speech alone (and especially the written word) accords emotion, and the back, open vowels of *doch, kommt, Wort, Aug, Grau, Hauch* convey the emptiness of absent feeling. The ʃv of *schwindet* blows the mood away in a fricative rush and recalls the contrasting *schwebt*, which stands at a parallel point in the previous stanza. The i vowels of *schwindet,* and *wie* similarly recall the principal vowels of the first two lines of the poem.

Comparing the three stanzas, we note that the principal word of each first line (*Melodien, Wort, Reime*) shifts toward the end of the line as the poem progresses:

Wie Melodien. . .
Doch kommt das Wort. . .
Und dennoch ruht im Reime.

Melodien begins on the first stress, *Wort* on the second, and *Reime* on the third. By positioning *Reime* at the end of the line after progressing through *Melodien* and *Wort,* the poet throws it into strong rhythmic relief which is reinforced by the sound of rhyme itself. *Melodien* lacks words, *Wort* lacks music, but *Reime* has both, and one manifestation of the music of poetry is the verbal consonance of rhyme. Thought and sound conjoin: of the three media, only *Reime* wins a rhyme, and it does so with *Keime,* a word that adds a new and deeper level of meaning. Together *Reime* and *Keime* form the crux of the poem: the lyric calls forth from the central bud of being the expressive form that moves the feelings.

The final stanza is a beautifully wrought summary of sound and meaning. The sonorous *r*s of *ruht, Reime, verborgen, ruft* color it with a new and resonant consonant, but the *l*s, *m*s, *f*s and *i* vowels, together with the words *Duft* and *Auge,* link the sound and tense of the first two stanzas closely to the third. The last line is particularly important. The first principal stress falls on *feuchtes,* a word that recalls *schwebt* and *schwindet* in both sound and position but replaces their strident fricative [ʃv] with a set of softer fricatives (*f,* [χ], and *s*) connected by a diphthong (eu) and final vowel (*e*). *Feuchtes,* with its firm but gentle, sustained and soft sounds, projects effectively the climactic image of a welling tear and humid eye. The quality of calm and fulfillment is maintained in the long vowels of *Auge* and *ruft,* the last two words of the line. Both words are tied to earlier images: *Auge* recalls the *Aug* of line 6 with the essential difference that the eye of line 6 is by implication dry in contrast to the moist eye of line 12. *Ruft* in turn picks up its rhyme *Duft* together with the *Duft* of line 4 and brings into play the important image of inchoate essence. *Ruft* also climaxes the chain of predicates that forms the poem's spine: *ziehen, fassen, führen, rufen.* The last three words tie up the motifs of the whole poem in a neat, expressive knot. They summarize the sounds and sense of an utterance that reflects on the aesthetic form of the lyric in the lyric medium itself. Perhaps, as we turn to Brahms's song on his friend's poem, we shall uncover an essay on the aesthetics of song.

STANZA 1

The stanza of "Wie Melodien" is a common species of the archetypal quatrain that consists of four lines each of four stresses and eight syllables. If the falling (or masculine) cadence dominates, the couplet is ideally:

$$- \; \acute{} \; - \; \grave{} \; - \; \acute{} \; - \; \grave{}$$
$$- \; \acute{} \; - \; \grave{} \; - \; \acute{} \; - \; \grave{}$$

where $\acute{}$ is a syllable with primary stress, and $\grave{}$ is a syllable with a secondary stress. But if the rising (or feminine) cadence is in control, the couplet is ideally:

$$\acute{} \; - \; \grave{} \; - \; \acute{} \; - \; \grave{} \; -$$
$$\acute{} \; - \; \grave{} \; - \; \acute{} \; - \; \grave{} \; -$$

The species of quatrain found in "Wie Melodien" has a couplet of thirteen syllables made up of a feminine sevener followed by a masculine sixer and is thus a variant of the masculine couplet above:

$$- \; \acute{} \; - \; \grave{} \; - \; \underset{\smile}{\acute{}} \; [\grave{}] \qquad \text{Wie Melodien zieht es}$$
$$- \; \acute{} \; - \; \grave{} \; - \; \acute{} \; [- -] \qquad \text{mir leise durch den Sinn}$$

The brackets enclose time units not articulated by syllables, i.e., syllable rests; $\smile$ indicates an unstressed syllable assimilated to a previous stressed syllable; and $[\grave{}]$ indicates a syllable with a secondary stress which, because it is preceded by a syllable with a primary stress, now functions as an unstressed syllable.

By assimilating the seventh syllable of the first line to the sixth, the fourth stress is joined to the third and is by contrast weakened to create a feminine cadence. The line now has three stresses instead of four and a feminine cadence in place of a masculine one. The second line is truncated by removing the fourth foot altogether, which produces another three-stress line, but with a masculine cadence. Thus, the two lines of the couplet are well contrasted in syllable count, cadence type, and rhyme, and group together closely to form a 13-syllable long line with a strong final cesura and a weaker median pause.

Poets of the day found this stanza useful for many purposes. Groth's own poems in this meter range from simple folklike lyrics to his elegies on the death of Robert Schumann and the singer Hermine Spies, and a poem to Hermine Spies on her singing of

Brahms's Alto Rhapsody. More germane to this study is the fact that Brahms set a number of other poems in this meter that range from a Scottish folksong translated and edited by Herder ("Murrays Ermordung" op. 14 no. 3) and a Slovak folksong published by Wenzig (op. 69 no. 2) to various poems by Uhland, Platen (op. 32 no. 6), Daumer (op. 57 no. 1), Candidus (op. 72 no. 1), Lemcke (op. 85 no. 6 and op. 107 no. 2), and another by Groth (op. 63 no. 7).

A comparison of the settings Brahms composed for these poems shows that he adheres closely to the archetypal stanza period of eight or sixteen measures, whatever the meter. Each couplet in the duple and quadruple meters has four measures (see fig. 15.1a–j), and each couplet in the triple meters has eight (fig. 15.1k, l). Furthermore, the declamation patterns are similar in many details. There is always an upbeat to the first measure which contains four syllables of equal length (fig. 15.1a, b, d, e), or two pairs of syllables where the first syllable of the pair may be two (fig. 15.1i), three (fig. 15.1d), and even five (fig. 15.1j) times as long as the second. In simple duple and quadruple meters dotted figures tend to reinforce the first primary stress of the line (fig. 15.1b, c, f, g, h). A constant feature of the archetypal declamation pattern of this stanza is that the sixth syllable of the first line always falls on the downbeat of the second measure, while the seventh usually falls on the third beat following. For special effects Brahms places the final syllable on the second beat as in op. 32 no. 6 ("Du sprichst dass ich mich täuschte"), where the short sixth syllable underlines the mood of impatience and despair (fig. 15.1h).

The declamation pattern of "Wie Melodien" stands apart from all the other settings Brahms made of this verse type. Instead of a one-syllable upbeat it has a three-syllable anacrusis, and instead of taking up four beats, the first five syllables take up seven beats. The result is that the first couplet receives a five- rather than a four-measure phrase (fig. 15.1m). The differences may appear slight at first hearing, but in a song aesthetic that hews so closely to the Volkston, any distortion of archetypal symmetries has a marked impact.

The three-syllable/beat anacrusis is very rare in Brahms's lieder; when it does occur, it is usually associated with the declamation of a ten- or eleven-syllable line (see fig. 15.2a, b, c). In figure 15.2a and b, the first principal stress occurs on the fourth syllable just before the cesura. The verse of op. 105 no. 4 is similar in length, but the cesura falls after the sixth instead of after the fourth syllable (fig.

15.2c). An upbeat figure of three eighths may also be found for eight-syllable verse in a triple meter, as in op. 47 no. 3 (fig. 15.2d), but for a seven-syllable line in duple meter, a three beat anacrusis is most exceptional, as is the succeeding measure in which two syllables are spread over four beats. The normal declamation rate for this verse type is four syllables per measure, thus a rate of two syllables per measure reduces the rate by one-half. But after the first verse, the declamation of "Wie Melodien" is perfectly conventional. There is a typical dotted pattern for line 2, which is reiterated for lines 3 and 4. It is the first line that sets the declamation of "Wie Melodien" apart from all other songs with a four-stress, four-line stanza. By stretching the first line over three measures, Brahms has created an exceptional song image that has important consequences as the song proceeds.

What is the meaning of this interesting departure from the norm? Some might hear it as a tonal image perfectly suited to the poetic image of *ziehen.* The lengthening of the fourth and fifth syllables and the consequent displacement and neutralization of the primary stresses might seem to create an image of attenuation, floating, relaxation, and ease. But then the classic problem of the strophic setting arises: the same phrase must also serve for lines 5 and 9 in conjunction with the actions of *fassen* and *ruhen,* respectively. Whereas an image for *ziehen* might do for *ruhen,* in these terms, it certainly could not be expected to illustrate *fassen,* and separatists such as Giebeler would say that the strophic design severely weakens the word-tone relation of the song. But to argue that the word-tone relation must exist on certain specified levels of the semantic/structural hierarchy of the song may be appropriate to certain idioms of song but not to others. Brahms prided himself on his ability to create strophic melodies that transcended immediate text images, and he scorned the through-composed declamatory setting that meandered casually from one image to the next without a larger sense of coherence. In light of the composer's evident preference for strophic settings (four-fifths of his lieder are strophic), we should interpret the opening song image as constitutive of the song as a whole rather than as illustrative of a particular line or stanza of text. Indeed, the last line/phrase of the stanza clearly compensates for the abnormal declamation of the opening phrase, and the setting of the third stanza will be seen to be a composing out of the tonal premises of the first line.

The reiteration of the fourth line of a quatrain is common in

Figure 15.1

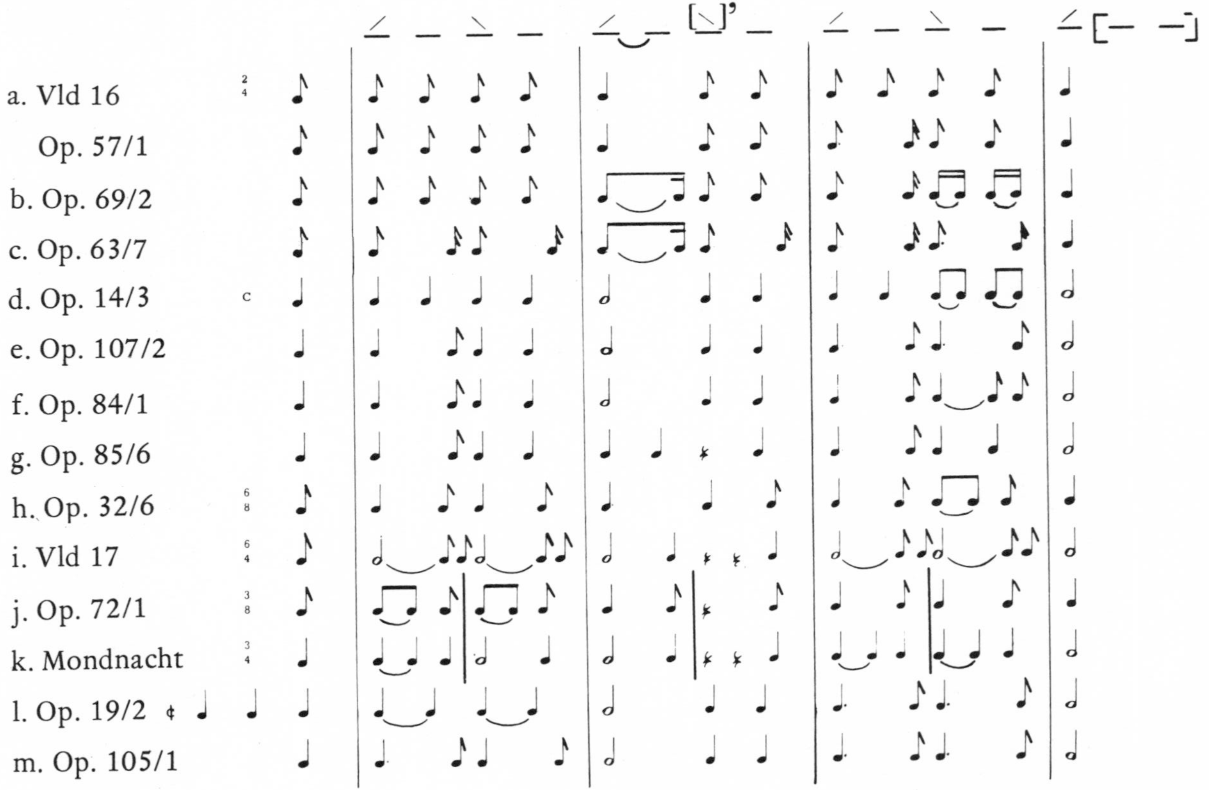

a. Vld 16

   Op. 57/1

b. Op. 69/2

c. Op. 63/7

d. Op. 14/3

e. Op. 107/2

f. Op. 84/1

g. Op. 85/6

h. Op. 32/6

i. Vld 17

j. Op. 72/1

k. Mondnacht

l. Op. 19/2

m. Op. 105/1

a. Vld 16	Wach auf mein Herzensschone zart Allerliebste mein.	
Op. 57/1	Im Finstern geh' ich suchen mein Kind, wo stechst du wohl?	after the Italian "Blinde Kuh"
b. Op. 69/2	O Felsen, lieber Felsen, was sturztest du nicht ein	from the Slovak
c. Op. 63/7	Wie traulich war das Fleckchen wo meine Wiegeging	Groth, "Heimweh"
d. Op. 14/3	O Hochland und o Sudland! Was ist auf euch gescheh'n!	from Herder's *Stimmen der Volker*, "Murray's Ermordung," Scottish
e. Op. 107/2	Es sass ein Salamander auf einem ku. 'em Stein	Carl Lemcke (1861)
f. Op. 84/1	Geh' schlafen, Töchter, schlafen. Schon fällt der Thau auf's Gras	Hans Schmidt (1854–1923) "Sommerabend"
g. Op. 85/6	Ich sass zu deinen Füssen in Waldeseinsamkeit	Carl Lemcke, "In Waldeseinsamkeit"
h. Op. 32/6	Du sprichst, dass ich mich tauschte beschworst es hoch und hehr	August von Platen (1796–1835)
i. Vld 17	Ach Gott, wie weh tut Scheiden, hat mir mein Herz verwund't	
j. Op. 72/1	Es kehrt die dunkle Schwalbe aus fernem Land zuruck	Carl Candidus (1817–72)
k. Mondnacht	Es war, als hatt der Himmel die Erde still gekusst	Joseph Eichendorff (1788–1857) "Mondnacht"
l. Op. 19/2	So soll ich dich nun meiden, du meines Lebens Lust!	Johann Ludwig Uhland (1787–1862) "Scheiden und Meiden"
m. Op. 105/1	Wie Melodien zieht es mir leise durch den Sinn	Klaus Groth

Figure 15.2

a. Op. 46/4

b. Op. 59/7

c. Op. 105/4

d. Op. 47/3

a. Geuss' nicht so laut/ der liebentflammten Lieder (4 + 7)
b. Mein wundes Herz/ verlangt nach milde Ruh (4 + 6)
c. Der Tag ging regenschwer/ und sturmbewegt (6 + 4)
d. So hab' ich doch die ganze Woche (4 + 5)

Brahms's art songs, but not in his folk songs. The "artistic" distortion of the archetypal quatrain lengthens the normal period by two measures to give a total of ten measures for the stanza/period (see, for example, other settings of the same stanza type: op. 14 no. 3, 32 no. 6, 72 no. 1, and 107 no. 2). In "Wie Melodien" Brahms departs even from the art song norm by inserting an extra measure between line 4 and its reiteration (mm. 9–10). The extra measure has two important functions: it balances the extra measure in line 1 by evening the stanzaic period to a total of twelve measures, and it makes room for an important figure in the piano—the descending parallel thirds in syncopated half notes in the right hand countered by a chromatically rising "tenor" line in the left hand—which plays a leading role in the process of strophic variation.

Turning to the tonal scheme, we should note that the one-measure extensions (mm. 2 and 10) are harmonically redundant and contribute to the sense of slow, leisurely movement. Measure 2 prolongs the opening tonic triad with a I^6, and the fourth beat of m. 10 could fall on the fourth beat of m. 9 without loss of continuity. In general, the harmonic background of "Wie Melodien" presents an unusual structure on another level. The most striking feature of the first couplet is its basic progression of a plagal cadence (see fig. 15.3f). Avoidance of dominant function in the first couplet renders the move to V in the fourth verse all the more decisive, and the reiteration of verse 4 firmly tonicizes V. The first stanza of some other songs with a similar stanza type are diagrammed in figure 15.3 for comparison. Notice their avoidance of IV in the first couplet and their consistent return to tonic at the end of the second couplet. The exploitation of subdominant function in the first couplet sets "Wie Melodien" apart from the usual quatrain period and presages some extraordinary events in the later stanzas.

A strong turn to the dominant at the close of the first stanza normally prepares a contrasting second stanza in a nontonic region and results in something like an *A B A* design (see, for example, "In Waldeseinsamkeit" op. 85 no. 6 and "Aug dem See" op. 106 no. 2). The first stanza of a strophic or varied strophic setting, by contrast, usually closes in the tonic. All the songs diagrammed in figure 15.3a–e close the first stanza in tonic function and all are strophic or varied strophic in design. Although "Mondnacht" closes with a contrasting stanza in the design *A A B,* the second stanza does duplicate the first.

Figure 15.3 Quatrain Periods in Five Brahms Songs with Versification
Similar to "Wie Melodien" (op. 105 no.1)

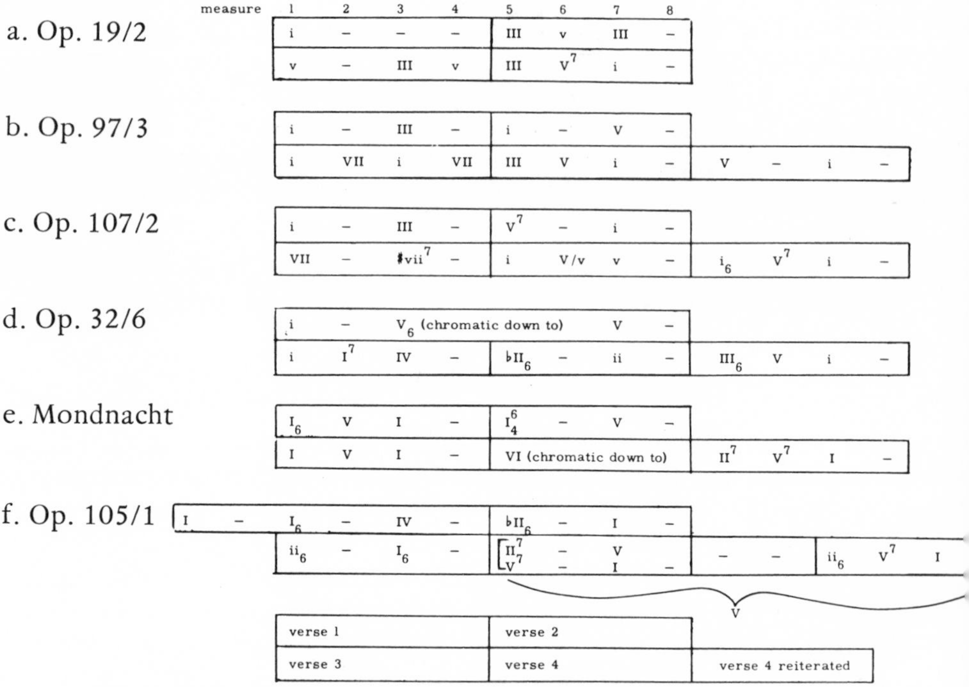

The move to V at the close of the first stanza of "Wie Melodien" leads the listener to expect something other than a strophic design, and although the design is in fact basically strophic it is of a quite unusual kind. The first couplet of each of the three stanzas is re-iterated almost identically, while the second couplet of the second and third stanzas departs increasingly further from that of stanza 1. This is manifest in the tonal realm by a move to IV then vi at the close of stanza 2 and then to the ♭VI in the second couplet of stanza 3 (see ex. 15.1). The wide ranging tonal scheme is kept firmly in check by the return to the tonic for each first couplet, but the decisive departures from tonic function in the second half of each stanza provide the basis for some magnificent imagery that could not have been achieved by the normal varied strophic design in which each stanza closes on the tonic. For other solutions to this problem, we can examine "Mit vierzig Jahren" (op. 94 no. 1), where both the first and the second couplet begin identically in all three quatrains. Occasionally, as in op. 32 no. 6, Brahms employs a tail- rather than

Example 15.1   Principal Chord Functions and Figured Bass in
                 Relation to the Stanza Periods

a head-motif so that the second couplet remains the same while the
first is varied. The varied strophic setting, which is so characteristic
of Brahms's lieder, admits a substantial element of through-composi-
tion, but never so much as to obscure the beloved Volkston of the
archetypal stanzaic period.

The interaction of line and chord in the first stanza of "Wie Melodien" also merits analysis as the textural patterns function strongly
in the song imagery. In Brahms's earlier songs the distinction between the successive and the simultaneous textural moments is
firmly and consistently maintained. The voice is given primary
responsibility for line while the piano accompaniment provides the
chords. When the piano doubles the vocal line, the distinction between line and chord is maintained and doubling functions on a
broad scale for major articulations. But in the later songs Brahms's
textures become more mobile: line and chord interchange, merge,
and dissolve in subtle shadings and colorings. In place of hard-edged

melodic outlines filled out with broad areas of block chords, we hear lines made of chords, chords generated from lines, and a rich variety of doubling relationships that range from the strongest possible linear emphasis to the most faintly shaded strokes.

The first couplet of the song is an extraordinary structure of textures. The vocal line extends from beginning to end in one unbroken arch that rises quickly to its crest and falls gradually to its starting point. Comparison with Brahms's other lieder shows that couplets of this kind usually have a break between the verses and that each verse has a distinct arch contour of its own (see op. 107 no. 2). A single, uninterrupted five-measure contour is unique and reinforces the image of length, flow, continuity, and easeful repose.

The motif itself is highly distinctive. A rising motion leads from the anacrusis of c-sharp^1/US (unstressed syllable) to the displaced downbeat e^1/PS (syllable with primary stress) and continues through two conjunct fourths (e^1–a^1–d^2) to an apoggiatura to c-sharp^2/SS (syllable with secondary stress) which falls to a^1 for the following US. In example 15.2, where we analyze the linear and chordal components of the first couplet, the motif e^1–a^1–d^2–c-sharp^2–a^1 is labeled *a,* and as we look further we discern the same motif projected on other levels of the phrase. In the right hand of the piano part the motif is extended over the first couplet, and in the left hand the bass line presents the succession a–d–c-sharp–a in retrograde. The three levels are presented more clearly in figure 15.2b. Reduced to basic intervals, we see that the rising fourth a–d is an essential constituent of the vocal line of the first verse, it defines the bass line move from the first to the second verse, and, on a still broader scale, it defines the bass line move from the first to the second couplet (see *x* in fig. 15.2b). The replication of motif *a* and of the interval *x* on three levels of the opening stanza period produces an extraordinary economy of material on several levels in the local and temporal fields. The effect is an image of a fundamental shape from which many levels of the song arise. To confirm the validity of the image, we might add that the overall shape of the third stanza similarly replicates at another level of magnitude the shape of the first couplet.

Returning to figure 15.2a, we note that the A triad is arpeggiated in falling eighth notes in the piano part and in rising quarters in the voice. This reflects in small the background structure of the piece as a whole, which is a falling arpeggiation of the A triad from the fifth degree to the first.

Example 15.2

Brahms's technique of doubling the vocal line in the piano is raised to a new level of functional importance in this song. In the first couplet the piano doubles the vocal line of the second verse very lightly and subtly (see fig. 15.2a, motif *d*). None of the piano pitches doubling the vocal pitches (f-sharp–a–f-natural–f–e) are attacked in sync with them, nor do the piano pitches appear consistently in the same figuration (f-sharp–a–f-natural are played in the right-hand dyads, while the following f-natural–e is played in the left hand). In verse 3 there is no doubling and the texture is lightened by rests and the reduction of the piano part to a series of dyads arpeggiated with open octaves and with a very static succession of interval steps (mm. 6–7). By contrast, verse 4 introduces heavy doubling by parallel thirds in the right hand, where it is important to note that the higher tone of the thirds is in unison with the vocal line. Reversing the arrangement by doubling the vocal line with the lower tone of the parallel thirds creates a striking image in the third stanza.

The vocal line of verses 3 and 4 has a rich interval collection—
falling fourths (perfect and diminished), a falling third, and a rising
fifth—which in a lively but gentle fashion guides the line down from
b² (m. 6) to a² (m. 7) to g-sharp² (m. 9) in two falling motions. Then
comes the extra measure of interlude between the fourth verse and
its reiteration: a series of three thirds falling stepwise in syncopated
half notes. Although we have just heard a series of stepwise falling
thirds in the previous measure, this is a new image. The thirds are not
doubling the voice, their attacks are syncopated against the *alla breve*
beat, and the left-hand figure is also new: rising and falling arpeggiation of V⁷ with a chromatically rising tenor line (b–b-sharp–
c-sharp–d) that creates a fine equilibrium with the falling thirds. The
reiteration of verse 4 (mm. 10–12), with the parallel thirds doubling
the voice as before, confirms the difference between that phrase and
the interlude motif and closes the stanza period with a cadence on e.
Two measures of dominant function arpeggiated in the manner of
motif *c* lead to the second stanza.

The first stanza period is loaded with a rich store of imagery. The
irregular phraseology, the motivic interlocking of structural levels,
the extraordinary attention to texture, the unusual dwelling on subdominant function, and the new accompaniment motif before the
reiteration of verse 4 create a richly modeled yet highly integrated
song stanza. But the powerful thrust of the poem's argument demands more than a purely strophic setting, and Brahms answers the
challenge by creating a first stanza that gives ample opportunity for
elaboration.

STANZA 2

The new stanza sets forth the music for the first couplet of the
first stanza with only very slight changes. The verbal emphasis in
the first line falls on *Wort* on the downbeat of m. 15, whereas in the
first stanza *Melodien* begins on the beat before *Wort*, and in stanza 3
Reime falls on the cadence of the line (m. 30). The effect of this
shift of the principal word is that *Melodien* is stressed least, *Wort* is
stressed more, while *Reime* is given the greatest stress of all. In m. 17
the dyads in the right hand are shifted ahead onto the beat, leaving
the voice with unaccompanied eighths on the second half of beats
2 and 4. This produces a rather bumpy effect that is carried into m.
18 with the piano dyads on the beat and the bass notes off it. The

effect of roughness, which is poetically conveyed by the density of hard, short phonemes in lines 5 and 6 and by the verbs *kommt, fasst, führt* is further reinforced by the g-sharp–g-natural cross relation between the tenor dyad and the voice in m. 17.

Variation is intensified in lines 7 and 8, where the vocal line is much reduced in melodic activity. The vocabulary of pitches and intervals is restricted to exclude fifths; fourths occur only between the phrases; and there are only two thirds, one minor and one diminished. Variety is reduced still further by sequencing the vocal line of verse 7 a third lower for the final verse of the stanza. Conjoined to poetic images of fading (*erblassen*) and gray mist (*Nebelgrau*), the minimizing of musical events in this passage produces a song image of bleakness and emptiness. For verse 8 the parallel thirds of verse 4 are abandoned and replaced by the open octave dyads of m. 19 with a diminuendo. The image of emptiness is underlined by the open fourths and fifths between the voice and the piano left hand on the fourth and last eighths of mm. 19 and 21. (In the first and third stanzas the intervals at these points are thirds and seconds. See mm. 6 and 33.)

The interlude before the reiteration of verse 8 is similar to that of stanza 1, which serves to heighten the absence of the parallel thirds, in the right hand, of m. 21 and their only partial reappearance in m. 24. For the second presentation of verse 8, the series of parallel thirds is broken down into pseudo-suspension figures preceded by eighth rests that indirectly double the vocal line in thirds over a static bass line that proves to be the dominant of vi and cadences on f-sharp. After so much subdominant function in the first couplet of each stanza, why does Brahms close the second couplet of the second stanza on IV and then move to vi for the reiteration? A variety of factors help to answer the question: the melodic sequence in mm. 18–22 is supported by a harmonic sequence, b–A^7–D to D–C-sharp^7–f-sharp; vi prepares the way for important tonal events involving submediant function in stanza 3; the subdominant and submediant have not appeared as cadential points before, and their color is appropriate to the second stanza. The submediant cadence is the first close on a minor function and has a desolate effect. Figure 15.3 shows that by moving from IV to vi the second stanza stands in a neighbor relation to stanza 1 with its emphasis on dominant function.

The harmonic rhythm, which has picked up some momentum at the cadence on vi, relaxes again in the interlude in preparation for the third stanza. The f-sharp root of vi is inflected to f-natural in m. 26, and the c-sharp moves to d to produce the minor subdominant function which is arpeggiated over two measures. Lengthening the interlude by one measure allows more time between the second and third stanzas to introduce another element of variation and to anticipate the figure that recurs in the postlude to close off the whole song.

The move from vi to iv involves an inflection of f-sharp to f-natural, which we have heard before and will hear again in still other roles. It occurs in each appearance of the first couplet, where it figures in a progression passing from IV back to I (see ex. 15.3). The second context is at the beginning of the second couplet of stanza 2, where f-sharp–f-natural–e occurs in a similar progression but at the beginning rather than at the end of a phrase (ex. 15.3b). The interlude between stanzas 2 and 3 is also controlled by the same movement, but this time it is articulated more fully and emphatically by the progression vi–iv–I and stretched over four measures rather than two or three (ex. 15.3c). The progression recurs in the third stanza in yet another fashion, and we might regard the tonal task of the final stanza as the recovery of the f-sharp.

STANZA 3

The first three lines of stanza 3 repeat the tonal setting of the first three lines of the first stanza without any of the modifications of stanza 2. We have already noted the important shift of word stress in verse 9 produced by the principal word *Reime* falling on the last primary stress of the line and thus on the downbeat of the cadential measure. The absence of change in the first three lines of the stanza is deceptive, for the succeeding passage to the end of the song is packed with a density of development that throws new perspectives on all the material heard before and gives the song as a whole an unexpected depth and breadth of imagery.

At the mention of *Keime* (m. 34) f-natural is heard in the right hand in preparation for a cadence on f-natural itself (♭VI). To manage this break with what has gone before, the bass moves down a half step from c-sharp to c-natural rather than the whole step it was accustomed to fall in stanzas 1 and 2. To secure the c-natural, it is reiterated in alternating octaves with the dotted pattern familiar from the parallel m. 21. An important variation is that this time the

Example 15.3 Five Contexts for the Inflection
or Progression F-sharp–F-natural

dotted pattern stresses the offbeats, not the downbeats. The shift of
metric stress in the bass is complemented in the right hand by arpeggiations of the $\frac{6}{4}$ and ♭7 sonorities over the c-natural that also stress
the offbeats with the highest tones of the arpeggio pattern. The
voice, on the other hand, retains the usual metric pattern stressing
the strong beats. The clash between the downbeat voice pattern and
the upbeat piano pattern is strongest on the third quarter of m. 35,
where the key word *Auge* is begun alone on a c-natural without a

simultaneous attack in the piano. Vocal pitches are rarely sung without simultaneous piano attacks, and a couple were noted off the beat in m. 17, but in m. 35 the "unaccompanied" vocal pitch falls on the beat rather than off and produces a quite different effect. The conflict between the downbeat and upbeat versions of the metrical pattern damps down the rhythmic flow to a node of relative stasis. The moist eye seems to be suspended, motionless at the still core of the song.

The melodic momentum is also reduced to a condition of virtual stasis. The voice holds to the a as though in hushed recitation, rises a minor third to *Au-* on c-natural (a new pitch class for the voice), falls a diminished fourth to g-sharp (a new interval class) for *-ge*, and returns to a for *ruft*. Thus the voice closes with a phrase that has fewer pitches and intervals than any other of the song but has new and striking elements nonetheless. The final note a is the third above the root of the cadential sonority, which reiterates the pattern established in the first two stanzas (in stanza 1 the g-sharp of m. 9 is the third of V, and in stanza 2 the f-sharp of m. 22 is the third of IV). The surprise of stanza 3 is that the third is not over the diatonic VI (already heard at the close of stanza 2) but is joined to an f-natural. Thus the first cadence on the prime scale degree closes in the context of the flat submediant, and the reiteration of the final couplet may be heard as returning the a from submediant to tonic function. The return is accomplished by a scalar descent through an octave started by the piano immediately in m. 36 and joined by the voice in the next measure, a descent that recovers the cadential a of m. 36 one octave lower in m. 43 as the root of the tonic triad and carries to completion the fundamental arpeggiation of the prime triad that began on the fifth degree at the opening of the song.

The return from flat submediant to tonic is centered about the now familiar inflection of pitch class f, but in this final transformation the f-natural returns to f-sharp (mm. 40–41). The reverse inflection of the f is accomplished by the word *feuchtes*, which we have seen is the only word in the song that is immediately reiterated. The first *feuchtes* resolves the f-natural to e (reaching the dominant degree), the second introduces the recovered f-sharp (see ex. 15.3d, e). *Feuchtes* is the key descriptive word of the last stanza. The moistness of the eye proclaims the arousal of emotion and hence the power of the lyric medium. This reveals the central image of the song, for it would seem that Brahms intends f-natural to be the tonal analogue of the still, secret core (*stillem Keime*). He prepares the inflection of pitch class f as a motif during the early stages of the song and then exploits it with unerring skill and power at the climax. By associating the poetic symbol *feuchtes* and what it symbolizes (emotion) with the inflection of f-natural to f-sharp, Brahms creates a song image that draws the symbolism of the song into a well-tied knot.

Other motifs which have been prepared along the way also find their fulfillment in the reiteration of the final couplet. The piano interlude following the cadence at m. 36 follows as expected with the bass resolving by fifth (f–b-flat) to begin the repeat of verse 11. In the third stanza, however, the syncopated half-note parallel thirds continue to fall diatonically through the octave from a^2 to a written g-sharp (m. 39) which actually sounds like a-flat until the f-natural resolves to e (m. 40). The syncopated parallel thirds replace the metrically consonant pattern of mm. 10–11 and in so doing contribute a fresh image to the closing stanza. Here, where word and melody unite in the lyric, the syncopated piano thirds (previously mere interludes) accompany an entire couplet. If the voice is an image of word, then perhaps the parallel thirds are an image of pure tone as they previously appeared only in between vocal phrases. Another feature appears to validate the symbolism beyond any doubt. In the first two stanzas, where pure tone and word are presented separately, the parallel third doubling of the voice is arranged so that the voice is in unison with the upper members of the dyads, but in the third stanza, where word and tone are united in the lyric, the voice is in unison with the lower members of the dyads. The tones enfold the word within the song fabric forming a new texture that symbolizes the nature of the lyric. Groth's poetic proposition that tone plus word equals the lyric is translated by Brahms into the song medium where the equation reads: absolute music plus lyric equals song.

The stepwise falling line recalls the final phrase of stanza 2 (mm. 23–25), but the descent is slower with two notes to a step in place of one. In m. 39 *Keime* takes two beats instead of three (as in m. 34) and so falls together with the syncopated thirds in the right hand pushing forward with more urgency to the last climactic phrase, which also climaxes the declamation pattern of the song. The declamation of the conclusion is characterized by the new, briefer pattern for *Keime* (m. 39), the half-note pattern of the ensuing *ein feuchtes* (m. 40), the reiteration of *ein feuchtes* set to the declamation pattern of the first line of the stanza, and the two-fold augmentation of the initial *Auge ruft* pattern in its final appearance. All in all, *ein feuchtes Auge* (mm. 34–35) is augmented three-fold in mm. 40–42, a written out ritard that is not mere cadence but climax as well. From m. 39 beat 4 it would have been possible to continue on the circle of fifths (c–f–b-flat) for one more step to arrive on e-flat in m. 40. But the last line had to recover the tonic function, so the bass moves up from b-flat to b-natural while the voice declaims *ein feuchtes* on f-natural. At that point what was really an a-flat in m. 39 becomes g-sharp and part of the home dominant that is fully constituted when the voice and right hand together resolve the f-natural to e. Arrival at last on the dominant requires a final reassertion, which Brahms provides when he repeats *feuchtes* with tonic and subdominant function in m. 41 and in so doing brings back the long lost f-sharp. The vocal line comes to a close by continuing the stepwise fall that was interrupted by the reiteration of *feuchtes,* and *Auge ruft* at last completes in brief the scalar motion 3–2–1 that is implied but never expressed in the body of the song. The tonal design of the last stanza is remarkable on yet another level, for it continues the motif of the replication of certain basic motifs on multiple structural levels. As example 15.4 shows, the tonal scheme of stanza 3 projects over a nineteen measure span the scheme of the first couplet, which extends for five measures. This explains the low density of dominant function and the high concentration of subdominant function in the third stanza and its postlude. A heavy dominant anticipation of the final cadence would destroy the pattern of a plagal cadence projected onto the whole stanza. It is no wonder that the postlude reiterates the plagal cadence in brief again. Frau Liesel heard the final A as the dominant of D and blamed Brahms for having too much subdominant. But the composer was only following through the premise of the first phrase of the song when he closed with a cadence that brought back the f-sharp in its original role in the subdominant context.

The postlude does still more, it recapitulates the interaction between line and chord that plays so important a role in the imagery of the song. The right-hand figure (m. 43) that rises out of the fundamental A with which the song begins also repeats the opening vocal figure. Carefully prepared in the two preceding measures (mm. 41–42), the figure emerges fully in m. 43 and leads to the motif

xample 15.4

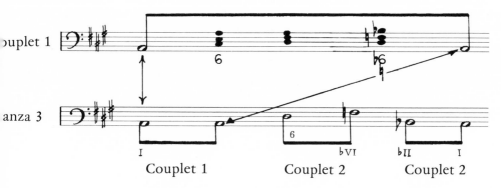

familiar from the other interludes. The figure now presents eighth-note arpeggiations of the tonic triad and at the same time outlines a descending arpeggiation of the tonic triad in half notes with the highest notes of the right-hand passage reinforced rhythmically by the left-hand chords. The recall of the motivic interlocking of multiple rhythmic levels that marks the first couplet of each stanza (see ex. 15.2b) is followed by the last appearance of the subdominant triad and the figure that had concluded the second interlude (m. 26). The difference, of course, is that f-natural is now f-sharp. Thus, restatement of IV at this point is not redundant; it clarifies and confirms the structure of the entire song.

NOTES

1. Max Kalbeck, ed., *Brahms im Briefwechsel mit Heinrich und Elisabet von Herzogenberg* (Berlin, 1907), 2:132.

2. Max Kalbeck, *Johannes Brahms*, 2d ed. (Berlin, 1915), 4:15–20.

3. Kalbeck, *Brahms*, IV/1:132f.

4. Walther Hammermann, "Johannes Brahms als Liedkomponist" (Dissertation, Leipzig, 1912). Max Friedländer, *Brahms' Lieder* (Berlin, 1922); trans. C. Leonard Leese (London, 1928), pp. 176–78.

5. Rudolf Gerber, "Formprobleme im Brahmsschen Lied," *Peters Jahrbuch 1931* (Leipzig, 1932), pp. 23–42.

6. Konrad Giebeler, "Die Lieder von Johannes Brahms" (Dissertation, Münster, 1959), p. 103.

7. Walter Wiora, *Das Deutsche Lied: Zur Geschichte und Ästhetik einer musikalischen Gattung* (Wolfenbüttel, 1971), p. 24.

16. A Schenkerian Approach

Edward Laufer

Brahms composed this beautiful song in the summer of 1886 in Thun, Switzerland, where he was to return the following two summers as well. It was certainly a very productive summer, and Brahms must have been working very quickly, for in a listing of his compositions for the summer of 1886 Brahms notes:

> Comp. August: Lingg "Immer leiser" cis m [op. 105 no. 2]
> Flemming "Und gleichwohl" A dur [op. 107 no. 1]
> Lemke "Verrat" h m [op. 105 no. 5]
> Groth "Wie Melodien" A d [op. 105 no. 1]
> Groth "Im Herbst" für Chor a moll [op. 104 no. 5]
> Violencellsonate F d [op. 99]
> Trio c moll [op. 101]
> Violinsonaten in d moll u. A dur [op. 108 and 100] .[1]

Amazing, even if the list is, as seems likely, a casual one, including compositions not yet finished. The set of songs op. 105, "Fünf Lieder für eine tiefere Stimme mit Begleitung des Pianoforte," was first published by Brahms's friend and regular publisher, Simrock, in 1889.

The text is by Brahms's friend, the plattdeutscher poet, novelist, and short-story writer, Klaus Groth (1819–99),[2] and comes from the collection of poems entitled *Hundert Blätter, Paralipomena zum Quickborn* (1854); it is the concluding poem in the opening sequence of thirteen poems subtitled "Klänge":[3]

(approximate literal translation)

Wie Melodien zieht es	Like melodies it flows
Mir leise durch den Sinn,	Gently through my mind;
Wie Frühlingsblumen blüht es,	Like spring-flowers it blossoms,
Und Schwebt wie Duft dahin.	And hovers along like a fragrance.
Doch kommt das Wort und fasst es	But yet the word comes and grasps it
Und führt es vor das Aug',	And presents it to the eye,
Wie Nebelgrau erblasst es	Like misty grey it pales
Und schwindet wie ein Hauch.	And vanishes like a breath.

Und dennoch ruht im Reime	And yet there dwells in rhyme,
Verborgen wohl ein Duft,	Concealed, a fragrance,
Den mild aus stillem Keime	Which, softly from its quiet core,
Ein feuchtes Auge ruft.	A moist eye calls.

If, in the art of poetry, the formal structure and divisions of a poem, its manifold verbal techniques (associative, rhythmic, prosodic, metric, or whatever), and the theme underlying the discourse are all, each with the others, intrinsically one inseparable unity, one can ask first how a musical setting may reflect this.

The simple formal structure of Groth's poem—the three quatrains with parallel beginnings (*Wie, Doch, Und*) and alternate rhymes—gives rise easily to the form of the song: strophic with modifications (modified, as changes in the meaning of the text call for corresponding musical changes). The alternate rhyme scheme (*a b a b, c d c d, e f e f*) is taken care of, too (ex. 16.1). (One notes the final rhythmic enlargement of mm. 31–32 in m. 42.) Various poetic word associations can be considered later. (Regarding the meter, see also n. 6.) But more importantly and perhaps less obviously, as elsewhere in vocal works of the great masters, the poetic idea, too, is composed. The words are not merely set: the poem, its structure, and the thought behind the discourse as well become organically part of the composition.

Example 16.1

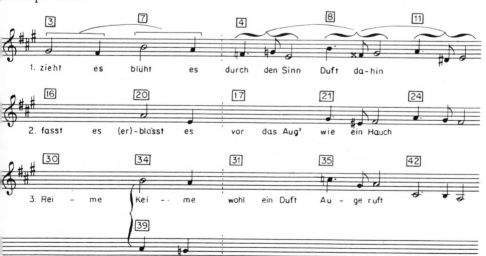

It may be well to consider first, then, what the underlying poetic idea or meaning is in Groth's poem[4] and how Brahms has expressed this musically.

First stanza: The poet feels in his imagination what might be called the idea of beauty—the spirit of beauty (*es*)—ineffable and indefinable, though like a melody or fragrance which hovers about.

Second stanza: But the poet cannot grasp this feeling with words, for it eludes verbal description or depiction (*vor das Aug'*) and seems, in this futile attempt, to vanish like a fading mist.

Third stanza: Only when it has become art (*im Reime*) can the feeling of beauty in the poet's imagination find expression and attain fulfillment and communicability: what was only in the poet's mind (*Sinn*, first stanza) has achieved realization through art (though an art concealed, and invoked by ein *feuchtes Auge*, third stanza; cf. in the second stanza *das Aug'* that has looked in vain when words without art were not evocative). Symbolically, the poetic message is itself mirrored in the structure of the poem: the first two stanzas refer only to "it" (*es*, the indefinite, impersonal pronoun); but finally the third stanza, now expressing the arrival at the goal, art, replaces the hitherto unnamed "it" with substance ("Concealed, a fragrance"; cf. first stanza, "*like* a fragrance").[5]

Brahms has composed this poetic meaning (the thought that only when the idea of beauty has become art can it achieve expression and fulfillment) in a number of ways; these have to do with (1) the thirds in the piano (mm. 7/8-11, 22-24, 36 *et seqq.*)—to be discussed in more detail presently; (2) the greater complexity (symbolizing art) in the setting of the third stanza, which brings about (3) the repetition and resetting of the last *two* lines of the text just in this last stanza (not only of the last line as in the previous two stanzas) the conclusiveness of which now suggests the textual sense; (4) the role and difference in structural function, programmatic and musical, of the note d^2 (mm. 2, 15, 29, 40 and implied in mm. 3-4, 15-16, 22-23, and 30-31—to be discussed in connection with the voice-leading sketches); and (5) the significance of tonic closure only at the end, m. 43, in contrast to the endings of the two preceding stanzas, which, because of the meaning of the text, had to move towards other goals.

The thirds which appear in the piano at the last line of the first stanza are indeed striking, being the first (and only) kind of melodic gesture, as distinct from the arpeggio figurations, in the piano part; moreover, they double the voice here. These thirds seem to appear, without preparation, only to break off suddenly in m. 11. (See ex. 16.2a. One notes the continuation in m. 9 by rhythmic enlargement.) In the second stanza they reappear in m. 22 (ex. 16.2b); disintegrating by nonsimultaneous statement in m. 24, they are once again discontinued. In the third stanza they make their final and longest appearance in m. 36—when the complete text and the poetic message have already been stated, thus before the restatement of the last two lines of the text, which the thirds therefore now reinforce (ex. 16.2c). Then the thirds continue through m. 40 and in some sense are picked up in the voice, and indeed in the piano coda, m. 43 (e^2–c-sharp^2). The fact that the thirds appear and break off in the first and second stanzas but continue through in the third stanza is too salient a feature to have occurred by chance; there must be a deeper compositional meaning. In this way Brahms has composed the thought behind the poem. The thirds correspond to what was paraphrased as the spirit of beauty (*es* in the poem), present in the first and second stanzas but incomplete, starting but breaking off (see

Example 16.2

"and hovers" in the first stanza, "and vanishes" in the second); only in the third stanza when the idea of beauty has finally become art do the thirds symbolically convey this by continuing—in a sense to the end of the song. In this sense, too, the thirds were present already in the opening (ex. 16.3), thus connecting the two points (m. 2 and m. 41) musically and textually, associating *Melodien* (m. 2) with art (m. 41; and incidentally also *Wort,* m. 15, and *Reime,* m. 30) to link that which was only implied, at first, to that which is now realized and explicitly stated.

Example 16.3

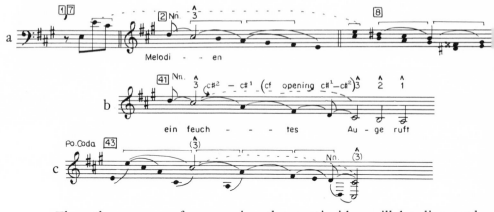

The other means of composing the poetic idea will be discussed later, in connection with the voice-leading sketches. Examples 16.4, 16.12, and 16.16 are sketches of stanzas 1, 2, and 3, respectively; example 16.18 covers the whole piece. These sketches are intended to be self-explanatory. One must, however, go beyond voice-leading sketches, since, unlike a purely instrumental work, the text and the way the text is expressed, being organically part of a vocal composition, must always be taken into account.

Example 16.4 Brahms, op. 105 no. 1, stanza 1 (voice-leading sketch)

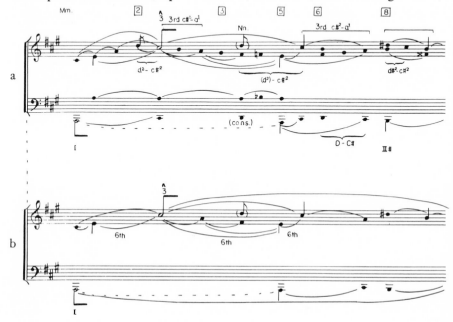

Example 16.4 (*continued*)

STANZA 1

Measures 1–5: The word *Melodien* is represented by the rising and falling (particularly melodic) opening measures of the vocal line (itself suggested in the piano figuration, which thereby becomes organic), by the "melodic" embellishments (the neighbor note d[2] and the passing note b[1]), and particularly by the successive rhythmic augmentations,[6] which also correspond to one meaning of the word *zieht* ("draws out") (ex. 16.5). The word *leise* ("gently") is marked by the further "gentle" slowing of the rhythm and is expressively evoked as the third a[1]–g-sharp[1]–f-sharp[1] (mm. 2–3) turns to the minor (a[1])–g-natural[1]–f-natural[1]. (The neighbor note g-natural[1] also

Example 16.5

Melo - di - en   zieht   es   leise.

tends to break up the fifths [ex. 16.6], and the flatting of the b
neighbor note avoids the diminished fifth b-natural–f-natural[1].) The
minor coloring for *leise* is pointed up by the change in rhythmic
detail to ♩·♪ . The e^1 of the opening voice arpeggiation—because
of its metric position, the word assigned to it, and the supporting

Example 16.6

e^1 of the piano—suggests the rising sixth e^1–c-sharp^2 (see ex. 16.4),
which is answered by the descending sixth back to e^1 in m. 5. This
descending sixth assumes significance as a kind of middleground
motive (see brackets, ex. 16.7). As a rising sixth e^1–c-sharp^2 in m. 5,
it connects to the opening and takes care of the parallel beginnings
(comparisons) *Wie . . . wie. . . .* The d^2 indicated in parentheses in
the sketch is not actually stated in the music, but contrapuntally it
would be the upper voice above the f-sharp^1, the motion to f-sharp^1
being a descent into an inner voice. Here d^2 may be understood,
present in the imagination (cf. text, *durch den Sinn*). Although this
d^2 is not related structurally to the d^2 in m. 2—merely an upper
neighbor note to the c-sharp^2—the pitch association is there and is to
take on significance later (m. 41).

Measure 6: The piano accompaniment subtly underscores the
change of thought in the text. Here the new comparison, *wie Frühlingsblumen,* receives a fresh impetus by the change in the piano's
accompaniment pattern, though the octave leaps are retained.

Measure 7: The piano accompaniment figuration picks up m. 1,
supporting the reading (ex. 16.4a) of the parallelism c-sharp^2–a^1
(m. 2) and c-sharp^2–a^1 (mm. 5–7). The connective sense of *und*
(e^2) is also composed. The principal top voice is still c-sharp^2 here:
the e^2 is merely superposed, effecting a connection between the third

Example 16.7

c-sharp^2–a^1 (mm. 5–7) and its parallel d-sharp^2–b^1 (m. 8) (ex. 16.8), and also preparing for the thirds in the piano (mm. 9 *et seqq.*). The placing of the e^2 above the principal tone also expresses *schwebt.*

Measures 8–9: The d-sharp^2 (m. 8 and again in m. 11) is not re-

Example 16.8

solved in register, again expressing *schwebt* and also perhaps the sense of unfulfillment implicit in the text. Just as in m. 6 a new melodic start corresponded to a new comparison in the text, so here the new comparison *wie Duft* requires some musical change, and the piano brings in the thirds, mentioned earlier. (The piano accompaniment, preserving the same textual thought, accordingly maintains a similar left-hand pattern through m. 12.) Example 16.9 shows how the motivic reference associates the words *Frühlingsblumen* and *Duft,* suggesting not only a "hovering fragrance" (m. 8) but also enhancing the poetic meaning with the suggestion of the "fragrance of spring-flowers." The f–double-sharp perhaps alludes to the pitch g-natural of m. 4, now revalued.

Example 16.9

wie Duft   wie Früh - lings-blu - men

There is also a kind of chiasmus[7] to be noted, in the following sense: Example 16.10, which would have as its raison d'être the association of the verbs *zieht* and *schwebt,* assimilates their meanings by connecting the opening phrase (mm. 2–3) with a rhythmic variant (m. 8) and enlargement (mm. 9–10). As regards the syncopation in m. 9, compare (in the score) m. 2 where main tones are on the weak beats 2 and 4.

Example 16.10

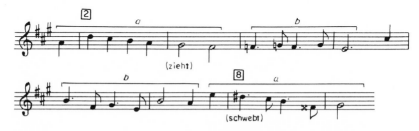

(zieht)

(schwebt)

Measures 10–11: The principal tone c-sharp[2] is approached from both sides (cf. *schwebt*) by the thirds (ex. 16.11); what a beautiful and expressive touch that the thirds g-sharp[1]–b-sharp[1] and b-natural[1]–d-sharp[2] should thus be juxtaposed, but not connected!

Measure 12: The inner voices seem to disappear (cf. *schwebt wie Duft dahin*) as the opening accompaniment figuration is restated,

Example 16.11

now arising, as a kind of rhythmic acceleration, out of m. 11. (The octave leap E–e in the left hand becomes the seventh e^1–d-natural^2 in the right hand, the seventh avoiding a conclusive cadence on V and aiming to its resolution in register in m. 15.)

STANZA 2

The motion to VI (m. 25) (as a I substitute)—while not in itself so unusual,[8] and beautifully mixing and superimposing a minor coloring upon the major mode (vice versa for a work in a minor key)—might here convey a programmatic meaning: that the poet has not yet achieved his real goal (ex. 16.12).

Example 16.12 Brahms, op. 105 no. 1, stanza 2 (voice-leading sketch)

Measures 18–28: The change in piano accompaniment (prepared by the change at m. 17) goes along with a change in the voice-leading: now not just the third c-sharp^2–a^1, mm. 18/19–20, as in mm. 5/6–7, but the third and a fourth, c-sharp^2–a^1–g-natural^1, mm. 18–21. Note the reassertion of the bass octave A^1–A of m. 18 in m. 21. Note also that the inner voice f-sharp^1–f-natural^1–e^1 in mm. 16–18, is picked up in mm. 19–20 (piano) and begins the third f-sharp^2–e^2–d^2 in m. 22, and again in mm. 25–28 (ex. 16.13); and note the f-natural^1 revalued

Example 16.13

as e-sharp^1 in m. 21 (coming from the e-natural^1 in m. 18) and m. 24. The word *schwindet* finds musical expression in the breaking off of the piano's thirds, m. 24, into the thinner texture of mm. 25–27, and in the underlying F-sharp–F-natural–(E understood) motion of mm. 25–28—the E disappearing into a low inner voice. One notes also the motivic tenor in m. 24 (ex. 16.14), which, supporting the cadence, has come most immediately from the thirds in m. 22 but refers to

Example 16.14

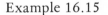

the motive in m. 2 and m. 15 and prefigures m. 29. How subtly beautiful is the linking of the close of the vocal line here, m. 24/25 (ex. 16.15a) (cf. m. 29), with the restart of the piano figuration, m. 25 (ex. 16.15b). Some kind of link was due here, since there had been a link in the analagous spot, mm. 11–12; the same kind of connection could not, however, recur.

Example 16.15

STANZA 3

Measure 28: If the cadence on F-sharp in m. 25 might possibly have led one to expect a later motion to a goal on a different degree of the scale (such as to V as a goal, as in I–VI–V, or I–VI–IV–V), then the return to the tonic here not only follows the strophic overall form but also coincides with and points up the word *dennoch* ("nonetheless").

Measure 34: The reference of *stillem Keime* back to *Blumen* in mm. 6–7 is pointed up by the same vocal setting, but the difference in thought at this point in the text calls for a new direction in the composition.

As will be seen from the voice-leading sketch (ex. 16.16), mm. 33–40 represent the composing-out of the bass by the arpeggiation, D–F-natural–B-flat[1], of which each of the notes is itself further prolonged (see the top-voice sketch). While this reading makes sense in terms of voice-leading, it is also the compositional reason for this more difficult and complicated prolongation that must be considered. As suggested earlier, the point would be that this very complexity expresses the message of the text by symbolizing the art which has, only at this time, been accomplished.

Measures 38–39: The word mild is now associated with *leise* in m. 4. The same sound (B-flat-major triad) returns, and in a certain sense the b-flat of m. 4, only an embellishing neighbor note, is also "fulfilled" or "realized," having become the final note of the bass arpeggiation as shown in the voice-leading sketch.

Measure 40: Although the low B-natural[1] in m. 40 is a chromatic passing note to "correct" the B-flat[1], one notes its downward quarter-note stem. Thus Brahms clearly marks the end of the bass arpeggiation and (literally) with the same stroke links the bass, through this quarter-note transition (♩-♩-♩) to the half-note bass tones in mm. 41–43.

The word *ein,* unaccented in normal declamation, here notably receives the pitch accent and significant harmonic support. One asks why this should be so, and what its significance is.[9] This d^2 becomes now a subtle realization of the *es* of the beginning: the implied becomes reality. For this particular pitch d^2 had not previously assumed harmonic or contrapuntal significance. When stated earlier it had been either an incomplete upper neighbor note, embellishing the principal primary tone c-sharp[2] (mm. 2, 15, 29)—only a fore-

Example 16.16 Brahms, op. 105 no. 1, stanza 3 (voice-leading sketch)

ground feature without harmonic or structural function—or else, as
shown in parentheses on the sketches and in example 16.17, the d²
was only suggested, being an implied upper neighbor note of the
f-sharp¹ (mm. 3–4, 16–17, 22–23, 26–27 above an f-natural¹, and 30–
31). It would be understood, contrapuntally, as still belonging to an
upper voice neighbor-note motion (perhaps on a middleground level),
embellishing the c-sharp². But finally here, m. 40, the d² is explicitly
stated, on a higher structural level, strongly asserted by the unusual

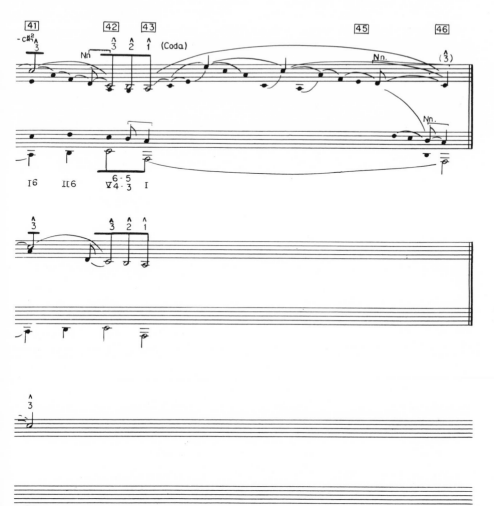

and deliberate accentuation of *ein,* its placement within the repetition of the last two lines of the text, and the harmonic support $\left(V_3^4\right)$—the end of the bass arpeggiation; note also the voice exchange in the sketch. (Harmonic support was, of course, always lacking when d^2 simply embellished the c-sharp^2 in mm. 2, 15, and 29.) The d^2 in m. 40 is in a structural sense also the highest pitch of the vocal part. (The e^2 of m. 7 merely embellished by prolongation the lower c-sharp^2, expressing *schwebt* and *und,* and the d-sharp^2 of m. 11 represented a motion through a third to the main tone b^1, giving rise

Example 16.17 Brahms, op. 105 no. 1, voice-leading sketch

to the parallelism marked in the sketches, exs. 16.4a and 16.8; the d-sharp in m. 11 embellished the c-sharp^2). And here, too (m. 41), as already pointed out, the d^2 signals the return of the opening melodic gesture (ex. 16.3).

The point of this emphasis is surely, then, to express once again the poem's message, realization through art, through the "realization" of the d^2 by endowing it with structural weight. For, like the previously discussed thirds, the d^2 was always hinted at and virtually present, but not to be brought to fulfillment until called for by the text.[10] Not even in the beginning of the third stanza could it appear: in keeping with the strophic design, and perhaps also with the word *verborgen.*

As the opening melodic statement (ex. 16.3) is resumed in m. 41, the octave transfer of the voice c-sharp^2 to c-sharp^1 picks up the original register of the opening pitch c-sharp^1 and brings it to completion in the original register by the descent to a. The restatement and conclusion is underscored by the prominent half note cadential bass tones (N.B. the low E^2) supporting the closing $\hat{3}$–$\hat{2}$–$\hat{1}$, and the corresponding change in the piano right hand (to the half-note pattern ♪♩♩ , mm. 41–43); mm. 41–42 are echoed by the piano coda (ex. 16.3c), the thirds e^2–c-sharp^2–a^1 being emphasized by the left-hand syncopation. (Compare the previously mentioned syncopation in the piano in mm. 1–2, 6, and 9–10.) The d–c-sharp "motive" appears in an inner voice (m. 42/43) and at the very end (mm. 45–46, in octave coupling), thus suggesting once more, by superposing it over the $\hat{1}$, the initial $\hat{3}$ primary tone. The quick arpeggios in m. 43 in the left hand continue the ♪♩♩ pattern, and the eighth note arpeggio figuration (right hand) associates, also registrally, with that established at the outset, as does its final condensation into the arpeggiated last chord.

THE SONG AS A WHOLE

Example 16.18 Brahms, op. 105 no. 1, voice-leading sketch

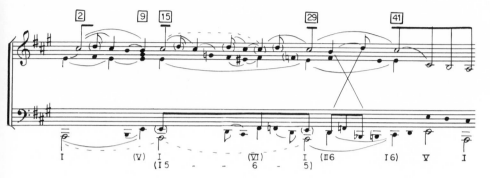

Certain foreground and middleground "motives," or parallelisms, should be mentioned here. The repetitions of the D–C-sharp "motive" (from *Melodien,* m. 2) are indicated by braces in example 16.4a at m. 2, at mm. 3–5, in the bass at mm. 6–7, and then at m. 8— d-sharp^2 (!)–c-sharp^2. The sketches of the second and third stanzas continue to indicate this programmatic feature (brackets in exs. 16.12 and 16.16). The opening descending sixth (mm. 2–5) becomes a basis for parallelism and continuation (compare, of course, the descending piano thirds), as indicated in example 16.7. The chromatic rising in the "tenor," b–b-sharp–c-sharp^1–d^1 (mm. 9–10), is composed in enlargement, as in example 16.4c. (Compare also the rising chromatic progression a–c-sharp^1 in the "tenor," mm. 16–18 and mm. 22–24, marked by brackets in ex. 16.12.) Although the enlargement does not reappear subsequently, its half-note rhythmic aspect may possibly, in the third stanza, have to do with the half-note values of mm. 41–42, ex. 16.19. Example 16.4d shows border tones, e^2 to c-sharp^2—not a voice-leading feature but rather a kind of registral line.

Example 16.19

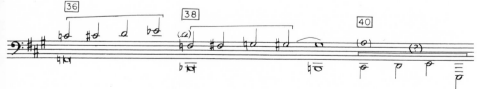

An alternate reading of mm. 6–8 may be considered quickly (ex. 16.20a). This interpretation would understand II⁶ as being prolonged, with the A-major chord in m. 7 only passing, not a return to the tonic. Such a reading can be supported only by the motivic reference in mm. 6 and 8 (ex. 16.20b), which occur at the beginning and ending of the prolongation II⁶–II-sharp, a procedure which, of course, is of frequent occurrence in passages that are to be understood as single prolongations. Also, the piano figuration changes in m. 6, though the octave leaps of the left hand are retained and do reappear in the left hand in m. 8.

Against this reading and favoring the reading given in example 16.4 speaks the fact that the piano figuration of mm. 1 and 2 certainly returns in m. 7, connecting these points and supporting the reading of a tonic return. Further, the rhythmic units are two-measure units: mm. 6–7 and 8–9/10 (with extension by the thirds motive), in which m. 8 corresponds rhythmically to m. 6, and m. 9 to m. 7 (and not m. 9 to m. 6). (See also ex. 16.20c for the rhythmic analogy between mm. 9 and 7.) The entrance of the thirds motive in m. 8, as something new—a new harmonic event—would also make a connection or reference back to m. 6 unlikely. The preferred reading (ex. 16.4),

Example 16.20

wie Früh-lings-blumen...wie Duft da-hin

shows the third c-sharp^2–a^1 of m. 2 in enlargement from m. 5 to m. 7, the extending of the word *Melodien* and then *zieht* subtly expressing "melody" and "drawing out." That the same third, c-sharp^2–a^1, should recur "drawn out" (in this enlargement) is a beautiful way of continuing the same thought. (The motivic reference, mentioned in ex. 16.9, and its connotation of course hold good in either reading.)

Perhaps great art demands not simplicity as such but a certain degree of inner complexity, however simple the appearance may be. This study would like to point out that the great art and beauty of this song results from the way the relatively simple background structure and other levels of greater complexity are linked through organically composed motivic and musical-poetic relationships. This very subtlety and inner complexity is expressive of the essence of that art invoked by Groth in his poem.

NOTES

1. Quoted from Max Kalbeck, *Johannes Brahms* (Berlin, 1914), 4:92.

2. Concerning Brahms's friendship with Groth, see (Brahms-Groth), *Briefe der Freundschaft*, ed. Volquart Pauls (Heide, 1956); H. Miesner, *Klaus Groth und die Musik* (Heide, 1933); also Kalbeck, *Johannes Brahms*. Brahms set many other Groth texts: op. 59 nos. 3 and 4 (also another setting of the same, without opus number, published 1908), nos. 7 and 8; op. 63 nos. 7, 8, 9; op. 66 nos. 1 and 2; op. 97 nos. 4, 5; op. 104 no. 5; and op. 106 no. 3; and all but two (op. 59 no. 4 and op. 97 no. 4) are from the same collection, *Hundert Blätter*, as "Wie Melodien." Brahms paid musical tribute to Groth in a number of compositions. The second subject of the first movement of the A Major Violin Sonata refers, almost literally, to "Wie Melodien" (composed earlier the same summer).

The opening of the same sonata alludes (possibly to extra-musical suggestion—cf. allegro amabile) to Groth's "Komm bald" (op. 97 no. 5); in the Finale there is a reference to "Auf dem Kirchhofe" (op. 105 no. 4), composed around the same time; and the last movement of the G Major Violin Sonata makes use of Groth's "Regenlied" (op. 59 no. 3). The personal and musical connotations of Brahms's testimonial in the case of "Wie Melodien" perhaps have to do with the text of the poem too: Brahms' personal gesture may symbolize the personal nature of the thought behind the poem and subtly suggest its theme of inner communication only through art, and completion of the poem only through the art of music.

3. Klaus Groth's *Gesammelte Werke* (Kiel and Leipzig: Verlag von Lipsius & Tischer, 1904), 4:177.

4. Groth's text is often held to be obscure; indeed, Brahms's friend and former pupil, Elisabet von Herzogenberg, who kept up a rather frank musical correspondence with Brahms, commented upon this (in a letter to Brahms, 2 December 1886; see *Brahms-Herzogenberg Briefwechsel*, ed. Max Kalbeck [Berlin, 1908], 2:133): "In the A-major song, with the singularly abstract text, the warm flow of the melody gives me much happiness, and I sing it to myself very gladly." She continues, "But the concluding strain—it, too—gave me real difficulty; I have played it to myself so often now that I have accustomed myself to it, and inwardly become A major myself, which at first, in spite of all my efforts, I was unsuccessful in doing. I felt the A still as the dominant of D. . . ."

5. Kalbeck's interpretation differs in letter but is the same in spirit: "In rhyme, the melodic element of verse [Groth says], resides perhaps that concealed fragrance which gives new color to the feeling that had paled in words, and which recalls the mood that had disappeared like a breath; and to this fragrance the musician is attracted, and only he brings the work to completion" (Kalbeck, *Johannes Brahms*, 4:19).

6. This extension results in a 5-measure phrase, grouped 3+2 in the voice. But the piano accompaniment groups the phrase into 2+3: thus both subdivisions are offset, each by the other, so as to fuse a single 5-measure unit in order not to interrupt the single thought expressed between *Wie* and *Sinn*. Schoenberg (in "Brahms the Progressive," *Style and Idea* [New York, c. 1950], p. 77) points out that often, at the outset of a Brahms song, the number of metrical feet corresponds with or is reflected in the number of measures in the phrase. Thus, the 3-foot verse of "Wie Melodien" would call for a 3-measure phrase—or subphrase—allowing of the subsequent 5-measure phrase. As to the upbeat sense that the first measure might convey, see Heinrich Schenker, *Der freie Satz* (Vienna, 1956), sec. 296, pp. 200–01; Schenker's discussion of rhythm and meter begins on p. 191.

7. Another instance of chiasmus: the opening three measures of Brahms, Intermezzo op. 76, no. 4 in B-flat.

8. A large-scale I–VI–I–V–I progression may, for example, be seen in Chopin, Etude op. 10 no. 1 (Schenker, *Der freie Satz*, ex. 130, 4a); Schubert, "Der Schiffer" (ibid., ex. 39, 1); Brahms, Symphony no. 1, Andante sostenuto (ibid., ex. 88, 4a); Beethoven, Sonata op. 14 no. 1, Allegretto; etc.

9. For a short study concerning questions of word accentuation in Brahms's "Das Mädchen spricht" op. 107 no. 3, see H. Federhofer, "Zur Einheit von Wort und Ton im Lied von Johannes Brahms" in Kongress-Bericht, Gesellschaft für Musikforschung (Hamburg: Bärenreiter, 1956), p. 97.

10. A somewhat analogous mode of composition occurs, for example, in Schubert's "Der Neugierige," where the pitch f-sharp^2 never appears as a tone with true harmonic significance: it is always only an embellishing tone. The f-sharp^2 expresses the "yes" which the poet wishes to hear from his beloved; that this note never really occurs with any structural force indicates, with beautiful subtlety, that the wished for response is not forthcoming.

PART 3

A SCHENKER BIBLIOGRAPHY

David Beach

Introduction

Heinrich Schenker has emerged as one of the most significant individuals in the history of Western music. His contribution to the field of music theory is unique—that is, his theories represent the only instance of what might properly be labelled a theory of tonality.[1] Because his conception of musical structure, which resulted from his detailed investigation of the works of the great tonal composers, differed so radically from those preceding him, it seems now that the controversy that has surrounded his works was inevitable. Nevertheless, whether one is willing to accept all, part, or none of Schenker's ideas, it cannot be denied that they have exerted more influence on musical thought in the twentieth century than those of any other theorist.[2] As Schenker would have hoped, this influence has by no means been limited to the fields of music theory and pedagogy.[3]

The fact that Schenker's ideas are so often misunderstood is a direct result of his revolutionary approach to musical structure. To put it bluntly, many musicians, assuming they have the desire, simply do not possess the patience nor the intellectual stamina necessary for the comprehension of an approach so foreign to their own. It is impossible to grasp the real significance of what Schenker intended without detailed study of a number of his works. The earlier works contain his most significant concepts only in their embryonic stages, yet it is almost impossible to understand the contents of the later publications without first reading the earlier ones. To this one must add the further obstacle presented by Schenker's often difficult style of writing.

Most of Schenker's works are no longer in print. Very little is available in German and even less in English translation. (More specific information about this will be provided later on.) This means that many musicians (I am thinking especially of students, here) are forced

I am indebted to Ernst Oster and Allen Forte for their invaluable assistance and advice in the preparation of this bibliography.

275

to rely on secondary sources. Unfortunately, very few of these
sources help to clarify his ideas, and in fact they often propagate
popular misconceptions about them. Such a situation does little to
facilitate the understanding of the profound insights with which
Schenker interpreted the inner workings of great musical works of
art.

The influence of Schenker's ideas on music pedagogy in this
country is witnessed by the number of courses offered at institutions
of higher learning which purport to deal, at least in part, with what is
commonly called Schenkerian Analysis. All too often, the only
relation between such courses and Schenker is his name. Thus students are often faced with second- or third-hand information about
concepts attributed to Schenker, without being made aware of the
proper sources. The primary purpose of this bibliography, then, is to
provide as complete a listing as possible of both primary and secondary sources. In most cases, the important features of each entry
are mentioned, especially when it is necessary to clarify the position
of an author or to point out an obvious misconception. It is hoped
that the information contained herein will be especially useful to the
inquiring student as well as provide additional source material for
those who are already acquainted with Schenker's ideas.

The bibliography itself is divided into two main sections: the first
is concerned with Schenker's own publications, both theoretical and
practical. This information involves a listing of Schenker's major
publications, including editions of music, as well as a partial listing
of his articles and reviews. The availability and projected publication
of specific works in German or English translation have also been
indicated. The second section deals with writings by others about
Schenker and his method of analysis. This body of literature can be
divided into the following categories:

1. Works which attempt to explain or interpret his theories.
   Some of these are major publications but most are simply
   surveys of his work.
2. Criticisms of his concepts. These are usually directed toward
   specific ideas with which the author disagrees.
3. Applications of his ideas. These include applications to Gestalt
   psychology and to the analysis of music other than that of the
   eighteenth and nineteenth centuries.

Of course there are some publications which do not fit neatly into any of these categories and others which fall into more than one. An attempt has been made to clarify such situations when necessary.

An effort has also been made to be as thorough as possible in compiling this bibliography. To the best of my knowledge, all pertinent material in English has been listed. However, I am fully aware of the fact that the listing of sources in German and other foreign languages is incomplete.[4] It would be virtually impossible to track down all of Schenker's minor publications (e.g., short articles and reviews appearing in newspapers) as well as many articles published in foreign periodicals. I would appreciate learning of additional sources from readers and apologize in advance for omissions.

About Schenker's Works

For the sake of clarity, I have divided Schenker's works into the following three categories: (1) theoretical works (see Appendix A for a chronological listing), (2) editions of music (see Appendix B), and (3) articles and reviews (see Appendix C for a partial listing by source). A brief discussion of his unpublished works (books and sketches in various stages of completion) is also included. Finally, I have indicated which of Schenker's publications are currently available, or will be available in the near future, either in German or in English translation.

THEORETICAL WORKS (See Appendix A for
complete bibliographic information)

Ein Beitrag zur Ornamentik (als Einführung zu Ph. Em. Bachs Klavierwerken mitumfassend auch die Ornamentik Haydns, Mozarts, Beethovens, etc.), 1904. New revised and expanded edition, 1908. This extended essay on ornamentation is based on C. P. E. Bach's *Essay on the True Art of Playing Keyboard Instruments* (*Versuch über die wahre Art das Clavier zu spielen,* 1762); it was written in conjunction with, and partly as an introduction to, his edition of the *Klavierwerke* (discussed later). Schenker considered C. P. E. Bach to be one of the greatest composers and musical thinkers and points to his influence on Haydn, Mozart and Beethoven. The title of this essay is somewhat misleading since it deals with other aspects of Bach's works (e.g., form and performance) as well as ornamentation. The comments on form hint at Schenker's concept of the scale-step (*Stufe*), first stated in his *Harmonielehre,* as it relates to his conception of tonality. The main portion of the essay is devoted to discussions of the various ornaments.

Instrumentations-Tabelle von Artur Niloff [a pseudonym] , 1908. This short publication is divided into the following four sections: (1) the classification of instruments, (2) the production of musical pitch, (3) emergence of instruments into families, and (4) transposing instruments. Also included is a large table which shows each instru-

278

ment (with examples from the literature), its range, and its transposition.

Neue musikalische Theorien und Phantasien: vol. 1, *Harmonielehre,* 1906; vol. 2, *Kontrapunkt* (part 1, 1910; part 2, 1922); vol. 3, *Der freie Satz,* 1935. This series, published intermittently over a span of thirty years, represents the full cycle of development and transformation of Schenker's conception of musical structure. The growth of his most important concepts can be traced from their initial statements in his *Harmonielehre* to their final form of expression in *Der freie Satz.* The importance of many of these ideas to Schenker's central thesis becomes clearer with each subsequent volume; others lose their relevance and quite naturally disappear. It is absolutely necessary to be aware of this continual process of growth and development within "New Musical Theories and Fantasies" if one is to arrive at a fair evaluation of any or all of its parts. In fact Schenker intended it to be, among other things, a documentation of these changes. One should be aware of the fact that these volumes were also designed to instruct in the traditional disciplines of harmony, counterpoint, and form. For it is in Schenker's approach to this material that we find a radical departure from the past.

At the time of the publication of his *Harmonielehre,*[5] Schenker was partially under the influence of conventional concepts. But the real importance of this publication lies in the fact that it contains many of his less conventional ideas in their initial stages of development. Of primary importance here are his concepts of the scale-step (*Stufe*) and the process of "compositional unfolding" (*Auskomponierung*), which has been documented by Oswald Jonas, as follows:

> The chief merit of Schenker's early work consists in having disentangled the concept of scale-step (which is part of the theory of harmony) from the concept of voice-leading (which belongs to the sphere of counterpoint). The two had been confused for decades. . . . The theory of Auskomponierung shows voice-leading as the means by which the chord, as a harmonic concept, is made to unfold and extend in time.[6]

Scale-step, then, is a far more inclusive term than *chord* (synonymous with *triad* in conventional theory) as the basic unit of harmony. A scale-step might encompass any number of "chords," all of which serve to prolong that harmony in time. (It should be pointed out here that this process of prolongation can apply to melodic phenomena as well.) The application of these ideas to increasingly broader levels of compositional structure eventually led Schenker to his concept of the "fundamental structure" (*Ursatz*) in *Der freie Satz*. Another important contribution contained in this volume is the distinction made between "tonicalization" (*Tonikalisierung*) and modulation. This, of course, is a direct outgrowth of the concepts of scale-step and Auskomponierung. The above-mentioned concepts are of basic importance to the development of Schenker's central thesis. Others are less significant; many were altered considerably in subsequent publications and others wisely dropped.

Kontrapunkt, the second volume in this series, is a complete treatise on species counterpoint.[7] Included are numerous references to the classical treatises (Fux, Albrechtsberger, Bellerman, Cherubini) as well as criticisms of the existing approaches to the subject. It is, in fact, a history of counterpoint pedagogy as well as a systematic study of fundamental problems of voice-leading within the framework of strict composition. Of primary significance here is the fact that Schenker incorporates his concepts of musical structure and motion, first stated in his *Harmonielehre,* into this discussion. Part 1 of *Kontrapunkt* is devoted to detailed discussions of cantus firmus and principles of two-voice composition. Part 2 begins with a continuation of procedures discussed in Part 1 as applied to three-, four-, and multi-voiced composition. The last section of this part, "Übergänge zum freien Satz" (Transition to Free Composition), is probably the most significant single section in the development of Schenker's conception of musical structure. Here Schenker shows the relationship between strict and free composition, by approaching the latter through so-called mixed species, which, by convention, belongs to the former. As the title suggests, Transition to Free Composition contains the seeds of what is to follow. For that matter, many of the ideas presented throughout the *Kontrapunkt* volume appear later in *Der freie Satz* in condensed forms.

Schenker's final work, *Der freie Satz,*[8] was published in 1935 shortly after the author's death. It is divided into two partial volumes; the musical figures are contained in the "Anhang," separate from the text. Although the title might suggest a book on compositional method, in reality it is a study of structure in tonal music. Schenker shows how counterpoint combines with harmony, and other musical elements such as rhythm, to form musical composition. He arrived at his theory of tonal structure through detailed analysis of compositions by the great masters. His method of analysis is the result of this life-long study, and the concepts presented in this work are the final synthesis of those contained in his earlier publications. The contents of *Der freie Satz* are divided into three main sections, corresponding to Schenker's concept of three levels of musical structure (fore-ground, middleground, and background). Starting with the back-ground, Schenker shows how it is prolonged by the content of the middleground, and that of the middleground is prolonged by the content of the foreground. Viewed in this manner, a musical work of art can be seen as the "interacting composite" of these levels; this is the central thesis of Schenker's conception of musical structure.

In his discussion of the background level, Schenker presents his discoveries of the fundamental line (*Urlinie*) and fundamental structure (*Ursatz*).[9] The Ursatz of a composition is its skeletal struc-ture, which one may arrive at through a process of reduction begin-ning with the foreground detail. As Jonas has observed:

> With the Ursatz concept, the circle of Schenker's system is closed: it opened, in *Harmony,* with the quest for a pattern in Nature for music as art. It closed with the discovery of the pri-mordial chord and its artistic recreation through the process of Auskomponierung.[10]

Much of *Der freie Satz* is devoted to the discussion of specific tech-niques of prolongation at the middleground and foreground levels. Also included are brief discussions of form, and meter and rhythm. Schenker's conception of form in tonal music is closely related to his concepts of Urlinie and Ursatz. All of the above-mentioned concepts are clearly illustrated in the "Anhang" to *Der freie Satz,* a collection of musical examples and diagrams drawn from the literature of tonal music. With the aid of the analytic sketch, one is more easily able to follow and appreciate Schenker's understanding of musical structure.

Beethovens neunte Sinfonie. (Eine Darstellung des musikalischen Inhaltes unter fortlaufender Berücksichtigung auch des Vortrags und der Literatur), 1912. Schenker dedicated this study of Bee-thoven's Ninth Symphony to "the memory of the last master of German composition, Johannes Brahms." As might be expected, the analytic approach exhibited in this study is quite traditional in comparison with his later works; yet it contains a number of deep musical insights and was a unique effort for the time. A clear outline of the form is provided at the beginning of the detailed discussion of each movement. Each part contains a "literature" section (discussion of available sketches and comments on other analyses) and a section in which problems of performance are discussed. Especially interesting are Schenker's comments on rhythmic detail and instrumentation as it relates to structure. Numerous musical examples and reductions are included but the sketch technique used in later analyses is not evident. This early example of Schenker's analytic approach provides an interesting comparison with his later analyses of Beethoven's Fifth Symphony (1925) and Third Symphony (1930).

Der Tonwille (Flugblätter zum Zeugnis unwandelbarer Gesetze der Tonkunst einer neuen Jugend dargebracht von Heinrich Schenker), 10 issues, 1921–24. Contained in these ten monographs are numerous essays on music and its structure, over twenty-five analyses of compositions, and a number of miscellaneous comments relevant to Schenker's work. Of particular importance are the two essays concerning his concept of the Urlinie, and two related to questions of performance ("Der wahre Vortrag" and "Wirkung und Effekt"). Other essays are: "Von der Sendung des deutschen Genies," "Gesetze der Tonkunst," Geschichte der Tonkunst," "Die Kunst zu hören," and "Beethoven zu seinem Opus 127." Analyses contained in *Der Tonwille* are of compositions by Ph. Em. Bach, J. S. Bach, Beethoven, Brahms, Handel, Haydn, Mendelssohn, Mozart, Schubert, and Schumann. Included in these analyses are a number of musical diagrams and sketches which are early examples of Schenker's method of graphic presentation. The analysis of Beethoven's Fifth Symphony, which originally appeared in *Der Tonwille* in three separate installments, was published separately in 1925.

Das Meisterwerk in der Musik. Jahrbücher: I, 1925; II, 1926; III, 1930. These three volumes constitute a continuation of *Der Tonwille.* Included are seven essays, approximately fifteen analyses of separate compositions, and comments and miscellaneous thoughts (concerning the relationship between art and the world in general). Of special significance is the essay on the art of improvisation ("Die Kunst der Improvisation"), in which Schenker states his views that improvisation underlies the creation of a masterwork, and that free composition is based on the strict and elemental contrapuntal forms. Also included are further observations on the Urlinie concept (two separate contributions), essays on organic structure in fugue and sonata form, one titled "Weg mit dem Phrasierungsbogen" (Down with Phrasing Marks!), and the following essay in Jahrbuch III: "Rameau oder Beethoven? Erstarrung oder geistiges Leben in der Musik?." Analyses contained in the Jahrbücher are of compositions by J. S. Bach, Beethoven, Chopin, Haydn, Mozart, Max Reger, and Domenico Scarlatti. With the exception of the one essay mentioned above (and a few miscellaneous remarks), the entire Jahrbuch III[11] is devoted to a detailed analysis and discussion of Beethoven's Third Symphony. Included in the analysis are the following: detailed dissection and discussion of each movement, comments on Beethoven's revised copy and the original from 1806, discussion of questions of performance, a "literature" section, and diagrams of the entire composition. This is the most interesting and complete of all of Schenker's analyses of large-scale compositions.

Fünf Urlinie—Tafeln, 1932.[12] These "Five Analyses in Sketchform" provide further examples of Schenker's method of graphic presentation. The analyses were actually done by students of Schenker under his close supervision and published without additional commentary. The five compositions are: (1) Bach. Choral: "Ich bin's, ich sollte büssen" (Matthäuspassion); (2) Bach, Wohltemperiertes Klavier I, Praeludium I (C dur); (3) Haydn, Sonata Es dur, G. A. no. 49 (first movement, development section); (4) Chopin, Etude F dur, op. 10 no. 8; (5) Chopin, Etude C moll, op. 10 no. 12.

Johannes Brahms, *Oktaven und Quinten,* edited by Heinrich Schenker, 1933. This work is based on examples of parallel octaves and fifths that Brahms found in compositions of other composers. Schenker interprets Brahms's comments and adds some of his own. The significance of the study is pointed out by Allen Forte as follows:

> He [Schenker] makes clear that the significance of Brahms's collection of examples of parallel fifths and octaves lies in the composer's recognition of the contradiction between a theory which dealt with immediate relationships only, often of a transient nature, and his own highly refined sense of hearing, which encompassed large spans.[13]

EDITIONS OF MUSIC (See Appendix B for complete bibliographic information)

Ph. Em. Bach. *Klavierwerke* [Selection]. New critical edition. Vol. 1: Six sonatas; vol. 2, Three sonatas, four Sonata movements, and one rondo. This selection is taken from Ph. Em. Bach's Six Collections "für Kenner und Liebhaber." It is based on the Breitkopf und Härtel "Urtext Edition" and was done in conjunction with the *Beitrag zur Ornamentik.* Included are fingerings and footnotes.

G. F. Handel. *Sechs Orgelkonzerte* [op. 4] (Nach den Originalen für Klavier zu 4 Händen bearbeitet), 1904.

J. S. Bach. *Chromatische Phantasie und Fuge* [D Minor] (Kritische Ausgabe mit Anhang), 1910. In the appendix to this critical edition Schenker discusses principles of fingering, non-legato, dynamics, and problems of composition and performance. He also compares different sources and discusses different readings.

Erläuterungsausgaben der letzten fünf Sonaten Beethovens. Op. 109 (1913); op. 110 (1914); op. 111 (1915); op. 101 (1920). These critical editions of four of the last five piano sonatas by Beethoven (Schenker was unable to complete this series because the autograph of op. 106 was, and is, missing) are based on the autographs, first editions, and revised copies. The merits of each of these sources are discussed at great length by Schenker in his commentaries. (Schenker was one of the first to realize the importance of autograph study in relation to one's conception of dynamics, phrasing, rubato, etc., in a specific piece. In fact he considered himself, justifiably so, the founder of that science.) Also included are quotes from the literature, by such as Bülow, Marx, and Reinecke, and critical discussions of their views. The music itself is presented with a minimum of editing—fingerings, measure numbers, and short footnotes only. However, analyses are provided (least in op. 109, more in op. 110, and extensive ones in op. 111 and op. 101), which include comments on form, performance and rhythm, and articulation. Special attention is given to rhythm and harmonic progression, and (where applicable) the significance of Beethoven's own fingerings is discussed.

Beethoven. *Klaviersonaten.* 192?. This critical edition of the complete piano sonatas of Beethoven is based on the autographs and first editions. The sonatas were first published in single editions and later in four volumes. Aside from a few footnotes, only Schenker's fingerings are added. Beethoven's own fingerings are made recognizable by the use of italics.

Beethoven. *Sonata op. 27 no. 2* (facsimile reproduction), 1921. Contains a foreword and three of Beethoven's sketches.

FURTHER INFORMATION

Articles: Schenker published a number of short articles, essays, and reviews in various newspapers and periodicals between 1892 and 1935. A few were published after his death in *Der Dreiklang—Monatschrift für Musik* (edited by Oswald Jonas and Felix Salzer), 1936–38. As was mentioned earlier, it is almost impossible to track down all of these short contributions; a partial listing by source is given in Appendix C.

Unpublished material: When Schenker died in 1935, he left behind a large number of unpublished sketches and manuscripts in various stages of completion. An incomplete book on interpretation, "Die Kunst des Vortrags," is in the possession of Oswald Jonas and is to be published in Germany by Universal Edition under his supervision. The following two manuscripts are in the possession of Felix Salzer: "Von dem Stimmführung des Generalbasses" (Aus dem Nachlass), and "Kommentar zu Ph. E. Bach's Versuch..." (incomplete). Numerous sketches were left unpublished, most of which are in the possession of Ernst Oster. The following is a partial list of sketches which he is preparing for publication. All are in his possession except for the Handel, which is in Salzer's possession.

Bach.	French Suite in E
	Brandenburg Concerto no. 5 in D
	Motet: Singet dem Herrn
Beethoven.	Several piano pieces, especially op. 106 (and particularly the Fugue)
Brahms.	Paganini Variations op. 35
	Waltzes op. 39
	Piano Pieces, op. 76, 79, 116, 117, 118, and 119
Chopin.	Preludes and Nocturnes
	Scherzo in D-flat op. 31
	Finale of Sonata in B-flat minor op. 35
	Etudes (complete)
	Mazurkas
Handel.	Suite no. 2 in F (Adagio I)

Availability of Works: The following of Schenker's publications are currently in print, all of which are published by Universal Edition: *Ein Beitrag zur Ornamentik* (UE 812); *Der freie Satz* (vol. 3 of *Neue musikalische Theorien und Phantasien*), second edition, edited by

Oswald Jonas (UE 6869/69a); *Oktaven und Quinten* (Brahms); Ph. Em. Bach, *Klavierwerke*; Beethoven, *Klaviersonaten.* Reprints of Schenker's analyses of Beethoven's Fifth and Ninth Symphonies (UE 26306 and 26307) will be available shortly. Universal Edition is also planning to publish the *Erläuterungsausgaben der letzten fünf Sonaten Beethovens*, revised by Oswald Jonas. The first two to be issued are op. 101 (UE 26301) and op. 110 (UE 26304). A forthcoming reprint of *Das Meisterwerk in der Musik* (3 vols. in 1) is listed in Bulletin 19 (Autumn 1968) of Blackwell's Music Shop (Oxford, England). Finally, *Fünf Urlinie—Tafeln* was reprinted by Dover Publications in 1969.

Translations: The only available translation of a major publication by Schenker is *Harmony,* edited and annotated by Oswald Jonas, translated by Elisabeth Mann Borgese (Chicago: University of Chicago Press, 1954).[14] A few sources mention a translation of *Kontrapunkt,* part 1, by John Petrie Dunn, but it is not available.[15] A translation of *Der freie Satz* by Ernst Oster should be published in the near future.[16] As was mentioned above, Oster is also planning to publish some of Schenker's sketches in his possession. Included in the first group of sketches scheduled for publication are: Bach, Inventions (selected); Chopin, Scherzo in D-flat (op. 31) and Finale of Sonata in B-flat minor (op. 35); Brahms, Waltzes (op. 39). A translation by Orin Grossman of Schenker's essay "Vom Organischen der Sonatenform" (*Das Meisterwerk in der Musik,* Jahrbuch III) appears on p. 38 of this volume. One would hope that more of these short essays will be translated and published in the future.[17]

About Works Concerning
Schenker and His Theories

This part of the bibliography is divided into the following three sections: (1) explanations and surveys of Schenker's work, (2) criticisms of his theories, and (3) applications of his ideas. A complete listing of sources which deal in some way with Schenker and his theories is provided in Appendix D.[18] Since this body of literature is quite extensive, only the most important of these works will be mentioned in the following discussion. Reference in the text to a specific book or article will be made by author and title only; complete bibliographic information can be found by referring to Appendix D.

EXPLANATIONS AND SURVEYS

The most complete explanation and discussion of Schenker's theories is contained in Oswald Jonas's book *Das Wesen des musikalischen Kunstwerks: Eine Einführung in die Lehre Heinrich Schenkers.*[19] The importance of this work lies in the fact that Jonas, a Schenker student, provides further information about his most important concepts, such as those of the Urlinie and Ursatz, in an effort to clarify and interpret them in Schenker's own terms. Unfortunately, there is no equivalent book in English.[20] Most of the articles written in an attempt to explain Schenker's concepts are too limited and end up simply as surveys of his works. Very few have contributed significantly toward the understanding of his ideas.

Two of the best introductions to Schenker's ideas, in English, are: Allen Forte, "Schenker's Conception of Musical Structure," and Adele Katz, "Heinrich Schenker's Method of Analysis."[21] In the former, Forte gives detailed explanations of Schenker's most important concepts and indicates their significance. Schenker's own works are discussed, as in much of the pertinent literature about him. The last part of the article is devoted to discussions of five unsolved problems in music theory and how Schenker's ideas might contribute toward their solutions. The five unsolved problems cited by Forte are: (1) constructing a theory of rhythm for tonal music, (2) determining the sources and development of triadic tonality, (3) gaining information about compositional technique, (4) improving theory instruction, and (5) understanding the structure of problematic modern works. Katz's article is divided into two main sections: (1) Tonality and (2) Harmony (which includes a section on counterpoint). Much of the article is concerned with a discussion of Schenker's most important concepts and the definition of terms associated with them. Katz also points out the difference between Schenker's approach to musical structure and those of the earlier theorists (Riemann, in particular, is noted). This difference is explained by her definitions of the words *analysis* and *syntheses* (Schenker's approach). "Analysis is the dissection of a work into its various parts. Synthesis is the re-assembling of a work whose various parts grow out of one principle" (p. 312). A further source of interest is the introduction and chapter 1 ("The [Schenker's] Concept of Tonality") of her book *Challenge to Musical Tradition: A New Concept of Tonality* (to be discussed later).

There are also a few articles of importance which are concerned with the clarification and amplification of specific areas of Schenker's conception of tonal structure. Two that warrant special mention here are: Ernst Oster, "Register and Large-Scale Connection" (see chap. 3, this volume) and William Mitchell, "Heinrich Schenker's Approach to Detail." The first of these is based on Schenker's view that register can have structural significance; that is, it can play an important role in establishing the larger connections in a musical composition. (Schenker devotes a chapter of *Der freie Satz* to a discussion of obligatory register [*obligate Lage*].) Oster goes on to show "a number of instances where register contributes in an essential way to clarifying certain contrapuntal, structural, or thematic-motivic connections and relations". The primary value of Mitchell's article is that it points out Schenker's concern with detail. This fact is too often overlooked, especially by those who have criticized Schenker's ideas concerning large-scale connection. Mitchell makes the point that "no valid appraisal of his theory of the whole can be made before complete familiarity with his theory of detail has been gained."

CRITICISMS

Responsible criticism is a difficult task. It demands at least two things of the critic: (1) thorough understanding of the object of criticism and (2) constructive suggestions for change and for alternate solutions. Unfortunately, most of the criticisms that have been leveled at Schenker's ideas are characterized by the opposite traits. Specific concepts have been isolated from their context, occasionally out of ignorance but more often to the deliberate advantage of the critic. This is most noticeable in those criticisms that have been aimed at Schenker's earlier publications and at his concepts of the Urlinie and Ursatz. Rarely in these instances can one find any solutions, especially constructive ones, offered as alternatives. I do not mean to imply that Schenker's ideas are above criticism. They are not. But when questioning specific concepts one must always relate them to their proper context and criticize them within this context.

One must also keep in mind the fact that Schenker's ideas went through a continual process of development and transformation during his lifetime. It is quite natural that some of the ideas presented in his earlier publications became obsolete and simply disappeared, while others were changed considerably in subsequent publications. An example of the former is Schenker's preoccupation with the number five (e.g., the first five partials of the overtone series, the interval of a fifth, etc.) in his *Harmonielehre.* Although he dropped this line of investigation later on, it has still been the object of much unfavorable criticism.[22] The process of growth and development associated with Schenker's thinking is clearly reflected in his analyses. An excellent example of this is his analysis of Beethoven's Fifth Symphony (1925), originally published in three separate installments in *Der Tonwille* (1921–24). Not only does his method of notation change from first installment to last, but a clear change in thinking as to what musical events constitute the background of the piece is evident. The later publications, especially *Der freie Satz,* contain a number of analyses of pieces that Schenker had discussed in earlier publications. These later analyses show a more highly developed way of musical thinking and a more rigorous application of his principles. In the large number of analyses published by Schenker, there are naturally some that are questionable and a few that are simply wrong. (One can only point to all those that are excellent and allow for human error!) One criticism that centers on an analysis of a specific piece (Bach's Prelude in D Minor from his *Twelve Little Preludes* no. 6; BWV 940) can be found in Walter Kolneder's article "Sind Schenkers Analysen Beiträge zur Bacherkenntnis?." (Schenker's analysis was published in *Das Meisterwerk in der Musik,* Jahrbuch I.) There is good cause to question Schenker's interpretation of this piece, but unfortunately Kolneder does not come up with a better solution. In this sense, the criticism is empty and meaningless.

By far the most popular targets for criticism have been the concepts of the Urlinie and Ursatz. Schenker arrived at them, or more precisely discovered their existence, after years of searching for the fundamental and natural laws of tonality. They did not come into being, as is often implied, as theoretical abstractions or fabrications from which Schenker derived the rest of his ideas. They are, rather, the final stage of development, chronologically and conceptually, in the evolution of his understanding of tonal structure. They are truly meaningful only when one considers them in relation to other levels of musical structure. But those who have criticized the Urlinie and Ursatz most often have divorced them from this context and treated them as isolated theoretical constructs. This mistake has resulted in such misconceptions as the characterization of Schenker's ideas as "static." One who has criticized the concepts of the Urlinie and Ursatz on this basis is John Daniskas in his book *Grondslagen voor de analytische Vormleer der Musiek*.[23] The inaccuracy of this view has been pointed out by Milton Babbitt as follows:

> Nothing could be less accurate than Daniskas's characterization of Schenker's methods as embodying a "static" notion of tonality. Schenker's essential concern is with the means whereby the inceptually static triad is activated in time in accord with the principles of structural polyphony, which makes possible the unfolding through various levels of the total temporal-spacial unity which is the musical composition.[24]

Another who criticized Schenker's concepts of the Urlinie and Ursatz is Roger Sessions. He gives the following two objections:

> The first is that it [the Urlinie-Ursatz concept] is far too primitive as a description of the actual events which constitute a musical work, or the sensations and apperceptions that constitute the ultimate comprehension of that work [p. 176]. [The second] is in essence the Alexandrian or "ex post facto" conception which envisages creation as the painstaking and meticulous embodiment of principles that were once vital and in process of development, but whose very definiteness and, so to speak, formulability proclaim either their insufficiency or their exhaustion. . . . It is precisely when Schenker's teachings leave the domain of exact description and enter that of dogmatic and speculative analysis that they become sterile [p. 177].[25]

An objection similar to Sessions's first one is stated by Walter Riezler in his article "Die 'Urlinie'." This is pointed out by Michael Mann as follows:

> He [Riezler] takes great pains to show by analogy with the other arts that an analysis of any art work proceeding from a given framework can never give evidence of specific traits contained within the framework without supplementing the basic structural principle by specific ideas such as are found in music in the concepts of motives, rhythmical patterns, etc.[26]

The most obvious fault in these criticisms is that both Sessions and Riezler have separated Schenker's concept of the whole from his concept of the parts. They have failed to grasp the real significance of the Urlinie and Ursatz in relation to middleground and foreground events. Sessions is particularly vehement in his condemnation of these ideas, yet he acknowledges the fact that Schenker's earlier publications contain a number of clear and profound insights.

The most extensive critique of Schenker's theories is contained in Michael Mann's article "Schenker's Contribution to Music Theory." Although he quotes Sessions (and Riezler) extensively, Mann differs from him on the following point: "Schenker's work must be accepted or rejected in its entirety" (p. 7). Later in the article, he states:

> we have found ourselves compelled to reject Schenker's analytic method in all its phases as inseparably bound up with the fixed conservatism which characterizes his view of music history, and as therefore essentially sterile in tendency: a negation, rather than an explanation, of musical realities. [p. 26]

In this statement, we find a common objection to Schenker's view of music history, namely his preoccupation with the music of the eighteenth and nineteenth centuries. This objection has been answered in two ways: There are those who have attemped to apply certain of Schenker's ideas to the analysis of contemporary and "pre-tonal" music. (This will be discussed more fully later on.) These attempts have been condemned by others on the grounds that Schenker was exclusively concerned with the fundamental laws of tonality and therefore his ideas do not and should not be applied to music other than that of the tonal period. Since these laws manifest themselves in their purest or most perfect form through the masterworks of the eighteenth and nineteenth centuries, it is only natural that he was concerned almost exclusively with that period in music history. And although Schenker had little regard for contemporary music, this should not affect our evaluation of his ideas as they apply to tonal music. We must meet him on his own ground—the music of the eighteenth and nineteenth centuries.

Mann points out a further objection to Schenker's ideas—what he calls "an accusation of coldness and dogmatism." This particular view is the basis of Paul Henry Lang's editorial in the Musical Quarterly.[27] What begins as a review of Donald Francis Tovey's *Beethoven* and Adele Katz's *Challenge to Musical Tradition,* ends up as an irrational and emotional attack on Schenker. Lang makes a distinction between a "technical expert" (Schenker) and an "esthete" (Tovey). In essence, he thinks that Schenker's approach lacks feeling and is too cold and calculating. He goes on to say that "Schenker—and his fervent disciples ever more—attack all those who find beauties that cannot be proved by logic or be reduced to their constituent atoms" (p. 300). This is, of course, ridiculous and a complete misrepresentation of Schenker's approach to music. It is especially surprising coming from a man of Lang's stature and influence. One possible reason for this characterization of Schenker's approach as "cold and dogmatic" may be related to his self-assured and often offensive manner of presentation. It is understandable to be irritated by this manner, but it should not affect one's evaluation of the meaning and significance of his ideas. Schenker's primary concern was with real music, not theoretic formulation. The latter was a by-product of his investigation of the music he viewed as living art.[28]

APPLICATIONS

As was mentioned earlier, a number of attempts have been made to apply Schenker's ideas to the analysis of contemporary and "pretonal" music. The extent to which these ideas have been borrowed and the success of their application has differed from one author to another. Some of Schenker's ideas are infinitely more "usable" than others in this context. For example, concepts such as those of structural levels, large-scale connection, and reduction can be made flexible enough to apply to most any kind of music, while others (e.g., Urlinie and Ursatz) are inseparable from the laws of tonality. As mentioned previously, these attempts have been condemned by others on the grounds that Schenker's total concern was with the fundamental laws of tonality as manifested in the masterpieces of the tonal era. Any applications to music other than that of the eighteenth and nineteenth centuries is viewed as a misinterpretation (or misrepresentation) of his ideas. This controversy has resulted in major disagreements even among Schenker's students.

One of those who has applied certain of Schenker's ideas to the analysis of contemporary music is Allen Forte in his book *Contemporary Tone Structures.*[29] Forte acknowledges his indebtedness to Schenker "for the notion of the analytic sketch and for certain terminology" (foreground, middleground, background, spans of structure, functional relationships, etc.). The basic technique used in this study is reduction, and "aid is provided by the analytic sketches, which constitute a visual means for comprehending structure, a means which is often more direct and more valuable than the verbal commentary" (p. v). Techniques and terminology are borrowed but never is an attempt made to apply a tonal concept in a non-tonal context. The major works discussed are: Bartók, Fourth String Quartet; Schoenberg, Phantasy for Violin with Piano Accompaniment; Stravinsky, *Petrouchka.* The shorter works analyzed are: Stravinsky, Larghetto from the Five Fingers; Milhaud, "Midi" from *Une Journée;* Sessions, *From My Diary*, no. 3; Copland, *Four Piano Blues,* no. 3; Bartók, Fourteen Bagatelles op. 6 no. 8; Hindemith, Fuga undecima in B from *Ludus Tonalis.* Scores of the shorter pieces are included for ease in following the analyses.

Analyses of contemporary pieces employing certain of Schenker's ideas can also be found in Adele Katz's book *Challenge to Musical Tradition: A New Concept of Tonality.*[30] Beginning with chapter 2 (chapter 1 is an explanation of Schenker's conception of tonality), the book is divided into discussions of the following composers: J. S. Bach, P. E. Bach, Haydn, Beethoven, Wagner, Debussy ("first challenge to the bulwark of tonality"), and Stravinsky and Schönberg ("representatives of the new order in music"). These particular composers were chosen because they "offer a well-rounded picture of the possibilities afforded by the tonal system, as well as an introduction to the techniques of the polytonal and atonal systems" (p. xxi). These latter "systems" are investigated in an effort "to find the new concept of tonality they express." Throughout the book, the basic terminology associated with Schenker's ideas and a sketch technique derived from his method of graphic representation are both in evidence.

The most well-known and also the most controversial of the works based on Schenker's theories is Felix Salzer's *Structural Hearing:*

Tonal Coherence in Music.[31] Some have condemned it vehemently while others have accepted it as the main source of Schenker's theories in English. Its external layout is similar to that of Schenker's *Der freie Satz:* It is published in two volumes, the first containing the text and the second containing numerous analyses of compositions from the Middle Ages to the present. The contents of volume 1 are divided into three parts, as follows: part 1 (definition of the basic terms used throughout the book and their implications); part 2, "The Pedagogic and Systematic Approach to Structural Hearing" (includes: The Contrapuntal Concept; The Harmonic Concept; Structure and Prolongation I, II, III; and the Concept of Tonality); part 3 ("the implications and consequences of structural hearing as they concern problems of musical understanding, interpretation and musicology"). Many of Schenker's ideas are used by Salzer in the discussion and analysis of "pre-tonal" compositions as well as modern works.[32] To those who are already acquainted with Schenker's works, his influence is clear throughout. To others, it is often difficult to tell whether a particular idea should be attributed to Schenker or to Salzer.

The primary motivation behind *Structural Hearing* was the organization of Schenker's ideas into textbook form. This is pointed out by Salzer, as follows:

> This book is based on Heinrich Schenker's revolutionary conceptions of tonality and musical coherence. . . . My purpose is to mold his conceptions into a workable, systematic approach for use by teachers, students and performers, as well as by anyone seriously interested in the problems of musical continuity, coherence, and structure. [Dover Edition, p. xv]

Until recently, *Structural Hearing* has been the only textbook in English which deals extensively with Schenker's theories.[33] As a major source of reference for serious students of harmony and counterpoint, it has been extremely influential. But for many it has become the sole source of information about Schenker. This is an unfortunate situation. The result has been that ideas are often associated with Schenker's name when, in truth, they have little or nothing to do with him. One may blame Salzer for not clearly differentiating between his and Schenker's ideas, but the real blame should rest on those who have never bothered to consult the primary sources. In its own terms, *Structural Hearing* is a serious and valuable contribution to the understanding of tonal structure.

Attempts to apply certain of Schenker's ideas to the analysis of contemporary music have also been made by Roy Travis in his articles "Towards a New Concept of Tonality?"[34] and "Directed Motion in Schoenberg and Webern." Both are strongly influenced by Salzer's *Structural Hearing.* The contemporary compositions discussed in the former are the opening of Stravinsky's *Le Sacre du Printemps* and two pieces from Bartok's *Mikrokosmos.* Analogies are made between the structure of these pieces and selected compositions from the eighteenth and nineteenth century literature. Most striking is Travis's definition of tonality: "Music is tonal when its motion unfolds through time a particular tone, interval, or chord" (p. 261). This concept of tonality is also applied to the analysis of Schoenberg's op. 19 no. 2 (from *Six Little Piano Pieces*) and Webern's Piano Variations op. 27 (second movement), in his second article. The extension of the meaning of *tonal* to include a particular tone or interval is a radical departure from Schenker's concept of tonality. It is also a major point of difference between Travis and others who have attempted to apply "Schenkerian analysis" to the understanding and interpretation of modern music.

An interesting discussion of the relationship between Schenker's theories and Gestalt psychology is provided by Hellmut Federhofer in his collection of five essays, *Beiträge zur musikalischen Gestalt-analyse.*[35] Federhofer's approach to Schenker's ideas is basically scientific. One thing he is concerned with is the "scientification" of Schenker's technique of reduction. (Schenker would have opposed this as he would have opposed the "scientification" of anything associated with art.) In the third essay, Federhofer discusses in detail the connection between Gestalt and musical form. The last two papers ("Der strenge und freie Satz und sein Verhältnis zur Kompositionslehre von Heinrich Schütz in der Fassung seines Schülers Christoph Bernhard"; "Tonale und reale Beantwortung bei Johann Sebastian Bach") are devoted to discussions of certain problems in the older music in relation to Schenker's ideas. Sketches of pieces by Bach, Mozart, and Brahms are provided in the "Anhang."

Many of the recent studies concerned with the rhythmic structure of music have also been influenced, at least indirectly, by Schenker's theories. The most detailed of these is the study made by Cooper and Meyer.[36] In it, a technique of reduction is applied to the analysis of the "rhythmic organization of phrases, periods, and section." The authors also may have been influenced by Schenker's concept of structural levels in the formulation of their concept of "architectonic levels," although there is no direct correlation between the two. The importance of Schenker's concept of structural levels to the formulation of a theory of rhythm has been pointed out by Forte in "Schenker's Conception of Musical Structure." He states that although Schenker did not attempt to formulate a general theory of rhythm, certain of his statements suggest that rhythm, like pitch, may exist at different levels of structure. He goes on to say that the following two questions need answering before a general theory of rhythm can be formulated:

> (1) At what structural level do rhythmic events begin to determine the tonal structure of a given work? (2) What is the nature of the relationship between the constituent rhythmic levels in a given work? Clearly, the analytic techniques developed by Schenker would be indispensable in the answering of these questions. [p. 21]

In "Some Problems in Rhythmic Theory and Analysis," Peter Westergaard discusses both Forte's comments and the ideas contained in the Cooper-Meyer book. Although he likes the flexibility of the Cooper-Meyer approach, he feels that it is inadequate and points to Forte's suggestions for the formulation of a theory of rhythm for tonal music. Once this is accomplished, Westergaard suggests that it might be possible to apply Schenker's concepts to the study of rhythm in contemporary music. He points out that contemporary music and music of the eighteenth and nineteenth centuries are more closely related with respect to rhythm than pitch structure. He also notes that Schenker's ideas have already been applied to pitch structure in contemporary music. The rest of the article is concerned with an analysis of the rhythmic structure of Webern's Piano Variations op. 27 (third movement).

Two interesting and unique studies which employ Schenker's basic approach to music are: "The Fantaisie-Impromptu—A Tribute to Beethoven" and "The Dramatic Character of the Egmont Overture," both by Ernst Oster. In the former, Oster compares Chopin's Fantaisie-Impromptu with parts of Beethoven's *Moonlight* Sonata. After detailed analyses of both compositions, he comes to the conclusion that Chopin consciously and deliberately modeled his piece on some of the main features of Beethoven's finale. It is probably for this reason that Chopin kept it from publication. (It was published by Jules Fontana after the composer's death.) The major portion of the second article is devoted to a detailed analysis of Beethoven's *Egmont* Overture. Oster shows how Beethoven built an entire composition on a minimum of material and how he developed and shaped this material in a musical way to achieve a dramatic effect. In this context, he points out the necessity of considering music and drama on their own terms, not in terms of one another (as Wagner has done). In both of these articles, Oster states his belief that detailed and meaningful analysis is possible only with the use of Schenker's approach to music. Only in this way is it possible to discover the structural relationships which exist in a work of art.

It is difficult to determine the extent to which Schenker's ideas have influenced musical thought and practice in the twentieth century. The publications that have grown out of his work are testimony to the importance of his concepts but this alone is not an accurate measure of their influence. One can only guess at the impact they have had on music performance and pedagogy. Many musicians have openly stated their indebtedness to Schenker but few have done so in print. Two that have are Wilhelm Furtwängler and Bruno Walter (see n. 3). A discussion of the importance of Schenker's ideas in relation to performance is contained in "Heinrich Schenker und grosse Interpreten," by Oswald Jonas. Schenker's ideas have also greatly influenced the teaching of harmony and counterpoint, analysis, and even the composition of tonal music. There are numerous courses offered at colleges and universities in this country which are based to some degree on his approach to music. In a few of these the subject matter is approached from Schenker's point of view, but in many there is little correspondence between Schenker's ideas and what is actually taught. This latter situation is reflected in Israel Silberman's article "Teaching Composition via Schenker's Theories." Silberman states that "any course of instruction in composition that purports to deal with classical style must take cognizance of the theoretical findings of Schenker" (p. 301). His approach to teaching composition in this style is to analyze a given composition and then use its basic structure as a model for creating new compositions. (This approach is not really new. Composers have been writing music this way for centuries.) The composition used as a model in this article is the exposition of the first movement of Beethoven's Piano Sonata op. 2 no. 1. One can overlook the fact that Silberman uses certain of Schenker's ideas and rejects others; many of them simply cannot be applied to the act of composing. What cannot be overlooked is his analysis of the Beethoven piece. Here it is evident that Silberman, despite all he has to say about Schenker, does not really understand the significance of Schenker's analytic approach. Nowhere in his examples 1 and 2 (diagrams) is there any indication of the relationships which exist within and among the different levels of structure in this piece. Also both reductions show the piece beginning on f^2 rather than a-flat^2![37] It is unfortunate that Schenker's analysis of this piece (*Der Tonwille*, no. 2) was not available to the author. Of course there are also many good ideas contained in this article. But what is deplorable is that Silberman's "application" of Schenker's ideas does not give a fair representation of his approach to musical structure.

The number of publications based on Schenker's theories is one testimony to their influence. In some cases this influence is subconscious (or at least undocumented),[38] but most often it is clearly defined. Complete discussion of each of these publications is beyond the scope and purpose of this bibliography. The most important of these have been mentioned in the preceding discussion; others are simply listed in Appendix D. Before coming to a close, I would like to mention two further sources of interest. One is the "Analysis Symposium" (published in the Journal of Music Theory and reprinted in this volume). The purpose of this symposium is to publish two or three analyses of the same composition for the purpose of comparison. An effort is made to represent diverse analytic approaches, one of these being oriented toward Schenker's approach. The other is *The Music Forum* (edited by William Mitchell and Felix Salzer). In the first volume of this annual, the editors state their intent to publish, among other things, articles which are based on Schenker's approach to music. Both of these sources are helping to bring Schenker's ideas before the musical public. A particularly encouraging sign is the scheduled publication of some of Schenker's works that have not been generally available. Even more significant is the probability that translations of some of his works will be available in the near future. All of this points to an increasing interest in his work.

NOTES

1. An attempt to formulate a theory of the twelve-tone system analogous to Schenker's theory of tonality is mentioned by Michael Kassler in his article, "Toward a Theory That is the Twelve-Note-Class System," *Perspectives of New Music* 5, no. 2 (Spring-Summer 1967), footnote 53.

2. The word theorist should be emphasized here. In no way do I intend to belittle the importance and influence of composers like Schoenberg and Webern on twentieth-century musical thought.

3. Schenker, of course, intended many of his ideas to relate directly or indirectly to performance. The influence of his ideas on two prominent musicians, Wilhelm Furtwängler and Bruno Walter, is pointed out by Allen Forte in his essay "Schenker's Conception of Musical Structure" (chap. 1 in this volume). Furtwängler devotes a chapter to Schenker in his book, *Ton und Wort* (Wiesbaden: F. A. Brokhaus, 1954), and Walter acknowledges Schenker's influence in his autobiography, *Theme and Variations* (New York: Alfred A. Knopf, 1947).

4. A biography of Schenker by Oswald Jonas, to be published in Germany, is in preparation. I would hope that some of this information will be included in that publication.

5. *Harmonielehre*, the first volume of *Neue musikalische Theorien und Phantasien*, was first published anonymously—by an artist (*von einem Künstler*)—in 1906 by J. G. Cotta, Stuttgart. The publication rights were taken over by Universal Edition at a later date.

6. Oswald Jonas, Introduction to Schenker's *Harmony*, trans. Elisabeth Mann Borgese (Chicago: University of Chicago Press, 1954), p. ix..

7. Part 1 of *Kontrapunkt* was first published by J. G. Cotta (Stuttgart) in 1910; part 2 was published by Universal Edition in 1922.

8. Two of those who have reviewed this important work are Roger Sessions ("Escape by Theory," *Modern Music* 15, no. 3 (1939):192-97) and Carl Dahlhaus (*Die Musikforschung* 12 (1959):523-25).

9. The relationship between these concepts and the foreground of a composition has proved a stumbling block for many. It is impossible to grasp their meaning and significance without having followed, step by step, the process of reduction which led Schenker to them.

10. Oswald Jonas, Introduction to *Harmony*, p. xxiv.

11. Jahrbuch III has been reviewed by Oswald Jonas (*Zeitschrift für Musikwissenschaft* 15 (1932-33):92-94) and E. W. (*Music and Letters* 12 (1931):306-07).

12. "Five Analyses in Sketchform" was published simultaneously by the David Mannes Music School (New York) under the direction of Hans Weisse, one of Schenker's students. Weisse, an influential teacher himself, was really the first to introduce Schenker's theories to this country in the 1930s.

13. Allen Forte, "Schenker's Conception of Musical Structure," p. 3, this volume.

14. This translation has been reviewed by J. K. Andrews (*Music and Letters* 37, no. 2 (1956):180-82) and William J. Mitchell (*The Musical Quarterly* 41, no. 1(1955):256-60).

15. I have seen a copy of Dunn's translation of *Kontrapunkt*, part 2, owned by Ernst Oster. It is handwritten and reproduced by opolograph, University of Edinburgh.

16. Another translation of *Der freie Satz* was done by T. Howard Krueger (Unpublished Ph.D. Diss., State University of Iowa, 1960).

17. Translation of other essays and analyses by Schenker are scheduled for publication in future issues of the *Journal of Music Theory*. This is also the case with *The Music Forum*, edited by William Mitchell and Felix Salzer (New York: Columbia University Press).

18. The following three sources were particularly helpful to me in compiling Appendix D: Jeffrey Hest, "A Union Bibliography of the Works of Heinrich Schenker and Works Pertaining to the Schenkerian System of Analysis," Queens College of the City University of New York, February 1968 (first draft, unpublished), Paul Mast, "Heinrich Schenker," Eastman School of Music, May 1969 (bibliography unpublished); Sonia Slatin, "The Theories of Heinrich Schenker in Perspective," Ph.D. Diss., Columbia University, 1967 (bibliography).

19. A completely revised and enlarged edition of this book has been prepared by Jonas and was published by Universal Edition (UE26202) in 1972.

20. An attempt to organize Schenker's ideas into textbook form has been made by Felix Salzer (also a Schenker student) in his book *Structural Hearing: Tonal Coherence in Music*. However, many of the ideas presented in this book are either those of the author or his own personal adaptation of those of Schenker. For this reason, *Structural Hearing* was not intended nor should it be considered, as is often the case, as truly representative of Schenker's ideas.

21. Other informative introductions to Schenker's ideas are: Oswald Jonas, Introduction to *Harmony*, trans. Elisabeth Mann Borgese (Chicago: University of Chicago Press, 1954); Arthur Waldeck and Nathan Broder, "Musical Synthesis as Expounded by Heinrich Schenker" (*The Musical Mercury* 2, no. 4 (1935)); Milton Babbitt, "Review of Salzer's *Structural Hearing*" (*Journal of the American Musicological Society* 5, no. 3 (Fall 1952):260–65.

22. One such criticism appears in H. K. Andrew's review of Schenker's *Harmony*, edited by Oswald Jonas and translated by Elisabeth Mann Borgese, in *Music and Letters* 37 (1956): 180–82. Besides his objection to Schenker's "acceptance of an (albeit modified) acoustical basis for harmony," Andrews criticizes him for his "almost complete disregard for the history and development of music and musical technique before the time of J. S. Bach."

23. Another who has characterized Schenker's theories as being static is Leonard Meyer in *Emotion and Meaning in Music* (Chicago: University of Chicago Press, 1956), pp. 52–54.

24. Babbitt, "Review of Salzer's *Structural Hearing*," p. 262.

25. Roger Sessions, "Heinrich Schenker's Contribution," *Modern Music* 12, no. 4 (1935). A more vehement attack by Sessions on the same subject can be found in "Escape by Theory" (A review of *Der freie Satz*), *Modern Music* 15, no. 3 (1938).

26. Michael Mann. "Schenker's Contribution to Music Theory," *The Music Review* 10 (1949):16–17.

27. Paul Henry Lang. Editorial, *The Musical Quarterly* 32, no. 2 (April 1946):296–302.

28. In "Heinrich Schenker und grosse Interpreten (*Österreichische Musikzeitschrift*, December 1964), Oswald Jonas points out that Schenker was a practical musician (composer, performer, critic) as well as a theorist. He also indicates the impact Schenker's ideas have had on performance.

29. *Contemporary Tone Structures* has been reviewed by Hans Keller (*Music and Letters* 32, no. 2 (1956):187–89) and Howard Boatwright (*Journal of Music Theory* 1, no. 1 (1957): 112–18). A rebuttal by Forte to the latter was published in the *Journal of Music Theory* 1, no. 2:201–05, and Boatwright's subsequent answer was published in the following issue, pp. 85–92.

30. *Challenge to Musical Tradition* has been reviewed by Percy M. Young (*Music and Letters* 28 no. 4 (1947):390–91) and Paul Henry Lang (Editorial, *The Musical Quarterly* 32, no. 2 (1946):296–302. The latter is more of an attack on Schenker than an evaluation of Miss Katz's book.

31. *Structural Hearing* has been reviewed by Milton Babbitt (*Journal of the American Musicological Society* 5, no. 3 (1952):260–65), Nathan Broder (*The Musical Quarterly* 39, no. 1 (1953):126–29), and Norman Lloyd (pro) and Oswald Jonas (con) (*Notes* 10, no. 3 (June 1953): p. 438 and p. 439. In the Introduction to Schenker's *Harmony* (trans. Elisabeth Mann Borgese), Jonas criticizes Salzer as follows:

> Recently an attempt was made to offset this objection [that Schenker's theory is too "narrow" and "lopsided"] by applying Schenker's ideas to modern music and its interpretation: *Structural Hearing* by Felix Salzer (New York: Charles Boni, 1952). Such an attempt was possible only through misinterpretation of Schenker's basic theories, first of all his concept of tonality, and therefore is doomed to fail. [p. viii, n. 2]

32. Much of the third part of *Structural Hearing* is concerned with the analysis of older music. The application of Schenker's ideas to the analysis of this music was begun by Salzer in his earlier work, *Sinn und Wesen der abendländische Mehrstimmigkeit* (Vienna: Saturn-Verlag, 1935).

33. A textbook on counterpoint which is strongly influenced by Schenker's ideas has recently been published: *Counterpoint in Composition* (New York: McGraw-Hill, 1969), by Felix Salzer and Carl Schachter.

34. A response to this article by Ernst Oster marks the beginning of an interesting controversy. In "Re: A New Concept of Tonality?" (*Journal of Music Theory* 4, no. 1 (April 1960):85–98), Oster criticizes Travis on a number of points. His main criticism centers around Travis's total reliance on Salzer's *Structural Hearing* as a source of information and ideas. A number of errors in his analyses of the Chopin and Mozart pieces are detected, and Oster points out that Schenker's analysis of one of the same pieces was never consulted. He also criticizes Travis for his failure to indicate the differences between his approach and Schenker's. Along the way, Oster criticizes Salzer for making similar modifications in Schenker's ideas and his failure to document these changes.

In a Letter to the Editor (*Journal of Music Theory* 4, no. 2 (November 1960):274–75), Hans Neumann responds to Oster's criticisms of Salzer's *Structural Hearing*. He criticizes Oster for misrepresenting Salzer's intentions and for implying that Salzer had "belittled" Schenker's work. Neumann states that Salzer had given Schenker sufficient credit and therefore was under no obligation to "account for every single departure from dogmatism and orthodoxy." Otherwise he does not discuss the merits of Oster's criticisms of Salzer's and Travis's extensions of Schenker's ideas.

Oster's point of view is defended by Arthur Komar in his Letter to the Editor (*Journal of Music Theory* 5, no. 1 (April 1961):152–56). Komar points to the fact that Salzer departs from Schenker even in his approach to traditional music. He gives three examples of instances where their analyses of pieces by Beethoven and Chopin differ. And although he does not feel it was necessarily Salzer's responsibility to do so, Komar states that it would indeed clarify the situation if all departures from Schenker were documented. Komar's main objection is to those who "cite *Structural Hearing* as the published source of their knowledge of Schenkerian techniques." Roy Travis is included in those he mentions.

35. A review of this book by Mosco Carner was published in *Music and Letters* 32, no. 2 (1951):177–80.

36. Grosvenor Cooper and Leonard B. Meyer, *The Rhythmic Structure of Music* (Chicago: University of Chicago Press, 1960).

37. A better analysis of the opening measures of this piece is contained in "Heinrich Schenker's Method of Analysis," by Adele Katz, *The Musical Quarterly* 21, no. 3 (1935), example 9.

38. One example of this is "Unity in Music" (*Journal of Music Theory* 2, no. 1 (April 1959):97–104), by William H. Reynolds. Although Schenker's name is never mentioned, a number of ideas and terms generally associated with his approach to music are used by the author. In "Re: Analysis and Elementary Harmony" (*Journal of Music Theory* 2, no. 2 (November 1958):240–49), William Gettel disagrees with many of the statements contained in the Reynolds article. Gettel also makes use of a number of ideas and terms generally associated with Schenker's name. (Schenker and Salzer's *Structural Hearing* are mentioned in footnote 1.) In "Re: Analysis and Unity" (*Journal of Music Theory* 3, no. 1 [April 1959]: pp. 140–47), Reynolds replies to Gettel's criticisms.

A Chronological Listing of Schenker's Works

APPENDIX A: THEORETICAL WORKS

1904   *Ein Beitrag zur Ornamentik.* Vienna: Universal Edition.

1906   *Neue Musikalische Theorien und Phantasien.* Vol. 1, *Harmonielehre.* Vienna: Universal Edition.

1908   *Ein Beitrag zur Ornamentik.* New revised and expanded edition. Vienna: Universal Edition.

——   *Instrumentations-Tabelle von "Artur Niloff."* Vienna: Universal Edition.

1910   *Neue musikalische Theorien und Phantasien.* Vol. 2, part 1, *Kontrapunkt* (Cantus Firmus und zweistimmiger Satz). Vienna: Universal Edition.

1912   *Beethovens neunte Sinfonie.* Vienna: Universal Edition.

1921–24   *Der Tonwille.* 10 issues. Vienna: A. Gutmann Verlag. (Republished later in 3 volumes by Universal Edition).

1922   *Neue musikalische Theorien und Phantasien.* Vol. 2, part 2, *Kontrapunkt* (Drei- und mehrstimmiger Satz). Vienna: Universal Edition.

1925   *Beethovens fünfte Sinfonie.* Vienna: A. Gutmann Verlag. (Also Universal Edition, no. 7646).

1925–30   *Das Meisterwerk in der Musik.* Jahrbuch I, 1925; Jahrbuch II, 1926; Jahrbuch III, 1930. Munich: Drei Masken Verlag.

1932   *Fünf Urlinie—Tafeln.* Vienna: Universal Edition.

1933   *Johannes Brahms, "Oktaven und Quinten" u. A., aus dem Nachlass herausgegeben und erläutert von Henrich Schenker.* Vienna: Universal Edition.

1935   *Neue musikalische Theorien und Phantasien.* Vienna: Universal Edition. Vol. 3, *Der freie Satz* (book 1, text; book 2, musical figures). Second edition, edited and revised by Oswald Jonas, 1956.

APPENDIX B: SCHENKER'S EDITIONS OF MUSIC

1902–03   *Ph. Em. Bach. Klavierwerke.* Vol. 1: Six sonatas. Vol.

2: Three sonatas, four sonata movements, and one rondo. New critical edition. Vienna: Universal Edition.

1904   G. F. Handel. *Sechs Orgelkonzerte.* Adapted for four hands from the original scores for piano. Vienna: Universal Edition.

1910   J. S. Bach. *Chromatische Phantasie und Fuge* [in D Minor]. Critical edition with appendix [Anhang]. Vienna: Universal Edition.

1913–20 *Erläuterungsausgaben der letzten fünf Sonaten Beethovens.* Op. 109 in E Major, 1913; op. 110 in A-flat Major, 1914; op. 111 in C Major, 1915; op. 101 in A Major, 1920. Vienna: Universal Edition. (Schenker was unable to complete this series because the autograph of op. 106 was, and is, missing.)

1921   Beethoven. *Sonata op. 27 no. 2.* Facsimile reproduction including three sketches by Beethoven. Vienna: Universal Edition.

192?   Beethoven. *Sämtliche Klaviersonaten.* Reconstructed by Heinrich Schenker from the autographs. Vienna: Universal Edition. New edition revised by Erwin Ratz. Vienna: Universal Edition, 1947.

APPENDIX C: A PARTIAL LISTING OF ESSAYS AND REVIEWS BY SCHENKER

Die Zukunft (Berlin)

1892   "Mascagni in Wien" (October).
        "Eine jung-italienische Schule?" (December).
1893   "Mascagnis 'Rantzau'" (February).
        "Notizen zu Verdis Falstaff" (May).
        "Friedrich Smetana" (July).
        "Der Sonzongno-Markt in Wien" (August).
      *"Anton Bruckner" (October).
1894   "Ruggiero Leoncavallo" (January).
        "Konzertdirigenten" (April).
        "Deutsch-Oesterreichischer Musikverkehr" (April).
        "Verdis Falstaff" (May).
        "Tantiemen für Instrumentalkomponisten" (May).
        "Anton Rubinstein" (August).
        "Eugen d'Albert" (October).

1896   "Siegfried Wagner" (February).
         "Das Heimchen am Herd" [Rubin Goldmark] (April).
1897   "Johannes Brahms" (May).

Musikalisches Wochenblatt (Leipzig).
   1892 "Brahms, 5 Gesänge für gemischten Chor op. 105" (August).
   1893 *"Bruckner, Psalm 150 für Chor, Soli und Orchester."

Die Zeit (Vienna)
   1895 "Zur musikalischen Erziehung" (September).
   1896 *"Mozarts 'Don Juan'" (April).
        *"Über Brahms" (May).
        *"Anton Bruckner."

Neue Revue (Vienna)
   1897 "Epilog zur Schubertfeier" (February).
   ——   "Johannes Brahms" (April).

Wiener Abendpost
   1901 "Beethoven 'Retouche'" (January).

Der Kunstwart (Munich). Further articles can be found in *Deutsche Zeitschrift,* a continuation of *Der Kunstwart.*
   1929 "Eine Rettung der klassischen Musik-Texte: Das Archiv
         für Photogramme in der National-Bibliothek, Wien" (March).
   1931 "Ein verschollener Brief von Mozart und das Geheimnis
         seines Schaffens" (July).

Der Geist der musikalischen Technik. A brochure. Original brochure owned by the Gesellschaft der Musikfreunde in Wien.

*The starred articles, above, were republished in: *Der Dreiklang: Monatsschrift für Musik* (edited by Oswald Jonas and Felix Salzer). Vienna: Krystall-Verlag, 1936–38. Also included in this publication are the following short essays and analyses by Schenker:
   "Vom Hintergrund in der Musik" (from *Der freie Satz*).
   "Von der Stimmführung im generalbass" (from the earlier un-published version of *Der freie Satz*).
   "Von der Diminution" (from *Der freie Satz*).
   "Urlinietafel zu Haydns 'Chorale St. Antoni'."
   "Ein Kommentar zu Schindler, Beethovens Spiel betreffend."

A Listing of the Works Concerning
Schenker and His Theories

APPENDIX D

Books

Daniskas, John. *Grondslagen voor de analytische vormleer der musiek.* Rotterdam: W. L. and J. Brusse, 1948.

Federhofer, Hellmut. *Beiträge zur musikalischen Gestaltanalyse.* Graz: Akademische Druck- und Verlagsanstalt, 1950.

Forte, Allen. *Contemporary Tone Structures.* New York: Bureau of Publications, Teacher's College, Columbia University, 1955.

Jonas, Oswald. *Das Wesen des musikalischen Kunstwerks.* Eine Einführung in die Lehre Heinrich Schenkers. Vienna: Im Saturn-Verlag, 1934.

Katz, Adele T. *Challenge to Musical Tradition: A New Concept of Tonality.* New York: Alfred A. Knopf, 1945.

Roth, Hermann. *Elemente der Stimmführung (Der strenge Satz).* Stuttgart: Carl Grüninger Verlag, 1926.

Salzer, Felix. *Sinn und Wesen der abendländischen Mehrstimmigkeit.* Vienna: Saturn-Verlag, 1935.

———. *Structural Hearing: Tonal Coherence in Music.* 2 vols. New York: Charles Boni, 1952. Reprint. New York: Dover Publications, 1962.

Articles

Baker's Biographical Dictionary of Music and Musicians. 5th ed. S. v. "Schenker, Heinrich." New York: G. Schirmer, 1958.

Bamberger, Carl. "Das Schenker-Institut am neuen Wiener Konservatorium." *Anbruch* 18, no. 1 (January-February 1926):7–8.

Citkowitz, Israel. "The Role of Heinrich Schenker." *Modern Music* 11, no. 1 (November-December 1933):18–23.

Dale, Frank Knight. "Heinrich Schenker and Musical Form." *Bulletin of the American Musicological Society* 1–3, no. 7 (1936–41): 12–13.

Federhofer, Hellmut. "Die Musiktheorie Heinrich Schenkers." *Schweizerische Musikzeitung* 87, no. 2 (October 1947):265–68.

——. "Die Funktionstheorie Hugo Riemanns und die Schichtenlehre Heinrich Schenkers." Bericht über den Internationalen Musikwissenschaftlichen Kongress, Vienna, 1956, pp. 183–90.

——. "Heinrich Schenker." In *Riemann Musik Lexikon.* 12th rev. ed. in 3 vols. Vol. 2. Mainz: B. Schott's Söhne, 1967.

——. "Heinrich Schenker." In *Anthony van Hoboken Festschrift* Mainz: B. Schott's Söhne, 1962.

Geiringer, Karl. "Heinrich Schenker." In *Grove's Dictionary of Music and Musicians.* Edited by Eric Blom. 5th ed. Vol. 7. New York: St. Martin's Press, 1954.

Hartmann, Heinrich. "Heinrich Schenker und Karl Marx." *Österreichische Musikzeitschrift* 7, no. 2 (1952):46–52.

Hirschkorn, K. "Die Stimmführung als Leitstern des Geigers: Die Bedeutung Heinrich Schenkers." *Musikerziehung Zeitschrift zur Erneuerung der Musikpflege* 12 (1959):233–234.

Jonas, Oswald. "The Photogram-Archives in Vienna." *Music and Letters* 15 (1934):344–47. Translated and reprinted as "Das Wiener Photogramm-Archiv," in *Anbruch* 18, no. 1 (1936):6–7.

——. "Der Nachlass Heinrich Schenkers." *Der Dreiklang,* April 1937, pp. 17–22. Unsigned article.

——. Introduction to *Harmony,* by Heinrich Schenker, trans. Elisabeth Mann Borgese. Chicago: University of Chicago Press, 1954.

——. "On the Study of Chopin's Manuscripts." *Chopin-Jahrbuch 1956* (Internationale Chopin-Gesellschaft). Vienna: Amalthea-Verlag.

——. "Die Kunst des Vortrags nach Heinrich Schenker." *Musikerziehung,* March 1962, pp. 127–29.

——. "Heinrich Schenker." In *Die Musik in Geschichte und Gegenwart: Allgemeine Enzyklopädie der Musik.* Edited by Friedrich Blume. Vol. 11. Basel: Bärenreiter Kassel, 1963.

——. "Heinrich Schenker und grosse Interpreten." *Österreichische Musikzeitschrift* 19 (December 1964):584–89.

——. "Nachtrag zu Schenkers Aufsatz über Schindler." *Musikerziehung* 1965, pp. 205–09.

Katz, Adele. "Heinrich Schenker's Method of Analysis." *The Musical Quarterly* 21, no. 3 (July 1935):311–29.

Kaufmann, Harald. "Fortschritt und Reaktion in der Lehre Heinrich Schenkers." *Neue Zeitschrift für Musik* 126, no. 1 (1965):5–9.

Kessler, Hubert. "On the Value of Schenker's Ideas for Analysis of Contemporary Music." Periodical of Theory-Composition (Illinois State Teacher's Association), vol. 1 (1958):1–11. Mimeograph ed.

Kolneder, Walter. "Sind Schenkers Analysen Beiträge zur Bacherkenntnis?" *Deutsches Jahrbuch der Musikwissenschaft* 3 (1958): 59–73.

Lang, Paul Henry. Editorial. *The Musical Quarterly* 32, no. 2 (1946):296–302.

Mann, Michael. "Schenker's Contribution to Music Theory." *The Music Review* 10 (1949):3–26.

Mitchell, William J. "Heinrich Schenker's Approach to Detail." *Musicology* 1, no. 2 (1946):117–28.

Plettner, Arthur. "Heinrich Schenker's Contribution to Theory." *Musical America* 56, no. 3 (10 February 1936):14.

Reich, Willi. "Kant, Schenker und der Nachläufer." *Drei und Zwanzig,* no. 15–16 (1934):29–32.

Riezler, Walter. "Die Urlinie." *Die Musik* 22, no. 7 (April 1930): 502–10.

Salzer, Felix. "Die historische Sendung Heinrich Schenkers." *Der Dreiklang* 1 (April 1937):2–12.

Schmid, Edmund. "Autographe und Originalausgaben Beethovens." *Neue Zeitschrift für Musik* 119 (December 1958):746–47.

Sessions, Roger. "Heinrich Schenker's Contribution." *Modern Music* 12, no. 4 (1935):170–78.

———. "Escape by Theory." *Modern Music* 15, no. 3 (1938):192–97.

———. "The Function of Theory." *Modern Music* 15, no. 4 (1938): 257–62.

Siedel, Elmer. "Ursatz." In *Riemann Musik Lexikon.* 12th rev. ed. in 3 vols. Mainz: B. Schott's Söhne, 1967.

Silberman, Israel. "Teaching Composition Via Schenker's Theory." *Journal of Research in Music Education* 12, no. 4 (Winter 1964): 295–303.

Slatin, Sonia. "The Theories of Heinrich Schenker in Perspective." Ph.D. Diss. Columbia University, 1967.

Travis, Roy. "Towards a New Concept of Tonality?" *Journal of Music Theory* 3, no. 2 (November 1959):257–84.

Vrieslander, Otto. "Heinrich Schenker." *Die Musik* 19, no. 1 (1926–27):33–38.

———. "Heinrich Schenker." *Kunstwart* 9 (1930):181–89.

Waldeck, Arthur and Broder, Nathan. "Musical Synthesis as Expounded by Heinrich Schenker." *The Musical Mercury* 11, no. 4 (1935):56–64.

Wingert, Hans. "Über die 'Urlinie' und ihren Schöpfer." *Zeitschrift für Musik* 3, no. 5 (1950):244–46.

Wolf, Hans. "Schenkers Persönlichkeit im Unterricht." *Der Dreiklang* 7 (October 1937):176–84.

Zuckerkandl, Victor. "Bekenntnis zu einem Lehrer." *Anbruch* 17, no. 5 (May 1935):121–25.

——. "Urlinie, Ursatz." *Harvard Dictionary of Music.* Cambridge: Harvard University Press, 1960.

Further Sources of Interest

"Analysis Symposium." Published at irregular intervals in the *Journal of Music Theory*.

Beach, David. "The Functions of the Six-Four Chord in Tonal Music." *Journal of Music Theory* 11, no. 1 (Spring 1967):2–31.

Cockshoot, John V. *The Fugue in Beethoven's Piano Music*. London: Routledge and Kegan Paul 1959.

Der Dreiklang: Monatschrift für Musik. Edited by Oswald Jonas and Felix Salzer. Vienna: Krystall-Verlag, 1937–38. This publication contains a number of articles and analyses, a few of which have been listed above, which are related to Schenker's theories.

Eibner, Franz. "Chopins Kontrapunktisches Denken." *Chopin-Jahrbuch 1956* (Internationale Chopin-Gesellschaft). Vienna: Amal-thea-Verlag.

The Music Forum. Edited by William J. Mitchell and Felix Salzer. New York: Columbia University Press. Vol. 1 (1967): Peter Bergquist "Mode and Polyphony around 1500: Theory and Practice"; William J. Mitchell, "The Tristan Prelude: Techniques and Structure"; Felix Salzer, "Tonality in Early Medieval Polyphony: Toward a History of Tonality."

Kliewer, Vernon L. "The Concept of Organic Unity in Music Criticism and Analysis." Ph.D. Diss. Indiana University, 1961.

Oster, Ernst. "The Dramatic Character of the Egmont Overture." *Musicology* 2, no. 3 (April 1949):269–85.

Oster, Ernst. "The Fantaisie-Impromptu—A Tribute to Beethoven." *Musicology* 1, no. 4 (1947):407–29.

Reynolds, William. "Unity in Music." *Journal of Music Theory* 2, no. 1 (April 1958):97–104.

Salzer, Felix, and Schacter, Carl. *Counterpoint in Composition: A Study in Voice Leading*. New York: McGraw-Hill, 1969.

Thomson, W. E. "A Clarification of the Tonality Concept." Ph.D. Diss. University of Indiana, 1952.

Travis, Roy. "Directed Motion in Schönberg and Webern." *Perspectives of New Music* 4, no. 2 (Spring-Summer 1966):84–89.

Vrieslander, Otto. "Carl Philipp Emanuel Bach als Theoretiker." *Von neuer Musik*, 1925, pp. 222–79.

Westergaard, Peter. "Some Problems in Rhythmic Theory and Analysis." *Perspectives of New Music* 1, no. 1 (Fall 1962):180–90.